PRAISE FOR WRECK OF THE MEDUSA

"[McKee's] terse account of the original disaster opens out into a study of the ensuing cover-up and widening political scandal, which deeply embarrassed the French government. . . . Instead of exploiting the Medusa episode as a unique horror story, McKee searches out the paradigmatic elements of human behavior under stress. This is a first-rate piece of work."
— *Newsweek*

"A weird and tragic narrative . . . a spellbinding human drama that made its mark on history and art . . . haunting."
— *Publishers Weekly*

"Well-told. . . . The real horror comes in reading the lurid details of what the author calls '. . . the most horrible sea tragedy of the century, possibly the most terrible that has ever taken place . . .' It is also instructive on the seemingly eternal propensity of man to be inhumane to his fellows."
— *Business Week*

"An epic of horror at sea. . . . McKee talks of cannibalism in some survival epics of this century, but if anything makes that soccer team's ordeal in the Andes seem tame, this story does."
— *Chicago Daily News*

"An admirable addition to the literature of survival."
— *Kansas City Star*

WRECK OF THE MEDUSA

Mutiny, Murder, and Survival on the High Seas

Alexander McKee

Skyhorse Publishing

www.skyhorsepublishing.com

10 9 8 7 6 5 4 3 2 1

Library of Congress Cataloging-in-Publication Data

McKee, Alexander, 1918–
 [Death raft]
 Wreck of the Medusa : mutiny, murder, and survival on the high seas / Alexander McKee.
   p. cm.
 Originally published under title: Death raft. New York : Scribner, 1976, c1975.
 Includes bibliographical references and index.
 ISBN-13: 978-1-60239-186-4 (pbk. : alk. paper)
 ISBN-10: 1-60239-186-6 (pbk. : alk. paper)
 1. Miduse (Ship) 2. Shipwrecks—Senegal. I. Title.

G530.M5M32 2007
910.9163'75—dc22

                                    2007013433

Printed in Canada

Contents

v

WRECK OF THE
Medusa

1

LANDLOCKED

June, 1816

THE girl who ran impulsively into the fields to gather blooms was saying goodbye to France. Picking a few of the red poppies and the blue cornflowers, she hurried back to join her family on the road, overcome by a feeling of sadness. Perhaps it was only a brief homesickness, but afterwards she thought it might have been premonition. Like many others making their way towards Rochefort that day, she was destined to witness the most horrible sea tragedy of the century, possibly the most terrible that has ever been enacted.

It was June 12, 1816, less than a year after the final downfall of Napoleon Bonaparte at Waterloo. It is not fanciful to link the *Medusa* disaster with that critical moment when the Guard recoiled and the British bayonets began to move forward, the flanking Prussians driving deep into the ruined French Army.

The fate of the *Medusa*, both her original mission and its terrible end, flowed as a direct consequence. That French power which had dominated Europe for twenty years had been humbled. That monarchy which France had twice rejected was once more imposed upon her by victorious foes.

One of those enemies had returned to the restored monarchy what it had taken from the deposed Emperor. The French colony of Senegal in West Africa was to be handed back by its English captors as part of the peace settlement. And the mission to be led by the *Medusa* was that of re-establishing a French garri-

son and a French administration on that fly-blown
fever coast, still largely unexplored.

Charlotte-Adélaïde Picard, the girl who had so impulsively picked the flowers, was one of the 365 passengers
to be embarked in a four-ship convoy consisting of the
frigate *Medusa,* the corvette *Echo,* the transport *Loire*
and the brig *Argus.* Soldiers of a low-grade battalion
under an elderly Lieutenant-Colonel formed the bulk
of the passengers, but there were also engineers, ac-
countants, hospital staff, explorers, bakers, school-
masters and a solitary gardener. Some had been able
to bring their families with them, so that there were
twenty-one women and eight children among a largely
male throng.

Charlotte was one of about 240 people destined to
take passage in the *Medusa,* the flagship of the little
fleet. With her crew of 160, a total of four hundred
men, women and children were crammed into her
wooden hull. One hundred and forty nine of them
were destined never to reach Africa. Of those who
did, some did not long survive the terrible ordeal they
had undergone.

The girl was on the passenger list, not in her own
right, but as the eldest daughter of the official intended to become the new public notary of St. Louis,
the capital of the colony. She loved him dearly, although he was inclined to be outspokenly critical.
M. Picard had great responsibilities already, for he had
married a second time. Apart from the two grown-up
daughters from his earlier marriage, he was accompanied by his second wife and their much younger children, Laura, Charles and Gustavus. Laura was only
six years old while the youngest child was still a baby.
He had taken under his care as well a five-year-old
boy, Alphonse Fleury, who was Charlotte's cousin but
now an orphan. In any emergency this large family
would be peculiarly vulnerable.

Their journey to Rochefort was leisurely, almost a
seaside holiday for the children. They found that the

town lay on the river Charente, four leagues* from the wide roadstead off the isle of Aix where the ships were waiting. First they had to board a boat to take them down the winding river towards the sea. And then contrary winds delayed this craft so much that it was not until the next day that they approached the bulk of the *Medusa,* which was to be their home for the next few weeks. The journey might take a month, they thought. But it was exciting for the children, who had never seen a ship this close. Only their father, an old colonial "hand" who had been working a plantation in Senegal when the English took over, had been to sea before.

Charlotte-Adélaïde, a girl of good education steeped in the mystique of fashionable Paris, found provincial Rochefort monotonous and boring. Clearly, it was an important naval arsenal but the *Medusa* herself conveyed no warlike impression. To her, the frigate was just a great hulk of wood. Not for the first time, the first impressions of Miss Picard were to prove absolutely correct.

The *Medusa* had been a warship until recently and had carried a battery of forty-four (mostly eighteen-pounder) guns almost entirely on one deck. But she was far from being a battleship, for they had superimposed tiers of guns on two, three or even four decks; and most of those guns were of much heavier metal than the *Medusa* could mount. She was a long, low ship, lightly built; in modern terms a cruiser, designed for scouting, message-carrying, patrol and convoy duties.

However, she no longer ranked as such because, in order to turn a frigate into a troop transport, thirty of her forty-four guns had been removed. What had been the gundeck, running almost the full length of the ship, had been converted into a makeshift accommodation deck for hundreds of passengers. The real accommo-

---

*A league is usually taken to equal three miles. But a nautical mile (6,080 feet) is longer than a land mile and a marine league correspondingly so. Most of the witnesses appear to use the French marine league of 5,556 metres because they are referring to distances shown on charts.

dation deck below was too near the waterline to mount guns. A frigate had far more space per man than any other warship of the time, indeed compared favourably in this respect with many modern warships, which was the reason they were so often temporarily converted into fast transports.

It was true also that the *Medusa* did appear clumsy when seen close-to, with her bluff bows and wide, square stern and hull with its oddly inward-sloping sides. Contemporary pictures by male marine artists hardly hint at this aspect of the "wooden walls," but a frigate contemporary with and almost identical to the *Medusa* is still afloat to show what Miss Picard meant.* This vessel surprised everyone when in 1972 she had to be towed away for repairs; in spite of her apparent clumsiness "she slipped through the water like a racing yacht." Below the surface, her lines were as fine as her upperworks were crude. The Parisian girl could not appreciate what a fast ship the *Medusa* really was. But that part which she could see, she described with admirably blunt honesty. It will be important to remember this when disaster strikes and stories become conflicting.

The first impressions which the Picard family received when they boarded were disconcerting; nothing was ready and no preparations had been made to receive them. Including the baby, they all had to find places for the night on the bare planks, surrounded by their luggage, like refugees. Not until next day was a berth made available "near the main deck." Probably temporary cabins were erected. There was so little headroom that only the children could move about freely without fear of cracking their skulls on the deck beams above. The centres of the decks were crowded with all sorts of interesting objects, such as capstans,

*The forty-four-gun *Medusa* was built at St. Nazaire in 1810. The forty-six-gun *Trincomalee* was laid down at Bombay in 1816, a few weeks before the *Medusa* sailed for Senegal. But her design was based on the lines of a captured French frigate, the *Hebe*, copied by the British in 1812. Almost invariably, French warships were better designed than British.

bitts for running rigging and riding bitts for the anchor cables, and cut by hatchways and companion ways (the one for cargo, the other for people) which were a standing temptation to the more daring children. Even with the gun ports and hatches open, the sunlight was subdued and uneven, lending an air of shadowy mystery to the ladders which led further down to the darkness of the hold below the waterline, where the powder magazines were placed. There was indeed treasure down there—three barrels full of gold coins amounting to 90,000 francs and destined for the treasury of the colony.

They had plenty of time to get used to their new floating home; to the constant movement of the deck underfoot, the sounds of wind and water against the hull, a continual background of noise, now subdued, now insistent. Day after day the *Medusa* and her consorts swung at their anchors within sight of the green fields of France, for the great roadstead between the isles of Oleron and Ré is almost landlocked and now contrary winds penned the ships as if in a trap.

And a trap it was in truth. It was late in the year for a voyage to West Africa, even had all been well with the little expedition. On June 15 one officer was sufficiently worried to make an entry in his ship's log "for the record," just in case. . . . He was the commander of the corvette *Echo,* Frigate-Captain Francois-Marie Cornette de Vénancourt. He noted: "We have already wasted too much time . . . we shall arrive in a season very much advanced. I shall be able to serve on that coast for only a short while. This will be inefficient, especially in view of the unique nautical description with which I have been supplied by the Minister of Marine! As for the charts enclosed with the Hydrographie Français, they are so imperfect that it is hardly possible to use them. Further, the chronometer No. 131, issued to me at Rochefort, is decidedly erratic.* How-

---

*Roughly, an error of four seconds in the watch may result in a miscalculation of one mile in a ship's position.

ever, with such poor means and in such an unsuitable
season, I shall do my very best."

Although he had emigrated after the Revolution, de
Vénancourt was an experienced seaman, as his con-
temptuously critical assessment of the navigational
and hydrographic information given him shows. But
he had a black mark against him in the French Navy
and had had to wait twelve years before obtaining a
worthwhile position. And now, he had been passed
over for command of the whole convoy in favour of
an officer who, although of equal rank, was far less
fitted to command a single ship let alone a squadron.

The reason for the "black mark" on his record went
to the heart of the trouble with the entire expedition,
which merely reflected the divisions within France herself. While in exile, de Vénancourt had served as inter-
preter in the British battleship *Queen Charlotte,* Lord
Howe's flagship in the first major sea clash of the Revolutionary Wars, which the English refer to as "The
Glorious First of June," 1784. The French know it as
"the Fight on the Thirteenth of Prairial" and remember the engagement chiefly for the heroic revolutionary legend of the battleship *Le Vengeur du Peuple* which
fought until she sank, supposedly with all hands, supposedly after sinking three British ships. She did fight well
but there were many survivors from her and, by malignant chance, one of them was now commanding another
ship of the Senegal convoy. He was Lieutenant Auguste-
Marie Gicquel des Touches, captain of the transport
Loire. Now aged thirty-three, des Touches had served
in the French Navy from the time that he was ten years
old. Six of those years had been spent in an English
prison, following the battle of Trafalgar in 1805. He had
been awarded the Legion of Honour for bravery.

The naval command of the expedition had been
given to Frigate-Captain Hugues Duroy de Chaumareys, who was also the captain of the *Medusa.* At the
time of the Revolution he had been a lieutenant and
had faced the same choice as de Vénancourt—exile
or execution. He had chosen to emigrate rather than

be dealt with officially by the guillotine or informally by hanging from a lamp-post. He also had joined the Royalist forces fighting with the English against the Revolution and in 1795 had taken part in the landing at Quiberon in support of a Royalist insurrection which ended in failure and massacre. He had become something of a hero by escaping after capture and getting safely back to England, where he wrote a book about it.

Genuinely proud of his family name, he affected a dandified air of gallantry, particularly towards women, which was fashionable then among young aristocrats and the gentry. He had good reasons for not wanting to return to France under Robespierre and did not go back until 1804, whether from home-sickness or because he thought that the Bourbons had lost their chance, is not known. He applied for the quiet post of Customs Officer at Bellac, where he waited out the tumultuous last years of the Napoleonic Empire. His dislike of the upstart Corsican artilleryman was known to the secret police, who kept him under routine surveillance, without result.

But as soon as Napoleon abdicated in 1814, he moved. On May 3, Louis XVIII was king again and on May 12 de Chaumareys obtained an audience with the monarch's brother. He produced the records of his naval service and asked for an appointment. It was the greatest mistake he ever made. From it, all the other errors flowed. He was now fifty-three and had not been to sea for twenty-five years. In those days, now so distant that hardly anyone could remember them, he had been only a Lieutenant. He had never commanded a ship, let alone a squadron of ships. But he yearned to make a name for himself and an inordinate vanity blinded de Chaumareys to the reality of his position, which would have been difficult enough even had he, like de Vénancourt, possessed all the necessary qualifications and experience.

Veterans of the Nile and Trafalgar were not likely to take too kindly to a Customs Officer being set in command over them, even had there been no suppressed hostility between the largely Republican officers and the emigré aristocrats. But still, de Chaumareys would probably have managed well enough had he set out to enlist their aid. Sheer professional pride would have compelled them to help him.

However, that was not the way of the new captain. Lieutenant des Touches of the *Loire* recalled his first meeting with de Chaumareys. "He was a courteous gentleman, but not very serious-minded and he seemed to find it natural that I would be his obedient servant. First I made him understand that I was myself as true a gentleman as he was, and that I did not think that I had done wrong in serving my country during the time he had chosen to go into exile. Then, he changed his attitude towards me. This was quite characteristic of him. Was it just a gentlemanly reflex or did it show a basic lack of character? The latter, I think, for it seems that in spite of his 'show-off' manner de Chaumareys was easily manipulated, like all cocksure fellows."

He was also sensitive and hesitant below the debonair surface assurance and, after he had read his instructions from the Ministry, deeply worried. There would be no opportunity for heroic deeds with the Senegal convoy, but a fair chance of making a disastrous error and being prosaicly wrecked. He was warned that the coast of West Africa ranked as one of the least-known and most imperfectly charted areas in the world. In 1816 that was saying a good deal. The technical means of establishing an accurate position for any feature on the globe's surface were poor, particularly when the observation point was a ship. Little survey work had been done by governments and real hydrographic departments had only just begun to blossom from the old chart and map depots. Their charts were often based on early and erratic observations taken from commercial charts, which were not to be relied on for distant waters.

The principal chart given to de Chaumareys was just such a one. It had been compiled by Jacques Nicolas Bellin (1703–1772), the first hydrographer of the French Navy, compiler of *Le Neptune François*, 1753, a guide to European waters, and *L'Hydrographie*

Françoise, 1756, a guide to the areas outside Europe. As a pioneer, Bellin was notable for being one of the first chart-makers who attempted to be systematic in citing his authorities for the longitudes he showed. That is to say, the positions given were likely to be disputed. The Ministry warned de Chaumareys to navigate with caution and not to be surprised if he found himself well to the north or south of a cape which, from his own calculations, ought to be abeam. The positions were wrong and so were the distances given. It was vital that he use the sounding lead often, noting depths and types of seabed, in order to avoid running into shallow water unexpectedly. In particular, he was warned to be careful of the Arguin Bank, a vast uncharted sandbank stretching many miles out from the coast north of Senegal. In this area he should start to sound while still in water too deep for the sounding lead to reach and then, when the lead did touch bottom, immediately alter course out to sea away from the hazard.

To the inexperienced de Chaumareys this frank admission of the deficiencies of his charts was un-nerving. It had to be added to the hazards presented by the inaccuracies of the only navigational instruments available at the time, augmented by the fact that no ship, let alone a wall-sided sailing vessel, actually goes in the direction it is steered. Almost always, it is offset to one side or the other by the forces of wind and current, whose combined effect is hard to estimate with precision. The cumulative errors resulting horrified de Chaumareys. Already, he could see himself aground on that notorious sandbank. Its fatal reputation began to exert an hypnotic lure on him. Its terror was that of the unknown, for it was not outlined on any chart. Whereas in other areas the chart was busy with figures and symbols which meant that someone had been there before him, the Arguin Bank was depicted blankly white. There, the soundings ceased. No one knew where that bank ended and deep sea began.

When the worried captain discussed the matter with des Touches, a Breton who had been to sea since he was ten, the veteran laughed at his fears. He had good cause to do so, for the Arguin Bank is still unknown; in 1974, it is still white and undelimited on the charts. Anyone who took a big ship anywhere near it would be a fool. That, in effect, was what des Touches told de Chaumareys. Just give it a wide berth, leave it off your route altogether. He even offered to take over the navigation at that point. This would be easy to do, for the four ships were ordered to keep together in convoy and as the *Loire* was by far the slowest of the four, the others would have no difficulty in following the course she set.

Mellowed by their rapid reversal of roles, the Lieutenant wrote down for the Captain a summary of his navigational advice. It was pleasing to have his genuine superiority so quickly recognised. De Chaumareys could have used this human trait with most of his officers and if he had done so no-one would ever have heard of the *Medusa*; or, for that matter, de Chaumareys.

From the conflicting advice and instructions received at Rochefort, de Chaumareys chose the worst possible route to Senegal. He claimed that it was in accordance with instructions from the Ministry. All the practical seamen, like des Touches and de Vénancourt, understood that it is not the sea which is a danger to ships, it is the shore. The safe route to Senegal was out of sight of land from beginning to end. That is, the ships would sail past Finisterre to the westwards until they were far out in the Atlantic and then turn south on a track which would keep them well clear of, successively, the Gibraltar current, the islands of Madeira and Porto Santo, the dangerous Canary Island group, and the barren Sahara coast with its shallows and sandbanks extending well offshore. A final turn when opposite the estimated position of St. Louis in Senegal would then bring them straight in to a gently shelving coast, so that even if there was an error it was likely to be perceived in time.

The route decided on by de Chaumareys required

hardly any navigation; it was little more than glorified map-reading. It included a close approach to all the hazards which could possibly be encountered. All that could be said for this procedure was that it would give plenty of navigational "fixes" from recognised landmarks. There was no danger of getting actually lost, provided it was understood that the landmarks were not exactly where they were thought to be and that the position of the ship itself would be merely an estimate involving a degree of inaccuracy. The hazards lay in an approach at night or in bad visibility from one inaccurate position to another inaccurate position and, above all, that the West African coast for much of the time would be a lee shore. For a vessel dependent entirely on the wind, this route involved quite unnecessary risks. Although a competent and cautious seaman could manage it well enough, given good weather, even so he would be well advised to allow a very great margin for error when off the Arguin Bank.

Left to himself, de Chaumareys might have listened to the experienced seamen and taken the longer, but much safer route far out to sea. But he was not really the leader of the expedition, for he had a V.I.P. aboard the *Medusa*. This was Colonel Julien-Désiré Schmaltz, designated Commander-in-Chief and Governor of Senegal, a mysterious personality who soon had de Chaumareys under his thumb. The known facts about him were that he was of German origin but his mother was half-Irish. He had been to the Military Academy but after the Revolution had gone into business most successfully. The business involved shipping and in 1811 he was called up for the Navy. He was taken prisoner almost at once, when a British expedition beat a French expedition to Batavia by a short head. Oddly, he had his first glimpse of the *Medusa* then, for she was with the French squadron when it turned back off Sourabaya.

The English summarily returned him two years later as unfit for active service, and he vanished from sight until the return of the Bourbons, when suddenly hon-

ours, rank and rewards were lavished on him. He was
garrison commander, under Admiral Linois, of a town
in Guadalupe when Napoleon returned from Elba,
and as Guadalupe declared for the Emperor, Schmaltz
again had his career interrupted by an English sea-
borne invasion. Linois was accused of treason but
Schmaltz courageously wrote a memoir in his defence.
He was now a Governor himself (when the English
would be pleased to allow it) on an extremely high
scale of salary and expenses. He was taking his wife
and daughter out with him and one suspects that his
colonial and business experience fitted him for his
new post.

But he was a colonel who was no real colonel and
may have been a Royalist all along, even when serving
Napoleon. His nature was devious and complex, but
his self-confidence—amounting to tactlessness—was
absolute, unlike that of the apparently cocksure de
Chaumareys. He was a very strong-willed, dominant
personality and difficult for Chaumareys to argue with,
for part of what he said, even if amounting only to 20
per cent, was undoubtedly true. He gives the overwhelming impression of being gifted less with real intelligence than with a remarkable flair for promoting
his own interests.

And during the long days while the convoy lay
idling in the roadstead for want of a favourable wind,
he was pushing, pushing, pushing for speed. The route
was for de Chaumareys to decide, but his inner uncer-
tainty could not withstand this continual driving demand for efficiency. The safe and easy route was also
the longest, apparently. Against it, Schmaltz could
argue the Minister's warning concerning their late
start and the dangers of being caught by the storm
season. De Chaumareys could not deny this, but he must
have felt uneasy as he acquiesced, feeling perhaps that
Schmaltz himself was driving the *Medusa* towards the
Arguin Bank. Schmaltz was in an excellent position to
"needle" everyone, for he had had access to the personal files of all the officers while he had been visiting

the Ministry of Marine. Perhaps this was how he prevailed at last over de Chaumareys. Not only would
they take the shortest route but they would disregard
the Ministry's instructions to proceed in convoy, given
partly for safety reasons but also in order to arrive
together at Senegal as an imposing squadron rather
than as four straggling ships appearing separately.

De Chaumareys could not deny that convoy was
laggard. They would be tied to the speed of des
Touches' transport, the *Loire,* a slow ship anyway
without taking into account her ageing canvas. The
Minister had ordered them to keep together but no
doubt Schmaltz could argue speciously that this instruction contradicted the equal warning concerning
the lateness of the season and the necessity for speed.
In any event, de Chaumareys now openly declared, as
if he had thought of it for himself, that he had no
intention of waiting for any ship which lagged behind.
And so the die was cast. The ships would risk the
hazards of the short route and hug the unknown and
dangerous coast of Africa right down to the Arguin
Bank. And they would risk it separately and alone,
not as a united squadron able to afford each other aid.

Well, that was the plan. But des Touches was too
fly a seaman to take foolish risks. He took the *Loire*
well out on the route they all should have taken and
arrived safely, although his vessel was a very poor
sailer. De Vénancourt, with the fast corvette *Echo,*
stayed with the *Medusa* as long as he dared and then
escaped under the cover of darkness at the critical
moment. Lieutenant Leon Henry de Parnajon, commanding the little brig *Argus* which had a much shal-
lower draught than the *Medusa,* nevertheless also kept
well clear of that notorious coast where the furnace
of the desert sucked in the sea winds and also the
ships that sought to use them.

2

A Passage to Senegal

June 17 to July 2

A T last, on June 17, the winds blew favourably for the small squadron waiting in the roadstead. The passengers, few of whom had been to sea before, watched the men labouring at the capstans to haul in the wet, slimy anchor cables while others aloft prepared to set the sails. As the huge bow anchors rose dripping from the water the canvas was sheeted home and the vessels began to move slowly. It takes a long time and a large sailing ship covers many miles before all the sails are out and drawing properly. And all these ships were of different types with varying performances and handling characteristics. It was also the start of a voyage, when crews are not fully worked up; before they have settled down into a routine which soon becomes almost automatic, with the minimum of commands needing to be given.

Once the ships did begin to move they were steadier than a modern, powered vessel because of the balancing effect of the wind on the sails; they had a more natural motion. Nor could they be brutally bashed into a head sea, with the resulting jarring shocks to the hull and the passengers' stomachs. This was also their weakness, as was demonstrated almost at once. Before the squadron could escape from the windtrap of the roadstead they were brought almost to a standstill because the ebbing current which was slowly helping them out died away and the flood tide began to pour in.

Then the wind shifted again and the ships were now in danger of being forced down onto a notorious reef called Les Roches Bonnes. They had to tack across the wind to avoid destruction, thus losing still more time. Clearly the weather was breaking up and there was a gale on the way.

At midnight Charlotte Picard was still awake, listening to the shock of the waves smashing against the timbers of the *Medusa*. Above the roar of broken water and the creaking of straining woodwork sounded the high-pitched howling of the gusts through the rigging mixed with the clatter of blocks and spars. Unable to sleep because of an uneasy presentiment of misfortune ahead for the frigate and now thoroughly alarmed, believing that the moment had come, the girl ran up on deck. There she paused in horror at the scene.

The labouring vessel was almost broadside to the gale. Out of the night came marching rank on rank of great combers. They burst in fury over the bulwarks, white water washing along the cambered deck and roaring out of the scuppers back into the sea. One moment the vessel was lifted half up to the lowering sky and then she was wallowing down in the trough. Each shock seemed to split open her side while high above the sails bellied and cracked and protested noisily.

Gazing round in desperate hope of succour the girl noticed the other three ships of the squadron, sometimes half hidden by water, sometimes rising lazily on the crests of the combers. *Echo, Loire, Argus,* they were all there and all bearing sail. Evidently, there was no danger at all, as long as there was no land near. Much comforted, Charlotte went below again to rest.

Now it was June 18, 1816. The first anniversary of the Battle of Waterloo. A year ago this morning two great armies had faced each other across half a dozen fields in Belgium and the day's end had riven French society. Those who had been up went down, and those who had been down had climbed up again, uneasily. The lines of division, the stresses, still showed, not

only in France but in that part of French society which
was afloat in the *Medusa*. That they contributed to
her fate is certain. How much they did so may still
be debated.

It seems that a number of officers were hostile to
de Chaumareys from the first moment he came
aboard; indeed it would be remarkable if they had not
resented the fact of his appointment and the cocksure
manner in which he assumed it. Either from original
prejudice or because he sensed hostility, de Chaumareys did not trust his second-in-command and, ignoring
him, turned elsewhere for advice. The First Lieutenant
of the *Medusa*, Joseph Pierre André Reynaud, had
been a zealous and efficient officer in Napoleon's fleet.
His "big ship" experience included service in the 74-
gun *Duguay-Trouin** but Reynaud's real flair was for
small commands where initiative was valuable. He
could certainly have run the *Medusa* efficiently if de
Chaumareys had let him. Instead, he rejected Reynaud—his official second-in-command and a tried and
tested officer—in favour, not of another officer, but
a passenger. Indeed, he made a crony of this man,
M. Richefort, who had never served in the Navy and
was not now a member of the crew but who claimed
vast sea-going experience. In all societies one meets
people like this and they usually turn out to be bank
managers, postmen or butchers. Richefort was a member of the so-called Philanthropic Society of Cape
Verde; he was to be employed by the exploration team
in Senegal. He had no official status whatever on
board the frigate.

While Governor Schmaltz had slight justification for
interesting himself in some aspects of the expedition
which were not strictly his concern, his interference
was understood if not approved. But for de Chaumareys to degrade his second-in-command, the officer who

*This two-decker could still be seen in Portsmouth Harbour up to
1949. She had fought at Trafalgar but was captured shortly
afterwards.

would take over the ship if anything happened to the captain, by in effect promoting the incredible poseur Richefort to that position was to alienate Reynaud irrevocably and to set most of the other officers on the side of the First Lieutenant, against their Captain. The command structure of the *Medusa* was riven even before the squadron left France. But this fact did not become apparent to everyone on board, as a daily drama, until several weeks had passed.

The passengers were still settling down to their unaccustomed life. After a disturbed first night in a rough sea, which seemed to them a howling, dangerous storm, their nerves received another shock at ten o'clock the next morning. An appalling cry rang out from the upper deck, followed by the rush and thud of madly stampeding feet overhead. Charlotte Picard ran up on deck to find the whole crew in motion. They were scrambling up the rigging, pouring into the tops and inching out along the yards. Some began to bellow in unison as various teams pulled at various ropes, while others swore or whistled, the officers of the deck roared out above and below and the helmsman roared back. Charlotte detected some actual words although she could not recall their exact order. But Starboard! Larboard! Hoist! Luff! Tack! were among them.

The yards turned, creaking in their pivots, the sails were reset and the ropes tightened, then the raw crew came rushing down on deck faster than they had ascended. The motion of the vessel was now much easier and the noise of wind and sea less violent. The frigate had changed course and the canvas had been trimmed, to follow a shift in the direction of the wind. That was all.

Within a week the *Medusa* was clear of the Bay of Biscay and passing Cape Finisterre on the north-west coast of Spain. But only the *Echo* was with her, white with canvas in the attempt to keep up. The clumsy *Loire* and the little *Argus* were out of sight, left clean behind although the *Medusa* was not carrying her topsails or studding sails. Even so she was making nine knots, or more than 200 miles a day. De Chaumareys was not waiting for the remainder of his squadron. Bows slicing the water, the frigate raced on among a school of porpoises which plunged and surfaced in their play, the grey-blue bodies diving in succession with effortless precision to reappear a minute later still in formation.

Charlotte Picard was by now enjoying sea travel almost as much as she loved journeys by land. But she did not describe, perhaps did not witness, the first tragedy of the voyage. Passengers and crew alike had crowded to the poop, the bulwarks and the ports to watch the dolphins, shouting with excitement and pleasure. Amid the hubbub the cry of distress went largely unheard. A fifteen-year-old sailor lad, leaning too far out of a port to watch the shining display, had fallen overboard and was now clinging to a rope, buffetted by the foaming torrent of the wash, spray silvering his head. For a few moments he hung on, then was plucked from his hold and swept astern into the bubbling wake.

If there had been three ships astern of the *Medusa*, keeping close station, his chances of being picked up would have been better. But only the *Echo* was in sight, far off. A flag signal was run up to the *Medusa*'s masthead and a gun was ordered to be fired to draw the distant corvette's attention. Then it was found that none of the frigate's fourteen guns were loaded. However, the large marker buoy was ready and this was pushed overboard. About a yard (one metre) across, it was topped by a small mast and flag. It would be much easier for the searchers to locate than the head of a swimmer.

De Chaumareys did not stop his ship by immediately coming up into the wind but had the sails laboriously clewed up. Then he launched a rescue boat. Although intended to be rowed by six men, only three were ordered into it. The strong breeze tended to drive it sideways and as a rescue attempt it was hopeless. Both the frigate and her boat drifted to leeward

with the wind for such a distance that not even the
buoy was sighted again, let alone the seaman, who
had been swimming strongly when lost to view in the
wake. When the *Echo* at last caught up with the *Medusa* she reported that her lookouts had not seen anything either. De Vénancourt had lost a man overboard
from the *Echo* the previous day, but he was a non-
swimmer so almost any measures would have been
too late.

All the *Medusa*'s logs and charts were to be conve-
niently "lost" later on, so all occurrences on board
were subject to the vagaries of individual memory.
This particular incident was recorded in the joint narrative of two survivors, who became friends. They
were J. B. Henry Savigny, junior surgeon of the frigate, and Alexander Corréard, a geographical engineer
in charge of a party of twenty workmen intended for
exploration work in the interior of the colony. They
were careful to check technical points with some of
the surviving naval officers and the detail they give
here is probably based on that. It shows a lack of
preparation and precision in an emergency which is
not entirely unexpected in a ship which is still in the
"working-up" stage, particularly if the officers are fighting among themselves instead of getting down to the
main task.

Leaving a fifteen-year-old boy still swimming somewhere in the middle of the ocean, de Chaumareys
hoisted sail and the *Medusa* again began to draw
ahead. It seems that he was anxious to make his next
landfall at the islands of Madeira off the coast of Africa and would not wait for his squadron, although
there was a navigational hazard ahead, a cluster of
rocks about five leagues in extent, which would have
to be passed in darkness. His instructions from the
Ministry were quite precise on this point. All ships
were to keep together and not to separate. But if for
any reason they did become separated, de Chaumareys was to indicate rallying points where they would
meet. Contrary to what he had decided (under pres-

sure from Schmaltz) while still off Rochefort, de
Chaumareys did initially order this normal procedure
to be carried out. But then, seeing its difficulty and
the delays which resulted, he changed his mind again
(or had it changed for him) and charged on regardless
in the *Medusa*. Neither Savigny nor Corréard knew of
these instructions in fact, but they correctly assumed
their existence because there was no point in forming
a squadron unless the ships were to keep in company.
They did not know of the hesitations and vacillations
to which de Chaumareys was subject (although their
officer advisers did) and assumed a thoughtless and
headlong rush to destruction on the part of an incom-
petent captain.

The situation next morning certainly reinforced that
view. Madeira should have been in sight already but
there was no sign of the islands, only empty sea. When
the approximate position of the ship was calculated
by observation of the sun at midday it indicated that
the frigate was thirty leagues to one side of her intended track. That is, someone had made a small error
of ninety miles not along a given line, but off it. Some
thought this was conservative and that the real error
was larger; in excess of one hundred miles. Therefore,
the *Medusa* had to make an embarrassingly large turn
to bring her bows onto the right heading, or what was
thought to be the right heading, because it was assumed that the Gibraltar current had been the main
factor in off-setting the ship and possibly it was still
affecting her. In any event, there must have been some
very red faces aft on the quarter-deck that morning.

It was not until sunset that the masthead lookout
sighted land on the far horizon. That meant that the
navigational error amounted in terms of time to the
best part of a good day's sailing. It should have been
a sobering thought for anyone contemplating a run
down the coast of Africa towards a vast and poorly
charted hazard. Possibly it was this which pushed the
hesitant de Chaumareys towards his final, desperate
decision. He reached out to clutch at a straw.

On the morning of June 28, as the *Medusa* neared
Madeira, the development of the situation was clear
even to the passengers. De Chaumareys and Richefort
were happily paired. While de Chaumareys had last
sailed as a Lieutenant twenty-five years before and
was really a Customs Officer, M. Richefort was fresh
from an English prison, where he had spent the last
ten years. He could speak at great length of his pro-
found knowledge of the waters off the coasts of Africa
but even assuming that he was not indulging in a little
compensatory self-importance, ten prison years in wartime must have taken their toll. It is known that he
was a member of an organisation of international busy-
bodies, called the Philanthropic Society of Cape
Verde, which was engaged in an ill-fated attempt to
colonise the interior. There is also a note to suggest
that he was intended to serve as a Port Captain; that
is, as a harbour master. One of the worst boats aboard
the frigate had been shipped expressly for the use of
the port, an eloquent testimony to its importance, for
what little trade it did was in slaves.

Having previously declared his intention to put in
to the town of Funchal in Madeira for a boatload of
supplies, de Chaumareys turned to M. Richefort as
the man with local knowledge for advice as to how to
enter the bay. Richefort bloomed like a shrivelled
flower upon which the soft rain has suddenly fallen;
and from that moment began to take over the command of the *Medusa*.

Not even the decision to call at Funchal was really
made by the Captain, for the *Medusa* was not short
of supplies. The decision was made by Governor
Schmaltz, or Mrs. Schmaltz or Miss Schmaltz. All urgency to arrive quickly at Senegal vanished if it was
a question of satisfying their whims for fresh fruit or
other delicacies.

With the wind behind her the frigate was making
nine knots as she ran along the coast of the island,
close enough for the passengers to take in the comfortable air of the place, with its tended vineyards and

groves of orange and lemon trees. The strength of the wind was due in part to its flowing round the 600-feet high hills of the island but as soon as the *Medusa* tried to enter the bay of Funchal she entered an area of calm where the breeze was blanketed by the hills. The frigate's sails ceased to belly in the wind and her bow-wave dropped away to a gentle ripple; but she did not stop moving. Caught by a current which was setting onshore, the *Medusa* was no longer under control; not even the most knowing asides by M. Richefort could remedy matters. After three hours spent drifting outside the entrance to Funchal bay, the responsible officers took advantage of a faint breeze to move further out to sea and, de Chaumareys declaring that he would not now bother to send in a boat, they at last entered the area of the offshore wind and were soon speeding away again at eight knots.

It was still possible, as the officers advised, for de Chaumareys to escape his fate by sailing far out to the west, but the Captain had put his trust in the certainties of M. Richefort. Also, there were the whims of the family Schmaltz to be considered. So their next landfall was to be the Canary Islands, another unnecessary hazard at night or in poor visibility. However, so clear was the air that the great peak which crowns Teneriffe was visible on the horizon next morning although it took them until sunset to close the island. In that red light the summit of the volcanic mass, rising more than 10,000 feet from the sea, seemed to be crowned with fire.

They stood off during the night and in the morning followed the coastline towards the port of St. Croix at a distance of a few hundred yards. The black sterile rocks, gigantic in size and piled in fantastic confusion, rose steeply out of the sea and the more nervous passengers began to imagine that any stirring of the volcano would bring down the very mountain upon them. But the summit was quiet that morning and it was plain that the old travellers' tales of a crater continually pouring forth lava of molten metal into a surrounding field of snow could not be entirely true.

It was the sight of a small fort, the mouths of cannon still pointing from its embrasures, which raised most emotion. One passenger was literally leaping for joy as he recognised it and remembered.

"We raised it in haste," he cried. "Just a few of us! That was when the English under Admiral Nelson attempted to take possession of the Colony. It was there, just there, that a great fleet, commanded by one of the bravest admirals of the English navy, failed before a mere handful of French! They covered themselves with glory. They saved Teneriffe. We made Admiral Nelson take flight, and it was there he lost an arm!* Oh, yes, the conflict was long and obstinate, my friends!"

This was delicate ground indeed, recalling not merely the military glories of the recent past and the hatreds bred by more than twenty years of war against the hereditary foe; it was also a reminder that the captain, de Chaumareys, had fought for a time on the other side, had actually landed in France from English ships. It must have sounded ill in the ears of his new friend, M. Richefort, whose ten years as an English prisoner did not constitute a conqueror's record.

The *Medusa* put into the bay opposite St. Croix and sent a boat ashore to get wine, fruit and fresh vegetables for the family Schmaltz. Richefort stepped forward, saying darkly that it was very dangerous for the ship to remain where she was. Purpling with importance, he added that he was well acquainted with these

---

*Nelson was shot down on the shore at St. Croix by Spanish troops, among whom were a few French. His "great fleet" consisted of four battleships, three frigates and a cutter; they carried no soldiers, only seamen and marines. The attack was Nelson's own idea and he proved to be a very poor hand at managing amphibious operations, which require more skill than simple land or sea battles. The basic causes of the defeat were the wind and current factors, which were the same as those which had baffled the *Medusa* off Funchal.

rocky islands, indeed he had navigated in all these latitudes. The resentment of the ship's officers came to the boil and they protested to de Chaumareys, saying that it was shameful of him to put such confidence in a stranger and to ignore the advice of his own officers. They would not obey Richefort; he had no worth as a commander. The tense, raised voices were the first indication Charlotte Picard had of the unpleasant situation which had arisen. She distinctly heard the captain refer to Richefort as "a good and able seaman." The words stuck in her memory.

De Chaumareys, in turn inflamed at the threat to his authority, ordered all the officers and crew to obey Richefort as pilot; and to do it because he, the captain, said so. He was king in this ship, since it was the orders of the King that they should obey him.

Nothing could hold Richefort after that. The vain but amiable man suddenly began to imitate a holy terror, to bluster and to shout, volleying a string of orders; putting the frigate first on one tack, then on the other; then charging the reefs, then going about. All to demonstrate his mastery of the ship and of them, while the sailors snarled aloud that the old fool was a vile imposter. At length, beaming with satisfaction and declaring that he had saved the *Medusa* from certain shipwreck, Richefort assured de Chaumareys that he had often been employed to explore the shores of Africa and none knew better than he how to avoid the perils of the Arguin Bank which was now only a few days' sail away.

Now it may be that Charlotte Picard, whose account this is, was confusing the arrival at Funchal with the arrival at St. Croix; but her narrative reads at certain points as though it has been constructed on a diary. In any event, she has correctly and vividly depicted the situation which by this time had arisen among the officers.

During the day the *Echo* came into the anchorage, having caught up once more, and in the late afternoon Savigny and Corréard recalled that the *Medusa*'s boat returned from shore and that there was tension among the officers who had gone in it to buy fruit for the family Schmaltz and to post their own letters. The Canaries were Spanish and when Spain had changed sides the French soldiers there had become prisoners. Now they were free to go home they had pleaded to be allowed on board the *Medusa,* which would be returning to France after she had carried out her mission to Senegal. This had been refused by one of the officers, although another had pleaded the case of the ex-POWs. The harsh decision was a fortunate one for the men concerned.

Another tidbit for shipboard gossip was the reportedly depraved morals of the Spanish women of St. Croix. No sooner had they learned that some Frenchmen had landed from the frigate, than they stood in their doorways and made inviting gestures. And this in spite of the fact that in many cases their husbands were at home. Nor was this all. The husbands were actually forbidden to show their jealousy by the Holy Inquisition. It was shocking, but it seemed that the local monks had told the husbands that their feelings were mere "conjugal mania" sent by Satan to torment them and that only offerings to the Church could deliver them from it.

The French whispered among themselves that abuses were of course inevitable in such a burning climate, where passion was often bound to be stronger than reason. Others, of the anti-clerical party, took the view that these abuses were typical of the actual effects of a religion claiming to be sublime. Thus the gossip as reported by Savigny and Corréard. One of the officers who actually went ashore, Midshipman Charles Alexandre Léonard Rang, saw the Palace of the Inquisition and made some biting comments concerning the effect of superstition on the human mind. This was yet another division in France which was reflected in miniature aboard the *Medusa* and had more to do with the Revolution than the Reformation.

Already, as the *Medusa* and the *Echo* slipped away

from Teneriffe and left the chain of islands behind, the hot winds off the coast of Africa could be felt and at noon the sun was not in the southern arc of the sky but blazed down from directly overhead. On the last two nights of June the frigate twice caught fire between decks, both times in the kitchen where the master baker had been at work; neither fire proved serious, being discovered before it could spread from the brick-lined area of the oven. On the first day of July Cape Bojador was in sight and the edges of the Sahara, a wilderness of great sand dunes shimmering white in the heat. The ladies aboard, including the wife and grown-up daughter of the Governor, as well as M. Picard's eldest daughters, who had struck up a friendship with them, thrilled at the sight. This was the legendary and romantic great sand sea stretching right across the Dark Continent from west to east, the abode of lions and all sorts of strange wild beasts, peopled only by Moors accustomed to the fierce heat. Had these ladies been told that some of them were shortly going to have to walk across that desert or die, they would have been astonished.

At ten o'clock that morning the ceremony of "crossing the line" into the tropics was performed, some of the passengers remarking sourly that the sole nautical purpose of it was to procure the sailors some money. But the crude slapstick was amusing at first and the appearance of high ceremonial was well carried off, with de Chaumareys in great good humour, quite the old sailor, presiding over the baptism of the neophytes. Charlotte Picard much enjoyed it. Meanwhile M. Richefort strode the deck and guided the vessel as calmly as if the surrounding sea had been the Bay of the Seine instead of the Gulf of St. Cyprian.

This part of the coasting route to Senegal was certainly not recommended by the Ministry of Marine and was notorious locally as being almost impassable at low water except for small craft because of the numerous reefs. There was no reason to approach such a dangerous and inhospitable coast at all, but a voyage far out from land would be uneventful and give no indication of the skill of the navigator. With an almost theatrical indifference M. Richefort gazed at the waves breaking on the black fangs of the higher rocks already exposed by the falling tide and with equal disdain at the ominous swellings of the sea over still-hidden obstructions, at the current running inshore and at the distinct change in the colour of the water itself, which was no longer clean and clear and deep blue.

For most of the passage the frigate had been sailing in blue ocean water a thousand fathoms deep or more and even after leaving the Canaries and unwisely heading in towards the coast of Africa had always had at least a hundred fathoms under the keel. The sudden change from deep, clear water to the sediment-filled shallows was obvious to crew and passengers alike. The officer of the watch, knowing that a submerged reef extended one and a half leagues out to sea from the next headland, took emergency action. The frigate tacked away just in time to clear the danger. De Chaumareys got into a rage and reprimanded him for acting without orders, but it seems that the Captain and his crony had mistaken a dangerous cape which juts out into the middle of the Gulf of St. Cyprian for Cape Barbas, the headland which marks the end of the gulf. Recognition sketches of such landmarks, as seen from various angles to seaward, are part of a navigator's equipment.

The last great shoremark before the Arguin Bank was the long, southward-stretching promontory of Cape Blanco (the White Cape). De Chaumareys had declared his intention of sighting and then positively identifying this distinctive headland. It was to be his final "fix" before turning out to sea to steer a "dog-leg" round the Arguin Bank, which lay a short distance south of Cape Blanco and extended a great distance out into the Atlantic. His instructions were to turn on to WSW. and make good that track for a minimum distance of twenty-two leagues. Then he

should be safely past the bank and could turn onto
SE. for a direct run to Saint Louis. Providing no onshore gale was encountered, this was not too risky; if
correctly carried out, the procedure would nullify any
position error on the charts. If the ship was by direct
observation say, five miles due west of the actual cape,
then it did not matter in the slightest where that headland was located on a piece of paper. The notorious
bank must be to the south and a track from that point
of WSW., if continued for a sufficient distance, would
take the vessel clear of the hazard.

It was an enormous, uncharted area of shallow
banks and weeded gulleys, of warm water and bright
light, both a haven and a feeding ground for multi-
tudes of fish. It was reputed to stretch thirty leagues
out into the Atlantic and to have an uncertain but
steep slope. It had not been surveyed then, and it
has not been surveyed now; it was known only to the
fishermen who went there in small boats at certain
seasons of the year. For a ship it was deadly. She
would be bound to strike many miles out from shore
and that shore would be almost uninhabitable desert
known then only to the natives, for the nearest small
European settlements were hundreds of miles distant.

All day the *Medusa* and the *Echo* coasted southward along the African shore. De Chaumareys repeatedly told his officers that he had a mind to anchor a
cable's length from Cape Blanco, because the Minister
had ordered him to make certain of its position. The
southern extremity of the cape was distinctive, resem-
bling rather a ship with a ram bow, like a Roman
galley or a modern oil tanker, when seen from due
west. However, a cable's length is one-tenth of a nautical mile or some six hundred feet. According to the
modern charts (French and Spanish 1942–1950) this
would bring the frigate in among a maze of shoals and
currents to an area where the low water depth varies
between six and sixteen feet. The *Medusa* probably
drew about twelve feet, but that is not the measure
of the matter. The depths given on charts are correct

only for flat calm; they take no account of the crests and troughs of waves, which increase and decrease the depth alternately according to their height. Apart from that, the motion of a ship in very shallow water is affected by the interaction between the seabed and the water displaced by the hull immediately above it.

Given their inshore route, to anchor off the cape was a good idea; not only would this provide an accurate "fix" but if they were prepared to wait until noon next day, there would be the positive value to themselves and others of taking observations to establish more accurately the real position of this headland. But the distance of six hundred feet is astounding, particularly in view of the contemporary lack of knowledge of the area and that the vessel was powered only by whatever wind happened to blow.

However, this was the pattern of the navigation since the moment M. Richefort took over off Madeira. Risks were taken for no good reason, starting there. Even the sending in of a boat at Teneriffe, happily without incident, was an example. De Vénancourt of the *Echo* noted in his log: "A stiff breeze was blowing and I did not find it suitable for sending anyone ashore." The place was notorious; indeed, most of Nelson's boats had been smashed or come to grief in the surf during the British landings. Then there had been the pointless risking of the reefs in the Gulf of St. Cyprian, possibly fatal if the wind had dropped or changed direction. And now this.

In wartime, such chances may have to be taken, the risks weighed and accepted. But there was no emergency in any of these cases, nor does one have the impression that the hazards were recognised let alone calculated. It was rather as if Richefort was playing with a toy boat in the bath in a series of fits of boyish inconsequence.

An even more incredible occurrence followed. By evening, there was still no sign of Cape Blanco and notwithstanding what de Chaumareys had been saying all day, the course was altered out to sea, onto WSW.

An officer quoted by Savigny and Corréard wrote: "He continually repeated that the Minister had ordered him to make Cape Blanco; he talked of it till the evening, but on going to bed he thought no more about it." Perhaps de Chaumareys had become inwardly unnerved by the nightmare of the Arguin Bank looming somewhere dead ahead and on impulse shied away from it; away too from any chance to get an accurate "fix" before turning onto the first course of the "dogleg" designed to take the frigate round the bank at a safe distance. Perhaps he merely gave in to the hostility of his officers towards him, a hostility which now increased perceptibly in step with the rapidly closing distance between the frigate and the obstacle in her path.

As darkness fell on 1st of July the *Echo* was still keeping company with the *Medusa* and both ships were headed west-south-west. That is, angling slightly to the south of due west, going away from the coast of Africa very nearly at a right-angle. This was the recommended course but de Vénancourt was clearly not happy about their general situation and began to signal to de Chaumareys. Henry Savigny, the junior surgeon of the *Medusa,* was pacing the deck at the time and saw the corvette start signalling. She burst several charges of powder and hung a lanthorn at her mizen-mast. The only acknowledgement given by the frigate was to hang a lanthorn from the foremast, where it gleamed for only a minute or two before going out. It was not replaced and Reynaud, the officer on duty, did not bother to inform de Chaumareys. Savigny suggests that Reynaud knew well enough that de Chaumareys intended a fast passage and every time the *Medusa* had out-run the *Echo* and put her down the horizon, had rejoiced at the fact. So why wake him now?

At eleven o'clock the *Echo* was ahead and to the left of the *Medusa*. But her signals being unanswered, Savigny saw her silhouette alter. She was steering an intersecting course with the frigate and was about to pass her bows. She merged for a minute or so with the bowsprit and then Savigny saw her clearly off to the right, on the other side of the *Medusa,* and steering further away from the presumed position of the Arguin Bank.

In his log, de Vénancourt wrote: "No answer was had from the frigate nor was a signal given by her regarding the night course. Therefore I continued to steer west-south-west, which had been her route up to now, and a wise one, as it would take us safely clear of the Arguin Bank which spreads in a south-westerly direction from Cape Blanco and for a very great distance out from the land." He also noted that the Bank was actually situated much more to the west than was shown on the chart and that the *Medusa* had deflected from the safe course of WSW.

Conceivably, de Vénancourt may have meant that and nothing more. Or, he may have meant merely that the winds and African current would drive both ships sideways towards the bank, so that a compass course of WSW. would not in fact mean that the track of the ships was WSW., but pointed more to the south, into the danger zone. Just possibly, he may have known of the unholy trio in triple command of the frigate— Governor Schmaltz nagging for more speed, Captain de Chaumareys making decisions and failing to see them carried out, M. Richefort radiating glib self-confidence; opposed by almost all the officers, led by Reynaud, the second-in-command. The sane course, considering the known hazards to the south-west, the vagueness and inaccuracy with which the charts depicted them, the pointless risks taken by the frigate for the past week, was to use the cover of night to part company with the suicide and get well clear of the danger zone. In any event, in the morning the *Echo* was no longer with them, not even as a speck on the horizon.

During the night the *Medusa* had sounded every half hour while still on the move and had stopped every two hours to obtain a more accurate measurement. Each time the sounding line showed shallow

water and so the course was continually altered a little
more out to sea and towards safety, in the general
direction which the *Echo* must have taken, long ago.
The other two ships of the squadron, the *Loire* and
the *Argus,* had of course been lost sight of many days
before. They were well to seaward, taking the safe
route which did not approach the African coast at all
until opposite St. Louis in Senegal. De Chaumareys
and his frigate were now quite alone.

The captain came up on deck at about five or six
o'clock on the morning of 2nd of July and asked a
remarkable question: had Cape Blanco been seen yet?
Someone said that the White Cape had been sighted
the previous evening and most of the officers wanted
de Chaumareys to believe this. Otherwise, he might
turn due south directly onto the Arguin Bank in an
endeavour to find Cape Blanco. Several officers
pointed to a distant white shape over on the African
coast behind them and said it was Cape Blanco, still
in sight.

One of the passengers then on deck knew better.
This was Alexander Corréard, a geographical engineer
who had been born in the Alps and knew the difference between a mountain covered in snow and a distant cloud, gleaming in the sun. He told the officers,
privately, that what they were looking at was only a
cape of vapour. They laughed and agreed. But its position was not too far off that of the real Cape Blanco
and as they were probably ten leagues or so on the
wrong side of it already, the most urgent question of
the hour was to get their captain to believe that if he
stood away from the shores of Africa he would be
obeying strictly those instructions which he said he
had had from the Ministry.

De Chaumareys wanted to believe and was easily
convinced, which was success of a sort. Unfortunately,
this meant that the final "fix" for the first leg of the
seaward zig-zag, as officially calculated, consisted of a
movable cloud rather than a cape of rock. Even so,
the frigate was not yet wrecked. The weather was kind

and the wind not unfavourable. By steering well out
to the sea for a longer distance than that recommended by the Ministry, by leaving a wide margin for
error to the south, and by sounding carefully, the frigate should be able to skirt the bank.*

By six o'clock that morning they had escaped from
the shallows and were obtaining soundings of one hundred fathoms.† That is, they were over the lower part
of the Continental Shelf of Africa, where the seabed
rises steeply towards the land on the east and on the
west slopes steeply down to the abyss. On learning
that there was now more than five hundred feet of
water under the *Medusa* Richefort made the grand
and knowing gesture of altering course to south-south-
east. This was an alteration of nearly a right-angle
from their previous course of WSW. The course was
right but the timing was wrong. This was the second
stroke of the "dogleg" which should, if made at the
right moment from the right position, have led the
frigate directly to St. Louis. Made far, far too early, it
could have only one result. From barely standing clear
of danger they were now heading right into it and,
regardless of where Cape Blanco really was, they were
bound to hit the coast well north of St. Louis exactly
in the area of the notorious shallows of Arguin. If
they did not strike sooner, they would strike later.
There was no avoiding it.

Speculation is probably pointless. Momentary mental aberrations affect most of us at some time or another, when we are tired or distracted or upset or just

*On modern charts a course of WSW. from Cape Blanco gives a
series of soundings, showing the steep slope to safety: fifty to two
hundred fathoms, then seven hundred to eight hundred fathoms, finally
1,200 to 1,700 fathoms (more than 10,000 feet), with a few submerged
peaks coming up to seventeen and eighteen fathoms from generally
much greater depths. These are English fathoms of six English feet.

†French fathoms ("brasses") of five French feet, equalling just
under five feet four inches English. None of these measurements would
be at all exact, because a fathom is really just a rough and ready
way of measuring lengths of rope by using the outstretched arms.

digesting. When made by Admirals or Captains they have not infrequently resulted in terrible disaster.* A tidy mind would try to find a logical cause for so large an error and seek to identify the flaw in the navigator's reasoning. The only cause which suggests itself is the Bellin chart. The frigate, observably, had not covered anything like a sufficient distance to round the Arguin Bank, regardless of whether it extended twenty leagues or thirty leagues offshore. They were turning much too soon. But if at the back of some cloudy mind there was an idea that the western extremity of the bank lay at such-and-such a position, and that the ship from yesterday's sun sights was actually at a position almost clear of the (false) chart position for the bank, then that mind, suppressing the vital factor of the distance which must actually be run out from the actual coast to round the actual bank, might have momentarily slipped into a false conclusion. Even so, ordinary caution would advise waiting until noon before changing course, so that a sun "fix" could be obtained, for the real position of the frigate was as cloudy as the cape which was supposed to have been sighted. As it was now about ten in the morning, with only two hours until noon, the delay would not be considerable. But still Richefort ordered the course changed.

At once there were angry scenes, centred around M. Richefort. An officer who called him an imposter was put under arrest by the captain, whose faith in his good friend was utterly unshaken. They were safe enough, declared de Chaumareys, as Cape Blanco had been passed the previous evening and the good Riche-

---

*e.g. Admiral Sir George Tyron, Commander-in-Chief of the British Mediterranean Fleet in 1893. He formed his ships into two divisions six cables apart, then ordered them to reverse course by turning towards each other. Although warned the distance was insufficient to allow for the known turning circles of the ships and that a collision must result, he insisted on the order being carried out. The collision duly occurred, his flagship was sunk, and he went down with it.

fort knew what he was doing. When someone questioned the accuracy of the White Cape's sighting, de Chaumareys flushed up and denied furiously that any doubt was possible. Voices called for a return to the westerly course, but Richefort was unmoved; like a wise and patient father surrounded by silly children he seemed only amused.

After three of the more experienced officers—Lieutenants Reynaud and Espiaux and Ensign Maudet—had vehemently put forward the wisdom of a westerly course, and been brushed aside in the most infuriating manner, M. Picard had had enough. It was not merely his own life which was at stake, but those of his wife, his teenage daughters and the four younger children, two of them little more than helpless babies.

He advanced on Richefort, the French family man aroused, and told him that they were about to strike on the Arguin Bank. And raising his voice over the man's deprecating tones, said that he at least *did* know the Arguin Bank. He had twice been past it during a previous visit to Senegal and had once been aground on it, eight years ago, from the captain having stood in too close. But Richefort merely smiled.

"My dear sir," he said. "We know our business. Attend to yours, and be quiet. I have already twice passed the Arguin Bank; I have sailed upon the Red Sea, and you see I am not drowned."

The fatuousness of the man was more effective than any righteous rage. The protests were stilled. M. Picard went below and flung himself on his bunk, exhausted with fury.

Ensign Maudet, the officer of the watch, repeatedly ordered soundings to be taken at ever shorter intervals. The sailors cried out with delight, for the fishing lines which were hung over the side in the faint hope of a catch all of a sudden became alive. Fish after fish was hauled in, all of the cod species. The officers gloomily noted the dulling colour of the water, the masses of floating river grasses typical of the Senegal and Gambia rivers and the occasional whiplike length of *Zostera,* a seaweed which flourishes in coastal shallows. Even Midshipman Rang, who knew nothing of the African coast, had only to listen to the talk around him to become alarmed. He wrote: "The usual remarks from the seamen made us believe that, if we were not yet on the Arguin Bank, we certainly were on its abrupt slope." It was now about halfpast eleven.

After the noon sight had been taken, Charlotte Picard saw Ensign Maudet sitting on a chicken coop, which he was using as a table for working out the ship's position from this up-to-the-minute and more accurate evidence. It seemed to her that he appeared melancholy. Then the officer got up and formally reported to the "good and able seaman" Richefort, who still had no official standing whatever in the *Medusa,* except the all-important favour of her captain, that the frigate was on the edge of the Arguin Bank.

"Never mind!" beamed the navigator. "We are in eighty fathoms."

De Chaumareys nodded his approval, in spite of the lessening depth, from one hundred to eighty fathoms. "No cause for alarm," he told the officer of the watch. Then raising his voice so that all nearby could hear it, he repeated, "No cause for alarm!"

The *Medusa* was in fact seaward of the bank and closing it, not directly but at an angle, so that there was still time to turn away into deepening water. Until three in the afternoon the frigate coasted along, with a steadily rising wind and steadily flooding tide tending to drift her even further in towards the shallows. The ladies, until now bewildered by the mysterious male technicalities of rough seamanship, had hardly known what to believe. Now, even they remarked aloud upon the noticeable change in the colour of the sea and could guess what it meant.

A kind of stupor pervaded everyone on deck, except the captain and his appointed navigator. All eyes but theirs were gazing in melancholy and resigned fashion at the water just alongside. Then a cry of horror went up from them all, together. Just under the surface, rolling in the waves, they could make out tiny specks of sand.

Maudet ordered another sounding to be taken, and instantly reported the result to the captain.

"Eighteen fathoms!"

Early in the morning 533 feet. At noon 426 feet. And now, 96 feet.

De Chaumareys nodded imperturbably and ordered the ship to be put a little more towards the wind. That is, slightly away from the coast. At the moment of the order the frigate had the wind directly behind her and the studding sails set on the shoreward side. These sails were on booms extending beyond the normal reach of the yards and gave extra pulling power and speed. De Chaumareys now ordered them to be taken in. Everything was to be done in an orderly and seamanlike fashion.

The officer of the watch almost instantly ordered another sounding to be made. There was an anxious wait, not nearly so long as before.

"Six fathoms!"

Still uncertain whether or not he was dealing with an actual and unimaginable emergency, de Chaumareys hesitated. Then he ordered the ship to be hauled round as close to the wind as she would lie. It was now 3:13 p.m. on the 2nd of July, 1816, and that last sounding had shown thirty-two feet. There could be little more than fifteen to twenty feet of water below the keel.

Two minutes later, the *Medusa* gave a slight shudder. Sped on, bumped again. Came free and moved on through the water. Grounded a third time with a thump which resounded through the fabric of her timbers, began to shake and this time heeled over noticeably.

The sails still bellied out in the wind, the rudder was hard over, the waves still dashed at her side. But there was no longer any wake astern. Instead there were eddies and swirls of water around the bow, which spun ahead of the *Medusa* and steadily lengthened towards the shore. The frigate was not moving through the water, the water was moving past her.

Savigny and Corréard noticed a most extraordinary change come over familiar faces, so that they became hardly recognisable. For a moment, not a word was spoken. But one man's features seemed to shrink in, so that he seemed hideous with horror. Another face actually changed colour, becoming yellow and finally green as shock clutched his heart.

Gaspard Théodore Mollien, a young explorer on the Governor's staff, read on the faces of de Chaumareys and his staff "a silent fever . . . a great anxiety."

Almost everyone was trembling, though some tried to suppress it. The officers were still for a moment and then volleyed orders in voices high with agitation. The captain was totally deprived of speech and M. Richefort was the recipient of brutally direct insults and was very nearly assaulted. Some responsible officers were totally disoriented. M. Poinsignon, commanding some of the native troops, struck Charlotte Picard's sister Caroline a sharp blow, apparently under the impression that she was one of his recalcitrant soldiers.

While men who had known twenty years and more of war were profoundly affected by the grounding of the frigate, the wife and daughter of M. Schmaltz, Governor-designate of Senegal, appeared not to take in the event at all. They gazed across the heeling deck and at the frightened passengers from below pouring up the companion ladders with unconcerned placidity, as though these scenes could not possibly concern the family of so grand an official as a Governor and Commander-in-Chief. Someone would take care of it. Someone always had. Although up to now the worst that had been likely to happen to them was the wheel of a coach working loose.

3

STRANDED OFF THE SAHARA

Afternoon, July 2 to morning, July 5

SEEN from a distance the *Medusa* looked gaunt and strange. Her sails were down, her top gallant masts were down, her top masts had been lowered. Only truncated bare poles protruded from her deck, although her lower yards still spanned out over the water. The frigate's boats were out around her, the men heaving and struggling in the swell against a powerful current in their efforts to take out anchors and cables to a sufficient distance to be of use. It was the morning of July 3, the day after the ship had stranded.

The instant of striking had produced first a shocked silence and then uproar. It had woken M. Picard and catapulted him on deck where he had flayed de Chaumareys and Richefort with what his eldest daughter described as "a thousand reproaches." M. Richefort had very nearly been thrown to the sharks. Then, as it was realised gradually that the frigate was in fact not wrecked but merely aground, the tumult had died down. Two energetic officers had begun to have everything in sight which was movable thrown overboard, in order to lighten the ship and get her off. It may be that they knew that the stranding had occurred at the worst possible time of the worst possible period—on high water of spring tides. From now on, every high water would be a little lower than the last for nearly a week. The chance to refloat the *Medusa* was only fleeting.

But no sooner had these officers begun to organise correct and decisive action than they were forced to stop. De Chaumareys seemed reluctant to take any

desperately final measures which must eventually
prove his incompetence. He sanctioned only those
half-remedies which would not show on the inventory
of the *Medusa,* which would not indicate the near-
disaster to which he had brought the ship under his
command. And so the process of lowering the upper
masts and yards and then floating them alongside the
stranded hull was begun; but in half-hearted and hap-
hazard fashion. The sailors worked hard, but not
under any real direction; their efforts were not co-
ordinated. They paid little attention to the orders of
the officers in any case, for they had lost confidence
in the men set over them.

The following day, July 3, matters became worse.
Crew and passengers were milling about to little purpose. There were four distinct tasks to be undertaken.
Relays of men had to work at the pumps to lighten
the hull of water leaking in through strained seams;
seamen had to lower the masts and yards, swing them
overboard and secure them alongside, so as to relieve
the frigate of more unnecessary weight; large anchors
had to be swung out into boats and the boats had to
carry out the anchors to a distance and set them in
the ground; while other men had to labour at the capstans which would haul at these anchors so as to move
the lightened frigate. A good deal of organising skill
was needed for all these tasks to go smoothly, without
interfering with each other; and the taking out of the
anchors required in addition calm weather and slow
or slack water. The passengers took their turns with
the physically exhausting labour at the pumps and capstans to spare the seamen for the skilled tasks. But
almost all their hard work was wasted.

Being the period of the spring tides, the currents
were strong and the seas very rough. The tasks set the
boats' crews were hard to carry out and de Chaumareys was too easily satisfied. He had had a small anchor
taken astern the previous night but to a quite insufficient distance. As soon as the capstan began to turn,
it was the anchor which moved and not the ship. So

another heavier anchor had to be taken out and to a much greater distance in a very rough sea. This anchor proved to be too big for the boat and so it had to be floated out in tow of the boat and this meant fastening empty barrels to it as a means of flotation. After this long task had been completed the boat's crew laboured to take out the anchor to a very great distance where the water was still shallow; indeed they could go no further because the anchor itself grounded while the upper end was still above water, but in such an awkward position that neither of the flukes would bite. When the men put their weight to the capstan bars and the cable began to come dripping in, the *Medusa* did not move. All that happened was that the anchor came slithering back towards them through the soft sand and grey mud. All their efforts of the previous evening and all their labours this day had been to no purpose.

The efforts to lighten the ship showed a similar lack of thoroughness. The upper masts and yards and the booms were got down and secured alongside, so that they could be recovered, but the heavy main yards were left in place, spanning out over the water; this was a precaution against the unlikely possibility of the *Medusa* heeling right over. However, the log-like appearance of the lashed timbers floating alongside did suggest another use for them, in case the ship really was immovable, and it was M. Schmaltz the new governor of Senegal who suggested it.

Leaning on the main capstan and using the top of it as a desk he sketched out the plan of a raft which could be made by lashing together this collection of masts, yards and booms. Gathered around him were the captain and officers and some of the passengers. There were four hundred people on board the *Medusa* and only six boats. They were of varied types and some were in poor condition. They certainly could not take four hundred people simultaneously to the African coast. But, M. Schmaltz explained, a raft could be made from these timbers which would support two

hundred people, plus all the provisions for the entire
party, those in the boats and those on the raft. The
boats would tow the raft towards the shore in a regular convoy and be provisioned from it. Once ashore
weapons and ammunition would be handed out and
the whole party of more than four hundred persons
would march along the beach until they reached St.
Louis, their numbers being a deterrent against attack.

Others suggested a similar but less cumbersome
plan: simply to use the boats to ferry everyone ashore
in relays, plus provisions and weapons. However, the
captain and his close advisers decided against this sensible solution and in favour of the raft. Its construction
was ordered to be begun at once.

Neither plan was impractical although the details
had not been calculated, merely guessed at; but both
were defeatist. The best lifeboat is usually the ship
itself and this should not be abandoned except under
extreme circumstances. There was no lack of people
to point this out and to urge that the really decisive
measures usual in such circumstances should be taken.
There were on board fourteen twenty-four-pounder
guns each weighing several tons; to jettison these
would make a considerable difference. De Chaumareys shrank back in muddled horror from the suggestion. Throw the king's cannon overboard! He would
do no such thing! Charlotte Picard heard someone
mutter that the frigate also was the king's, which
would be sacrificed if the guns were not. Another
pointed out that the guns could be taken out to a
distance by the boats and would make admirable anchors for hauling the frigate off the bank.

Yet other voices urged that the bulk of the stores
be jettisoned, particularly the many barrels of flour
down in the hold. They protested that up to now the
officers had been merely playing with the problem,
lightening the frigate by a minute amount, twenty or
thirty centimetres at the most, a matter of a foot or less.
She would never come out of her bed that way. This
time it was M. Schmaltz the governor of Senegal who

squashed the suggestion with heavy-handed righteous-
ness. Did they not know, he declared, that the greatest
scarcity of flour prevailed in the European settlements
of the province? To do such a thing was unthinkable.

Surgeon Savigny pointed out that they did not necessarily have to lose all the flour if they put the barrels
in the water, for the moisture would form with it to
make a thick crust on the outside, preserving the bulk
of the contents. And if the barrels were all roped together, they could be recovered on board once the
frigate was afloat again. Grudgingly, it was agreed to
give this method a trial and some barrels were got
overboard; but the task of fastening them together
proved difficult and so the whole project of jettisoning
the heavy stores was abandoned. The guns also still
remained aboard.

That evening yet another anchor was taken to a
very considerable distance in spite of strong winds and
a heavy swell over the shallows. But when attempts
were made to work the capstan, still the frigate did
not move. Embarkation lists for the boats and the raft
were made out. One of those who found himself put
down for a boat was M. Bredif the mining engineer.
"Our mode of living, during all this time, was extremely singular," he wrote later in a private letter to
his sister. "We all worked either at the pump or at
the capstan. There was no fixed time for meals, we ate
just as we could snatch an opportunity. The greatest
confusion prevailed, the sailors already attempting to
plunder the passengers' luggage." All these exertions
took place in the heat of the tropics and in weather
which steadily grew worse and on tides which became
lower and lower and thus less favourable.

On July 4 some of the stores were got overboard,
a few barrels of flour and some barrels of powder;
some of the water casks were staved as well. But still
the guns and the bulk of the stores remained aboard.
The bulk of the effort this day was devoted to the
construction of the raft and the repair of the boats,
some of which were in poor condition. Just before

high water that evening the working parties began to labour at the capstans again, hauling in on a stern anchor designed to pull the frigate off and a side anchor near the bow which was intended to swing the ship so that she would be headed towards deeper water. After only a few minutes work the hull began to move, swinging slowly to the left.

Seeing success at last, the men worked with fury, full of hope. The first few slight tremors were succeeded by a definite swinging movement of the hull. The labourers redoubled their exertions. Reluctantly the bows of the *Medusa* veered round until she was headed into the open sea, held only at the stern and very nearly afloat even there. And at that point they had to stop, for they had hauled the ship round until she was almost over one of the anchors and the heavy sea and swell had prevented the boats from taking out a really long warp, right out into the open sea, which was what was needed now. Had it been possible to do that, the frigate would have come afloat that evening. She might still have come afloat, had she been lightened of her guns and stores even as late as this, the third day aground.

As it was, all that had happened was that the heavily-laden hull had been got out of the bed which it had dug for itself in the soft soil of the bank and moved about two hundred metres away, before the falling tide grounded her again. It was an omen that sent many people wild with joy, a token that another day or two of similar effort would see the frigate not only completely refloated but under sail once more. And indeed that might have come to pass, had nothing changed. But after dark the sky clouded over ominously and the wind began to howl in from seaward, driving great waves before it which began to beat the insecurely moored frigate further onto the bank. It was now too late to regret the wasted days and all the specious reasons for ineffective action.

There were plaintive and confused cries from the passengers who had been so joyful only a few hours before; so many sheep led in so many directions by uncertain shepherds, their despair held undertones of rage and suspicion. Others for the first time felt real fear, certain at last that the frigate was doomed and that her frames would split and her planks open at any moment. But the *Medusa* had been soundly built. She lasted intact until halfway through the night. Then in rapid succession came a series of blows which spelt catastrophe. The hull was breached and the water began to pour in; unheard on deck, it sounded like a torrent down below. Then the great keel snapped and the broken-backed frigate began to work horribly in the waves. The seas could now rage at the stern with greater effect and smash it up and down on the sand with shuddering concussion. The great mass of interlocked timbers which formed the rudder was driven up and out of its securing pintles and, held now only by the side chains, began to act as a giant ram, flailing against the stern with every sea that struck. In a few minutes the Captain's cabin was completely beaten in and the roaring breakers began to drive right into the ship itself.

Charlotte Picard, watching the mountains of water riding out of the black night and seeming to engulf the broken hulk of the *Medusa*, and fearing for the helpless children of her family, began to regret the spirit of adventure which had made them all eager to go out and see new lands and peoples. She would not miss Paris, she thought, but she vividly remembered the flowers she had picked in the field outside Rochefort before they embarked. Surely they had been mad to forsake France at all! What on earth could Senegal hold for them that would make the risks of a perilous ocean journey worthwhile? She began to pray. For her family, then for all the people aboard.

All work at the pumps was abandoned and a young sailor urged his comrades to take to the boats and at least save themselves. Some of the soldiers heard this and passed the word. They began to arm themselves and in a short time were in control of the deck, guarding every gangway and allowing no one up. They were determined that if the ship was to be lost the sailors would be lost with it, as well as the soldiers.

Down below, another passenger came up to M. Picard and asked if he and his family were ready to go. This was the first they had heard of it but they were soon convinced that a large part of the crew and some of the passengers were secretly preparing to leave immediately in the boats. The Governor, M. Schmaltz, went on deck to quell what he thought of as "mutiny" to find the soldiers in control above. He assured them that there was no intention of abandoning anybody. Everyone would depart in orderly fashion at dawn. He was told roughly that that had better be the case, because anyone who tried to leave the frigate in a hurry was going to be shot. The Governor descended, considerably chastened, certain coarse expressions having been used which left no doubt in any listener's mind that the Governor himself was regarded as the coward most likely to be fired upon. And as the news spread that the soldiers were guarding the deck against illicit escapes, certain other passengers seemed unaccountably confused and shamefaced.

In the midst of this mutual suspicion and anger came a tumult of shouting from above. The raft itself, supposedly destined to save two hundred people, had broken loose from the cable which fastened it to the frigate and was being driven off before the waves. But a boat was manned and, despite the difficult conditions, the raft was brought back and re-secured.

M. Schmaltz then called a council of all the officers and passengers and swore on the French flag that he would not abandon anyone. The boats would stay with the raft and tow it to shore, where they would all form up in a proper caravan and march as a body across the desert to St. Louis. That solemn declaration satisfied almost everyone, including the Picard family, and started a new train of thought. What should they take with them in the morning?

As the black seas broke over the dismasted, broken

and half-submerged hulk of the frigate, four hundred people reacted in all their individual ways, many of them ludicrous, all understandable. Some of them had all their wealth sunk in merchandise; without it they were penniless in a foreign land. But how to take it with them? Others had their fortunes in more portable form, in actual gold. These of course tried to secrete the heavy bullion in their clothing; in obvious places, such as the lining, or by sewing into the waistbands of their trousers. The sharp operators were in a rage: the contraband which they had so successfully smuggled through customs, and on which they had confidently looked to yield 200 or even 300 per cent profit, was in chests too bulky to move. There were even a few who fell into a wild and significant self-pity. In a destructive fury they hurled their money overboard, set fire to their belongings and laughing like maniacs surrendered to what tomorrow would bring. These were the happiest, when it was learned that no luggage of any kind could be taken.

The passengers who had been busily picking over their belongings in order to decide what to take with them were dismayed. The Picards would lose their trunks, their linen and their store of merchandise, but this seemed less important to them than the various manuscripts which M. Picard had been labouring on for a long time. They never thought to preserve part of their wardrobe by wearing two of everything and an officer who had opened his sea chest to offer clothing to anyone who wanted it had few takers.

The ship's boys had got at the officers' wines and liqueurs and were making merry of the best. Thieves were on the prowl, both in the cabins and the hold, for tempting personal possessions or stores, to be had for nothing. But the sailors and the soldiers generally, people who had nothing very much to begin with and no hope of being able to carry much with them, made for the spirit room. They broached the casks and lapped at the brandy like thirsty dogs. Some, more impatient, staved a cask in their hurry so that the spirits flowed out over the planks. Soon they were all roaring, reeking drunk; serious drunk, knitting their brows and mouthing oaths; friendly drunk, eventually collapsing hazily into a corner; aggressive and assertive drunk, reeling along the decks in search of bother. Charlotte Picard was to declare primly that "the tumult of the inebriated made us forget the roaring of the sea which threatened to engulf us." As the sky lightened with the dawn she heard piercing cries mixed with doleful groans. The frigate was being abandoned.

4

"WE ABANDON THEM!"

Morning, July 5

THERE was no shore in sight, the waves were steep, the means of escape fragile and insufficient. There was not room enough for all; some would be left behind. Those who went in a good boat might survive; those who took to the raft were probably doomed. A great unease swept the crowds of people on the heeled deck of the frigate. There existed lists meticulously detailing the place to be taken by every man, woman and child, but these were still kept secret—with good reason.

The raft would have seemed a godsend only to a lone swimmer who had all but spent his strength. Viewed from the waterlogged hulk of the *Medusa*, the construction was horrifying although on paper the dimensions might appear large. The outside timbers spanned a space some twenty metres long by seven metres wide, or roughly sixty feet by twenty feet. There was no form of flotation whatever, merely the negligible buoyancy of the topmasts, yards, fishes and booms of which it was framed, to which were lashed cross timbers and crudely nailed planks. The space was less than it seemed for at one end the affair had been sharply angled to form a kind of bow. This was weak, as was the flat "stern" of the craft. Only at the centre was the contraption at all strong.

The "bow" and "stern" were illusionary. Below the surface, the raft was simply an enormous sea-anchor, a drag in the water. A further critical defect was that solid timbers have little buoyancy and float low in any case. As a means of actual support for two hundred

49

people plus stores of food and fresh water for over four hundred, it was a cruel kind of joke. There were six boats in all. The best was a fourteen-oared barge appointed to take Governor Schmaltz, his family and their luggage in which only thirty-eight people embarked; as it had once carried seventy fully-armed and equipped soldiers, it was by no means overloaded on this occasion. Equally capable of an ocean journey was the captain's barge in which de Chaumareys intended to embark with one of his cronies and no less than twenty-six sailors chosen for their fitness at rowing; he could hardly avoid survival. Next was a fourteen-oared pinnace commanded by Ensign Lapeyrère in which the Picard family was supposed to embark; it appears to have carried forty-two persons. The largest but weakest craft was the longboat commanded by Lieutenant Jean Espiaux; the forty-five persons originally appointed to it included Captain Beiniére and his detachment of thirty-six soldiers. It had no oars at all, merely sails, and was therefore not so easy to manoeuvre; but because Lieutenant Espiaux would not abandon anyone left to die upon the frigate by the Captain and the Governor, eventually no less than eighty-eight persons were crammed into its thirty-foot length. Yet it was only a few feet longer than the 27½-foot boats of the Governor and Lapeyrère, both of which carried less than half that number. Ensign Maudet was given command of an eight-oared port boat intended for use in Senegal which had been damaged in collision with the raft the previous day and hastily repaired; even so, twenty-five people were taken off by it. Both this weak boat and the captain's excellent barge were twenty-four feet long. Finally, there was a small twenty-foot yawl which at one time had fifteen persons on board. The second-in-command, Lieutenant Reynaud, was appointed to command the barge which was to carry Schmaltz and his family to safety.

The small matter of who was to command the raft appeared to have been overlooked. The identity of this unfortunate individual was not at once announced because that would make too clear that the people

who had written out the lists appointing every officer
and man to his place had taken the best places for
themselves. It seems to have been by convenient design that the senior naval officer eventually to be discovered on board the crude raft turned out to be a
twenty-three-year-old midshipman, Jean Daniel Coudein, in great pain from a leg injury sustained earlier,
who also happened to be a Bonapartist not trusted by
de Chaumareys.

The fact that the raft sank completely below the
waves as soon as a mere fifty people had got onto it,
and that there seemed hardly any space for them to
stand let alone for any person to sit, was not helpful
for the injured officer who was to command it. Eventually, when an estimated 149 persons had got onto
the raft and it had sunk so much beneath the weight
that they were up to their waists in the sea, it was
grasped that the Governor's aim of embarking two
hundred men on it together with a mass of stores was
totally impractical.

The last man to get on it was an army officer, Lieutenant d'Anglas de Praviel, and he was most unwilling.
He recalled: "I was the 150th to get down. I did not
move. Then the captain, seeing me still standing on
deck, spoke abruptly:

'For heaven's sake, sir, do get down!'

'I would rather die on board the frigate, for then I
shall be able to choose my own way of dying,' I
replied."

This officer was not so brave as his words suggested
and at length he obeyed the order. "I tied myself to
the rope and with a tremendous effort succeeded in
getting down. But the raft was already crowded. All
the officers had occupied its centre, which was the
safest part of it, being less exposed to the waves. From
this privileged position, an impregnable fortress, they
were pushing back those who wanted to escape from
the edges of the raft. I got onto it, but in spite of my
assistance earlier, I found no better place than the last
planks of the raft, where the water covered half my

body and the waves went over my head. This bitter situation forced me to take a desperate resolution. I threw myself into the waves and struggled back to the frigate, with no hope of salvation but intending only to leave an undeserved position."

The officers had in fact grouped themselves in the centre, where they had better control of the struggling mass of humanity. At least two of them had no right to be on the raft at all, as they had been put down for a place in the boats. Surgeon Savigny did not record what his reason was but does say that his friend Corréard, the geographical engineer, felt it his duty to go because about ten men from his engineering detachment had been ordered on board and he felt that he could not separate his fate from theirs.

The bulk of the persons allocated to the raft consisted of soldiers, about 120 of them including officers. There was also a cantiniére, the wife of a sergeant. There was a small group of some ten sailors, so that the most unseaworthy craft of all was short-handed in the most important respect of all. Further, as those who built it were not to go with it, the construction lacked a mast to which a sail might have been attached. There were six wine casks and two water barrels, but no food, no tools, no water-tight chests for arms and ammunition; not even a compass and chart for consolation.

But this was true also of most of the boats. Barrels of wine, water and biscuit had indeed been brought up from the storerooms and placed on deck of the *Medusa,* ready for loading into the boats and the raft, but the embarkation took place in a rush and resounded with cries (from those in authority) of: "Every man for himself!" Consequently, casks were thrown over rather than lowered, and most fell into the sea. The movement of the broken-backed frigate in the waves, together with the marked heel of the deck down to the port side apparently convinced de Chaumareys that the *Medusa* was about to overset and that little time was left. As his command was where he had placed her, firmly aground and with her keel deeply buried in the mud and sand, this was a highly imaginative conception. Nevertheless, the fright he communicated was sufficient to produce a frenzy on the ladder down which people were scrambling to get into the boats as they came alongside and to urge others to throw ropes over the side and try to climb down that way. A number lost their hold and fell into the sea and were recovered; surprisingly, no bones were broken by those who arrived prematurely in the boats.

By about seven o'clock four of the boats had been loaded and were standing off. The Captain's barge was waiting ahead under the bowsprit, while the Governor's barge and the raft were still alongside. Men were still struggling for positions on the raft and in their desperation to find room knocked over or threw off some of the flour barrels which had now been added to its load; these, washing in the waves which swept the timbers to a depth of several feet, struck the tightly-grouped men feeling through the water under them for some insecure footing and with nothing to hold on to, for there were no rails or breastwork. They were so packed that it was almost impossible to move and Alexander Corréard roared out for the captain. De Chaumareys immediately came to the bulwarks above.

"Are we in a condition to depart?" he shouted. "Have we instruments and charts?"

"Yes, yes, I have provided you with everything you need," the captain called back.

"What naval officer is to come and command us?"

"It is I!" cried de Chaumareys. "In a moment I shall be with you."

He disappeared at once, heading in fact for his own barge lying ahead by the bow. This was soon joined by the fourteen-oared barge into which, quite unobtrusively, Madame and Mademoiselle Schmaltz had slipped together with three trunkfuls of luggage. The purpose of the move was to embark the Governor himself who, rather than climb daringly down a side-ladder, required to be lowered down in an armchair suspended by a rope from the overhanging bowsprit. Once the Commander-in-Chief was aboard, his barge was then rowed round the side to the raft and a towrope thrown out from its stern to the raft.

While this was being secured to the angled "bow" of the raft, two sails were at last thrown over from the *Medusa* to the unwieldy contraption; and then a bag of biscuit, which missed and hit the water but was got hold of with difficulty. The ropes which should have accompanied the sails were not thrown over. By now the first towrope, that linking the raft directly with the stern of the governor's barge, was firmly tied at both ends.

As the Governor's barge drew away, oars beating the water, two of the other boats came in and also passed towropes, not directly to the raft but to each other, so that a line of three boats laboured to move the raft slowly away from the broken, dismasted hulk of the once swift *Medusa*.

At this moment there were still about eighty people on board the frigate, including the numerous Picard family. It was then they realised that they were to be abandoned. Charlotte Picard had already wasted several minutes calling out to the officers in charge of various boats, and when the Governor's barge had come close alongside to take up the tow of the raft, she had tried to catch the eyes of his wife and daughter. These two ladies had promptly looked the other way. Charlotte had even made a motion to descend the side of the frigate above their boat, but they had ignored her. She had become very friendly with them during the last few weeks, but this friendship it seemed was as easily wrecked as the frigate.

Pleas to the captain were useless. Charlotte intercepted him on his way forward, but he told her that the Picard family positively would not be allowed into the Governor's barge; it would do no good to hail it. According to the embarkation list, the Picards had

been allotted places in the pinnace, but so secret was
the list that they were unaware of the fact. They did
however see the pinnace moving away from the frigate
rather lightly loaded, so they called out to the officer
in command, Ensign Lapeyrère, but he also chose not
to hear them.

A few minutes after they noticed a very small boat,
the twenty-foot yawl, clawing its way close to the hull
of the *Medusa*. As soon as it was near enough, M.
Picard shouted a cry for help. He asked the sailors
just to take himself and his family over to the pinnace,
so they could board it. It held only thirty-three people
at that moment and could embark the Picards with
ease. But the crew of the yawl refused to do even this
small service for the most helpless and vulnerable
group of all those stranded in the *Medusa*.

Public notary or not, so savage was the father's
anger that he snatched up a musket which had been
dropped on deck by one of the soldiers embarking in
the raft, levelled the barrel at the crew of the yawl
and swore to kill every one of them. Even then, his
legal background did not desert him entirely, for he
was at pains to point out that the yawl was the property of the king and that he was as much entitled
to have the use of it as they were. Muttering among
themselves, but convinced by one or the other of these
two arguments, the sailors reluctantly sheered in under
the side of the frigate.

The sullen, revengeful men threw overboard the few
personal possessions the Picards tried to bring with
them, including a small box of vital documents and
two bottles of wine. Everything the family really
needed would be found already in the pinnace, they
snarled.

Ready excuses met them when the yawl ran alongside the boat to which they had been assigned. They
did not believe a word of it, for it seemed to the
Picards that the arrival of such a large and ill-assorted
family as they were had proved as unwelcome to the
occupants of the pinnace as they had to the crew of

the yawl. Indeed, they were really two families, the grown-up daughters of M. Picard's first marriage who were able to shift for themselves, and the four very young children, one still at the breast of the young Madame Picard.

Exposure in an open and ill-provided boat to the burning sun and blazing heat of the tropics with such helpless creatures to protect and care for, should have seemed a terrifying prospect. On the contrary, at that moment the Picard family were very happy. Clearly, father's initiative on their behalf had been well timed. Had he not commandeered the yawl, they were certain that the gallant Sub-Lieutenant Lapeyrère would have sailed away without them.

M. Picard was jovial, too. He called out to the crew of the yawl, saying that he would be eternally grateful to them. Perhaps taking this for irony, the sailors replied with indistinct muttering and some open abuse. Raising his voice a little, as if in court, the notary turned to his family and explained gently:

"You can hardly blame these sailors for being without shame, when their officers blush at being forced to do a good deed."

The Sub-Lieutenant affected not to hear and busied himself with being charming to the ladies.

Meanwhile a theatrical comedy which at any time might have become a sordid tragedy had been enacted on the deck of the frigate. Lieutenant d'Anglas, lately of the *gardus-du-corps,* and even more lately of the raft, was the centre of it. We know, because he was to say so, that his feelings were tinged with spite. He cared nothing for the unfortunate soldiers of his unit who were on the raft, because he thought them so stupid as to be unable to appreciate the dangers of their position; but he had been bitterly hurt by being refused a privileged position in the centre. Now, on board the *Medusa* once more, he picked up a carbine and levelled it at the Governor's barge as soon as that craft had begun to move from the ship's side to take up the tow of the raft. To those who did not know of

the wound to his pride, this officer's actions seemed
to be those of a madman and may have precipitated
the captain's flight. In any event, under cover of this
uproar de Chaumareys embarked in his own barge
which was lying ahead under the bowsprit concealed
from most of those standing on deck.

With the departure of the captain in a well-found
boat not overfull, following that of the governor in a
similar craft similarly half-empty and towing the raft
slowly and awkwardly away from the *Medusa,* the last
of the boats had gone. But the deck of the frigate
was crammed with people, not less than sixty-three,
of whom some were women and children.

Lieutenant d'Anglas gave way to a furious despair.
To him, the prospect of having his life snuffed out by
the suffocating sea, instead of a noble death on the
battlefield under the admiring gaze of the army,
seemed unbearable. He now tried to kill himself,
rather than the governor, and on being forcibly restrained began to cry out for death. His hysterical reaction was in marked contrast to that of M. Bredif,
the young mining engineer, who had from the first
deplored the disorder of the embarkation. As he told
his sister, wryly: "I gave the example, and was near
being the victim of it."

With more deliberation than Lieutenant d'Anglas
had shown, some of the soldiers who had been abandoned began to load their muskets to fire a volley into
the departing boats, particularly the last to leave, that
of the captain, which was nearest. M. Bredif, and their
own ingrained submission to authority, prevented it.
But the engineer had to use more than forceful argument; he had to seize the firearms from their owners
and throw them overboard. He never doubted that it
was the right thing to do, but some of the survivors
from the raft, long afterwards, were still of the opinion
that it had been wrong of him to prevent the execution
of de Chaumareys.

A significant thing, however, is that in all this brandishing of firearms, starting with father Picard and

ending with the threat of a volley from trained soldiers, no weapon actually went off; not even accidentally. These incidents tend to show that there was no
widespread panic; they were demonstrations of anger,
not uncontrolled riots.

Apart from the temporarily deranged Lieutenant of
the Guard, those on board the hulk of the *Medusa*
quickly and quietly accepted that they had been abandoned and would have to rely on themselves alone.
Although water was washing about inside the hull it
was below the level of the upper deck and superstruc-
ture. Indeed the hollow noises made by the sea flowing
through the hold under their feet, as floating objects
below bumped against obstructions on the submerged
platforms, gave some kind of comfort to the marooned
men and women. Clearly, the frigate must be hard
aground and could sink no further. A full gale might
sweep it from end to end and perhaps break up the
structure completely, but for the moment they were
secure. There was time to plan, to do things as they
should be done.

Their initial move was to gather to make a solemn
pact. "We all joined together, officers, sailors and soldiers," wrote Bredif. "We appointed a master-pilot to
be our leader, we pledged our honour, either to save
ourselves, or to perish all together; an officer and myself promised to remain to the last." They talked
about making another raft and prepared to cut away
one of the masts which was now threatening to topple
and was straining an already weakened hull. They methodically lit the galley fire and put a cauldron of food
on to boil.

But de Chaumareys had not in fact abandoned them,
although he had no intention of rescuing any of them
in person with his own boat. He came up to the
longboat commanded by Lieutenant Jean Espiaux, informed him that there were no more than some
twenty people left on board the *Medusa*, and that he
was to sail back and take them off.

The weakness of this plan was that, of all the boats,

it was Espiaux's longboat alone which lacked oars, which was at the mercy of the current and the wind, both serving at this time to drive all the boats away from the wreck. Its strong point, although perhaps the captain did not realise this, was that Jean Espiaux was one of the bravest and most capable officers of the *Medusa.* Aged thirty-three, he was the Second Lieutenant (or third-in-command) of the frigate. He had fought at Trafalgar in the *Algesiras,* been wounded twice and promoted for bravery. The following year, 1806, he had been captured in Cadiz Bay by the British. In 1810, while being transferred with five hundred other officers from Spain to England, he had escaped while still at Gibraltar by diving into the sea and then made his way through Spain (terribly dangerous territory then for a French officer) until he encountered a French Army outpost. In 1811 he was promoted to Lieutenant for distinguished services at Guadalquivir. With the First Lieutenant, Joseph Reynaud, he had opposed the plans of de Chaumareys but in the catastrophe which had now occurred as a result of them the actions of these two officers were to be interestingly different.

There was now an exasperating delay because, although there was nothing wrong with what de Chaumareys was trying to do, as usual he bungled the execution by bad judgement. As the wreck was upwind of the boats, the oarless longboat could not by herself go in that direction. So one of the other boats was ordered to tow the longboat and when that manifestly proved impossible also, what might have been done first was attempted last. The powerful fourteen-oared pinnace of Ensign Lapeyrère was sent at length to the wreck; she secured a line to the frigate which she then paid out as wind and tide drifted her back to the longboat. Finally, by dint of much heavy hauling in on this line, the weak and unwieldy longboat was eventually dragged through the water to the side of the *Medusa.*

Climbing up her side, Jean Espiaux found himself faced by, not a mere twenty men, but a crowd of more than sixty passengers, of all ages and both sexes, many of them with tears running down their faces at the prospect of deliverance. Some of them threw their arms round his neck in gratitude.

Espiaux said promptly that he would take all of them and this embarkation, by far the most desperate, alone was carried out in the accepted way, known as "reverse order." That is, women and children first, then junior ranks, officers last. Two women and a child were the first to be lowered down to safety. When they were seated in the longboat, the most fearful of the soldiers and seamen followed quickly. As the crowd filled up the longboat the true nature of the situation became apparent. There was not room for all.

With nearly twenty men still aboard the *Medusa* the longboat was precariously as well as heavily loaded. It seemed incapable of reaching land, gave the instant impression that it would swamp or upset in the first heavy sea it encountered. Indeed, so terrifying a prospect did it present that some men in it began to get up and start to clamber back on board the wreck. Once on deck, three of these men slipped away and found hiding places down below. They were afraid that some interfering officer would order them back into the longboat and, having experienced its leaky condition for themselves, saw no salvation in it. Other men were already below, dead drunk and unable to make a decision either way. In all, seventeen men either refused to seek the refuge of the longboat, preferring to stay with the wreck, or were too intoxicated to move.

True to his word, the last man of the last *Medusa* party to leave the frigate was Bredif the engineer, followed by Lieutenant Espiaux. Their final action was to hoist the French flag above the wreck. The young engineer paused a moment before getting down the side, then threw his small parcel of personal possessions into the sea. Everyone else before him had done the same. It was tacit acceptance of the state of the

longboat. Crowded with what he estimated to be
ninety persons, she was riding sluggishly and low,
water from her leaks washing about inside her. It
seemed as if even the weight of a few small bundles
might be too much for the craft.

All this had taken time. The state of the longboat,
the enormous mass of humanity she was carrying, was
not known to the occupants of the other boats, which
had in the meantime moved away. The young explorer
Mollien, who was in one of them, described the scene
as they had left the frigate. The *Medusa* heeled over
forlornly on her larboard side, the densely-packed unfortunates standing to their waists in water on the raft
under the white flag of the Bourbons which someone
had hastily set up. He found it all very moving and
regretted later that they had not realised just how near
the African coast was, for then the boats could have
saved them all, by ferrying in relays.

The boats were now strung out in a line and going
southeast before the wind about a league and a half
away. They were not heading directly for the shore
but an angle to it. All of them with the exception
of the yawl were connected to each other by ropes,
the captain's barge being at the head of the line while
the governor's barge was at the rear, next to the raft.
The approach of the longboat threw them all into
some confusion.

Grossly overladen, there was no room for the crew
to trim the sails smartly. Its manoeuvres were erratic,
as Espiaux was trying to drive in close enough to shout
out to the captains of the better-found boats to take
off some of his passengers. He needed to get rid of
about twenty, a total which could easily have been
shared out. Reynaud and Lapeyrère one after the other
refused to take a single person, although the Governor's barge was carrying three heavy trunks, the luggage of the Commander-in-Chief, and the pinnace ahead
of it could have managed a few. The next in line was
the eight-oared Senegal port boat captained by Ensign
Maudet, too light, too laden and in too bad a state of

repair to take any more; but immediately in front, at the head of the line, was the captain's fourteen-oared barge.

Unfortunately, at this moment the longboat sheered in sharply towards the line and for a moment it looked as if it would blunder across the towrope or drive violently into Maudet's frail craft. The Ensign was forced to loose his towrope or risk an accident. Once it had dropped free into the water, the two leading boats—his own and that of the captain—drew swiftly ahead; while the two boats behind, left to tow the raft on their own, wallowed almost to a standstill and began to drift.

It was a minor mishap, easily repaired. Maudet prepared to do so. As soon as the erratic longboat was safely clear of them he brought the Senegal boat about in order to reform line and resume towing. The captain's barge was similarly wheeling round. Maudet called out to de Chaumareys, "Captain, take your towrope again." The reply was shouted back: "Yes, my friend."

Meanwhile the unwieldy raft was acting like a giant sea-anchor on the pinnace and the Governor's barge. They seemed to be tugging at it in vain, veering round it at the extremities of their ropes without apparently moving it at all. The impression of sheer futility, of a task far too great, was heightened by the swift mobility of the boats of Maudet and de Chaumareys as they manoeuvred in the distance and began to return. Lieutenant Reynaud, seated in the stern of the Governor's barge, directly in front of the raft, called out: "Shall I let go?"

M. Clanet, paymaster of the frigate, gave a defiant "no, no!" and was supported by several others.

Then the towrope connecting the bow of this barge with the stern of Lapeyrère's pinnace was slipped unobtrusively. Reynaud was to say that this was cast off by the crew of the pinnace; and Lapeyrère was to deny it. But cast loose it was, leaving only the Governor's barge to tow the raft alone for a moment or two.

Now Reynaud was in a difficult position, convinced that the whole idea of the boats towing the raft any distance in the open sea was a practical impossibility, and under pressure from Governor Schmaltz and his entourage to let the raft go. Schmaltz had always been impatient of slowness and inefficiency, and the deadly drag of the raft must have been a torment to him. Although reminded of the oath he took while still aboard the *Medusa,* not to desert anyone, he insisted that the rope be cast off; and was seconded by many.

Obediently, Reynaud began to loosen the towrope at the stern. Then he flung it into the water. He had to do this in clear view of many men standing to their waists in the waves, staggering for a foothold on the raft, which was now left to wallow on its own, two leagues from the *Medusa* but twelve leagues or more from the shore. The Governor was afterwards to tell a cunningly articulated story, of how the men at the front of the raft had pulled on the towrope to draw his barge nearer to them and how a wave had made them let go, and so the boats had too rapidly taken up the slack and stretched the rope so much that it broke. As Savigny was to remark: "This manner of explaining this last desertion is very adroit, and might easily deceive those who were not on the spot, but it is not possible for us to accede to it, since we could even name the person who loosened it." That person was of course Reynaud, who subsequently admitted the fact that it was done, and done at the orders of Governor Schmaltz.

The captain's barge and the Senegal boat were now approaching in order to resume towing. Seeing Reynaud's boat drawing ahead of the raft they passed close and de Chaumareys hailed the Governor's barge.

"What are you doing?"

Reynaud shouted back, too ashamed to admit the truth, "The rope has just broken."

"What do you intend now?"

Many persons heard Reynaud's shouted reply.

"We abandon them!"

Midshipman Charles Rang, who was in the captain's barge and was one of the few officers who had supported de Chaumareys, testified to this dialogue. At that moment, he added, "We could not see the least movement on board the raft, not even a cry was uttered. They seemed reduced to nothing. . . .

"There is no doubt that the handling of the pinnace caused the boats to scatter and to abandon the raft. But they alone cannot be blamed for this. The separation was taken as the signal for common escape. Everyone sailed ahead and took care of himself first. In a short while we were out of sight of the raft.

"When we left them, we all thought they were bound to be lost. We knew that they had not enough food and we could only hope that they might possibly meet a ship. It was the most fragile of hopes," Rang added, deadpan, "for it was most unlikely that a ship would sail in the area where we were then."

The sodden, weary men on the raft were unable to believe that they really had been left to die. Any excuse for hope was at once seized upon. The first evidence they thought they saw was in the movement of Espiaux's longboat, which had remained in the vicinity. They watched intently as her foresail was lowered to the halfway position. Then it came down completely, as if to slow her speed for the task of taking up the towrope.

This was in fact Espiaux's intention, a resolution only made possible by the cries of anger from his passengers as it became clear to them that all the other boats were leaving the raft and were not just reforming. But their resolution did not match his, for a closer approach to the raft revealed the dangers. To pick up the tow they might have to come so near that any desperate man could leap on board them. Certainly, a shoal of swimmers could strike out from the raft and grasp the gunwales to haul themselves up out of the water. That would mean the swamping of the longboat and the deaths of them all. There were muttered objections.

"I know, I know," pleaded Espiaux. "I haven't the least intention of coming in dangerously close, my friends. And I know we can't tow them on our own. But once *we* take up the tow, the other boats may follow our example," he paused, then added: "I promise you this, if the other boats don't come back and join us, I'll not risk your lives to save the people on the raft. I know I can't perform miracles."

But too many of his passengers were unwilling to face the risk. The spectacle of the other boats, all five of them, and all in better condition than they were, fleeing for the horizon, decided the matter. There went the Commander-in-Chief of the whole expedition, the Captain of the *Medusa,* and the First Lieutenant also. Obviously there was no hope.

"Very well," said Espiaux. "We are probably doomed, too, like those on the raft, but let's face it to the last. At least, we'll try. *Vive le roi!*"

The men began to cheer. Although some thought it madness, others found it sublime, a gesture of defiance and hope. The cry was heard far off by the men in all the other boats and they took up the shouting also. The calls echoed a long way over the sounding board of the sea.

The staccato chanting convinced many of the men massed on the submerged raft that rescue was only just out of sight, only just over the horizon; that the men in the leading boats had sighted a passing ship and were speeding away to attract her attention.

They rationalised their hopes. They thought they saw the explanation. For had the boats continued to tow their raft, progress would have been so slow that the distant ship might have passed before they had come close enough to be sighted by her. The actions of Espiaux's longboat provided a convincingly final touch, for had she not appeared to be about to take up the tow? Then she had hoisted her sails again and made off in the wake of the other boats towards the coast.

The men on the raft were patient, because they

knew that the onshore wind which so rapidly carried the boats away from them, would be unfavourable for the rescue ship, which would have to beat laboriously out to sea against it in order to locate them.

They gazed intently at the horizon for the first sight of her topsails, but none appeared. Steadily, the sails of the boats grew smaller as they drew away until they could be seen only now and then as a boat here or there reared to the crest of a distant wave.

Finally, there was no sign of any sail at all.

And then they knew.

5

"LAND, LAND!"

Morning, July 5 to evening, July 6

ABANDONED, buried to their waists in the sea, many of the shipwrecked men cried out in terror and despair. Endlessly, in every direction, the waves heaved and sparkled to the horizon. There was no glimpse of a sail, no sign anywhere of land. Above was the blazing sun of the Sahara, the oppressive, suffocating heat of the tropics. In the chaotic rages and emotions of the morning everyone had forgotten food; but it was becoming all too plain to each man that he had not eaten since the previous day. Curiously, it was hunger they felt now, not thirst, and it was hunger which terrified them all, for its insistence emphasised their utter helplessness.

Everyone experienced this first wave of despair which had succeeded the initial stupefaction at their desertion by the hierarchy of the ship. It was as though the world had crumbled. The officers abandoned on the raft felt this also, but concealed their emotions. They pretended to be unafraid and to see some hope still in the desperate situation. By degrees they produced a veneer of decent calm, although inwardly everyone trembled.

Alexander Corréard was gnawed by self-doubt and useless anxiety, for he had no one but himself to blame. Twelve out of his twenty civilian engineers had been set down to go on the raft, while he and the remainder had been listed for places in the boats. He had argued with M. Schmaltz that all his men ought to be with him, that they had promised to follow him wherever the service might require and that he in his turn could not desert the majority of them. Failing to persuade the governor, Corréard had taken his place with the dozen engineering workmen condemned to the raft, but without realising how fatal that course might prove. With only two exceptions, one of them the excitable Lieutenant d'Anglas, all the army officers had made the same decision as Corréard. If the men under them were listed to go in a boat, they would go in that boat and command them; but if the men were ordered onto the raft then their place also was on the raft.

As the officers strove to calm the men at the same time as they controlled their own fears and regrets, they found an ally. It was simply the gradual realisation that with the favourable wind, and the tide due to become favourable also within a few hours, the ungainly raft could have been dragged appreciably nearer to shore had the boats continued to tow it. They might not have been in sight of the coast that night, but the following day they surely would. At least, they would have been moving; there would have been hope. Instead, they had been sacrificed and deliberately; they were sure of it. As the thought sank in, there was now an outburst of hatred. They swore vengeance, if ever they should get out of this alive. Everyone felt the emotion, even the officers. And the officers encouraged it, fanning the men's feelings with their own genuine rage, thankful that the channelling outward of their tension could swamp their fear and bind them together in a union of the deserted.

Stupefaction—despair—revenge—that was the sequence of the first morning. And it was followed by a measure of acceptance, disturbed by outbursts of fury, as the more thoughtful among them began to think of what to do and then discovered that the raft was bare of necessities. There was no compass, no chart, no anchor. The lack of a compass, the least necessary item had there been a competent navigator or seaman on board, was what disturbed and enraged them most. There were renewed shouts for revenge against the men who had abandoned them without a thought, until Corréard remembered that he had seen a pocket compass in the possession of his foreman Lavillette, and asked him if he still had it.

"Yes, yes! I've got it with me," the man called back.

A tremor of hope and joy ran through the drenched, packed mass of humanity standing uncertainly on the submerged timbers of the raft. The ridiculous little instrument, about the size of a large coin, seemed a talisman promising safety. It was passed from hand to hand towards the nominal commander of the raft, the midshipman Coudein who was in great pain from the wound on his leg, now raw from the salt water in which he had to stand. A few hours later, the compass fell from his grasp into the water and disappeared forever between the openwork timbering of the raft.

The lack of a chart as well as a compass brought a sense of loss, of being utterly without bearings; of being unable to make the simplest calculations of distance and direction, except at dawn and sunset. How far away was the land and what sort of coast was it? Wasn't there an island of Arguin much nearer to them than the coast, where they might take refuge? How many leagues were they from it and which way did it lie?

In truth, given the clumsy, careless design of the raft with its rows of projecting spars—each one a drag in the water—compasses and charts were near enough academic. More important was the lack of an anchor, for the raft did drift with the winds and tides, and sometimes it drifted in the right direction. A good anchor, to hold the position gained when wind or current became adverse, would have been invaluable. Bit by bit, moving only when the natural drift was landward, the cumbersome construction would have come eventually to shore. Such a steady shoreward movement, although it might have taken some time, would have kept hopes alive. But there was no anchor.

There was not even a commander of the raft, for the unfortunate Coudein was in agony, unable to move, unable to supervise. His place was taken by two men, Corréard the engineer and Savigny the ship's doctor. The former attended to the rations. He made out a nominal roll, with everyone allotted a number (so far as was possible, the crowded conditions on the raft making a head count difficult). Then, because everyone felt hungry rather than thirsty, he shared out the contents of the flour container which had fallen into the water, together with a three-quarter measure of wine, which was to be the daily ration. The full measure was probably a pint. He does not specify, but remarks only that this was "the best meal we had the whole time we were on the raft."

Probably because of his experience at sea, Savigny the surgeon undertook to organise the setting up of a mast to take a sail. For a pole he used one of the *Medusa*'s masts which had been incorporated in the raft; he had it cut in two pieces to serve as their mast and yard. It was impossible to step it properly in a recess, but they managed to erect it more or less upright by using a lot of rope to make stays and shrouds. No rope had been included in the stores loaded onto the raft, but a long length of rope was washing round the raft—the towrope to the boat which had freed itself from them. They used that.

When the sail billowed out triumphantly, many thought they would soon be able to confront the men who had left them to die. In case they saw a ship sooner than they sighted land, pistols and gunpowder had been hung at the top of the mast as a signalling device. All that could be done had been done, and the very act of working to save themselves had produced a new attitude of determination and hope. But it soon became apparent that however well they trimmed the canvas the raft would move only crabwise and then only when the wind was directly behind the sail. The two spars interlocked in a V-shape at one end only gave the impression of being a bow because they were on top; there was no bow. Indeed, there was no hull. There were no lines at all to the contraption, for the spars and beams projecting far out from the sides made the width nearly equal the length, apart from causing turbulence and drag in the water.

Even so, although the hulk of the *Medusa* was still in sight it was only as a low-lying dark object at least five leagues away. And those leagues were in the right direction. One way or another, partly by towing, partly by the drift of the current, partly by pressure of the wind, the raft was by that much nearer the shore in the evening than it had been in the morning. Savigny and Corréard believed that the *Medusa* had struck some twelve or fifteen leagues from the coast, so that if the boats should return for them once they had lightened themselves by landing the passengers the ordeal of the shipwrecked might not be unbearably long. It might even be ended that night, if the boats had gone to unload at the island of Arguin instead of carrying on for Africa.

Before the coming of the night they prayed, alone on the sea. They prayed with fervour and with hope, gaining comfort from the belief that there was a protecting spirit; that God would not abandon them. This was the fragile unity which the more dominant characters among the officers had created out of nothing in the first day of their strange new command. The castaways were divided by nationality, by colour, by caste, by age, by occupation, by experience, and most dangerously of all by the marks of the branding iron which indicated from whence many of the soldiers had been recruited—the jails of France. They were divided also into the strong and the weak, but as events were to show it was not physical strength or weakness which would determine who would live and who would die, but more inward qualities.

With darkness came a rising wind and wild seas driving out of the night. Because only the upper parts of their bodies were above water, the castaways were battered and buffeted, hurled this way and that by the foaming waves. And as the raft swayed and tilted unsteadily beneath them, the soldiers particularly tended to lose their footing. This struggling, helpless mass of humanity might have disintegrated completely and been washed away in the darkness, had not Savigny found men still cool and determined enough to help him search for short lengths of rope and to tie these to the timbers of the raft. Now, with some of the castaways holding on to ropes, the formless mass of people struggling individually to keep their footing and stay above water was given cohesion and anchorage.

Some time after midnight the wind blew with even greater strength, the waves were higher. The castaways became like would-be swimmers struggling out to sea through surf, but very tired swimmers for they had had little to eat and no rest at all for nearly a day. Some were swept away over deep water but managed to struggle back; others simply disappeared into the night, helpless in the waves. Weary men fell among their struggling fellows and at last were too weak to claw themselves upright again. There were those whose feet became trapped in the openings between the timbers of the ill-constructed raft and in their exhausted state could neither free themselves nor stand upright. The night was very dark and no one could make out what was happening more than a yard or so away. The only relief was the glinting foam of the breaking wave tops all around them in the blackness.

Someone cried out in the night that he saw fires. Then others, staring at the horizon, thought they saw them also. A long way away, something seemed to be flickering repeatedly in the gloom. At once they thought of the gunpowder and pistols, hung for safety well above water at the top of the improvised mast. One after the other they lit gunpowder charges, which burned and sparked slowly. As one died out, feverishly they lit another. But there was no answering signal out in the night. If it was a ship out there, or one of the boats returning for them, they were not keeping a very good watch. Perhaps a noise and a bright flash might attract their attention. Several of the pistols were loaded and fired into the sky. The flame momentarily lit with an orange glow the exhausted, stubbly faces of the suffering men. The sound of the reports rang in their ears. Slowly, at deliberate intervals, the firing continued.

The longboat was in desperate straits, lying so low that the gunwales amidships were a few inches only above the sea. Every wave of any size came over and water washed about the floorboards. Bailing had to be continuous but few of the soldiers or sailors were prepared to do it. After abandoning the raft, they had struggled all day towards the coast of Africa, lagging behind the other boats. Indeed, none of the commanders of the other boats wished to have Espiaux's longboat anywhere near them. They were fearful on two counts, that Espiaux would try to unload some of his mass of passengers into them, and that this might be done by force. When the five serviceable boats had left the castaways to their fate on the raft that morning, they had heard several young army officers in the longboat shout out: "Let us fire on those who fly!" At least, that was the polite translation of their words given by one witness. "Shoot the cowardly bastards!" might have been a more strictly literal version. At any rate, this story had been passed rapidly along the line of boats. It was especially worrying for their commanders because a number of their own people took the same basic view and if given armed encouragement might have seized control from them and tried to aid the castaways on the raft.

Just such an incipient revolt occurred on the first evening, as soon as the leading boats sighted the coast of Africa. They had cast off from the hulk of the *Medusa* at about seven in the morning of July 5. The towrope to the raft had been loosed about two hours later. At about ten o'clock there was a distribution of provisions in the fourteen-oared pinnace commanded by Sub-Lieutenant Lapeyrère which now held the Picard family. A small glass of water and a quarter of a biscuit already soaked by the sea was handed out to each person. The water went down at a gulp but few could touch the biscuit yet. The heat was suffocating and the sun blazed down without mercy. The tender skins of the very young children began to redden.

This day the strong north-west onshore wind which had got up each day after sunset began to steepen the waves much earlier, howling at gale force. The sea became covered with the curious jellyfish known as the Portuguese Man-o'-War, which is really a colony of animals attached to a gas-filled float, pale blue and shot with pink, which serves as a sail. The boats were being driven towards the land, but the jellyfish were trying to avoid it. For them it meant death, not life. They could be seen presenting their sails to the wind at an angle, apparently in an attempt to escape, and seemed to be in a regular formation. The young midshipman, Charles Léonard Rang, who was in the captain's barge, was curious enough to lean over the side and scoop one of them out of the sea in order to examine it. Soon he felt a tingling sensation in his hand which grew to a burning heat. Some of the creature's tentacles reach a length of several feet and contain stinging cells which are very powerful, although not fatal to a human being.

The water was whitened also with the floating shells of dead cuttlefish. And almost every one of these was a lifeboat, for it was covered with flying insects which, unable to combat the gale, had taken temporary refuge on these drifting islands of dead bone.

The crisis came in the evening when from the gale-tossed boats the land was sighted, a thin line of white and burning sand beyond the breakers. All the boats except Espiaux's longboat, still labouring out to seaward of them and nearly swamped, gathered together. Safety of a sort lay just on the horizon and several officers proposed that the more overloaded and also less well-provisioned boats should run for the shore and disembark some of their passengers, who would form into a march party for a long walk towards St. Louis.

Other thinkers were more radical. They demanded that the bulk of the passengers from all the boats should be disembarked at the coast immediately ahead. And that while these people set up a temporary base camp, all six boats should be formed into a rescue force. Three should go back to the *Medusa*, take off the men left on board the hulk and as many provisions as possible, and then return to the base with the rescued men and these supplies. The other three boats should meanwhile go in search of the raft and rescue the castaways, bring them back to the base as well. Only then should a boat be despatched to St. Louis to bring a ship to their aid.

This was near enough what the Governor and the Captain had agreed to do, had solemnly sworn on the French flag to do, before ever they left the *Medusa*. It was, however, more practical because it dispensed with the raft as a means of transport. But now, Colonel Schmaltz and Captain de Chaumareys had second thoughts. Their barges were well-found, well-provisioned and far from overloaded. Their chances of making a run direct for St. Louis by sea were good. So they forbade anyone to land and ordered all the boats to go south in convoy with them to the mouth of the Senegal River. Some officers protested that the town of St. Louis, which is on an island near the river mouth, must be a hundred leagues away, a desperately dangerous distance for some of the boats to sail along this open coast.* And there were some voices to declare that this final abandonment of the raft was a shame and a dishonour to France. But there was no

---

*The distances and times given are those estimated by the witnesses. As their charts were poor and they did not in any case know where they really were, the figures must not be taken literally. This being the evidence, they cannot now be corrected, but the distance to go was probably in the order of 250 miles. The *Medusa* may have stranded as far as forty miles off shore. Only a modern discovery of the wreck could give an accurate position.

shaking the determination of their seniors. Both the Commander-in-Chief and the Captain, who was very much under the influence of the Governor's dominating personality, insisted that all the boats should anchor for the night where they were and sail for the Senegal River in the morning.

Night fell and as the boats plunged at their anchors there was little sleep, the people dozing fitfully in cramped and uncomfortable positions. One man in the pinnace cried out suddenly that he saw ghosts and witches out over the water, and uncanny, wavering lights. No one else could see them, although he pointed desperately. They assumed it was some phosphorescence in the water that he had seen, if in fact he had seen anything at all. Even a distant wave might cause that. They were now beyond scientific explanations, so M. Picard and one or two others also pretended to see the lights and pleasantly suggested that Arabic sorcerers must have set fire to the sea to prevent the infidel from approaching their coasts. Very likely it was just phosphorescence, although some doubt must linger. For at about this time the castaways on the raft were burning gunpowder flares and firing pistols to attract attention.

Meanwhile the ninety or so persons packed into Espiaux's longboat were in trouble many miles away from the five boats which had kept together in front. Later than the other boats they too had glimpsed that shimmering line on the horizon which was Africa and the cry of "Land, Land!" went up from them all. With the wind blowing strongly and the longboat moving rapidly towards the shore, their spirits rose. Then there was an ominous thumping, more a sensation than a sound, a slight shudder of the timbers below them. They were bumping on a sandbank covered by only three feet of water in the trough of the waves. Lieutenant Espiaux got the heavily-laden craft off into deeper water and by constantly sounding the depths worked his way further out to sea for the night.

M. Bredif at least was relieved, for he was more

afraid of Africa than the sea. The water could only drown him whereas the Arabs, he thought, would march him off over the desert to Morocco or Algiers as a slave.

The sea did its best that night, the waves running very high. With so little freeboard, the longboat was vulnerable to a single mistake, however slight. Unless the boat took each wave at exactly the right angle she would be swamped. As wave after wave came roaring down on them, the helmsman skilfully headed into it, so that the crests parted broken around the bows. Even so, several times an unpleasantly large amount of water came smashing aboard, and the men bailed frantically for their lives. Any other boat enduring those circumstances would have been lost, thought Bredif. It was a superlative performance to maintain the same unvarying skill hour after dark hour, within seconds of disaster.

As even the longboat, lagging well behind the others, had sighted land before sunset, it is probable that had all the boats towed the rafts towards the coast then the north-westerly gale, blowing obliquely towards Africa, would have proved a blessing. It would certainly have been moved many miles nearer the shore. Whether that would have made much difference we cannot know, because it was never tried. As usual with the command of the *Medusa,* half-measures had been employed half-heartedly and when any problem proved difficult, it was abandoned.

The gale which battered the group of anchored boats that night, which made the hours of darkness perilous for Espiaux and his men, which swept the raft from end to end so that the castaways seemed engulfed in the waves, also sent its spume soaring high over the black, shuddering bulk of the *Medusa* lying stranded far to seaward. There were seventeen men still alive inside her broken hull. Some were there from choice, because they thought she was a better refuge than the raft or Espiaux's longboat. Others had

been too drunk to make any rational decision. But by
nightfall they had scoured the hull thoroughly, climbing down into the darkness to where the waves washed
about underfoot to search for provisions. And they
came upon prize after prize: biscuit, bacon, wine,
brandy. Enough to last seventeen men for a long time.
Then they had sought out living quarters for themselves, each man finding his own "den" in the creaking
structure of the ship.

Although her keel was fractured, her holds flooded
and her stern gallery smashed in, the *Medusa*'s hull was
far from falling to pieces. The frames, beams and plank-
ing were solidly bolted and pegged together, with lavish
use of great timber brackets called "knees" to support
them at the angles. The ship's bottom was bedded down
into a hollow in the soft sand and mud, so that it could
not move, and the slope of the Arguin Bank seaward
served to break the force of the waves by degrees and
weaken them before they struck the wreck. The best
refuge of all that night was the ship, better even than
the best boats, immeasurably better than the doleful
raft. This night proved that there had been no valid
reason for the precipitate mass abandonment of the
wreck of the frigate. When dawn came on the second
day of the mass flight, July 6, 1816, her foam-streaked
sides still crested the waters like a cliff.

By daybreak the sea gale had died to a whisper and
the waves were flattening, although a swell still rolled
over the banks from the open Atlantic. From Lieutenant Espiaux's longboat, barely afloat, the land was distinctly visible. Soon the hot wind would begin to blow
out from the Sahara, carrying seawards with it tiny
particles of sand which would fall like rain upon the
boats. But the sight of that arid, burning waste
sparked hope in the sodden, despondent men. They
demanded to be set ashore at once, although virtually
without provisions. They were given most of what biscuit remained and also firearms as a protection from
the Arabs. Espiaux took the longboat in as close as

he dared and then anchored in the shallows. A mass of men and some women scrambled over the gunwales and splashed into the water. Then they began to wade ashore to whatever fate awaited them in the Sahara. There were sixty-three of them in all.

Lightened of two-thirds of its heavy burden, the longboat now rode higher and more easily in the water. Bredif, who preferred the terrors of the tumultuous sea which had driven the majority ashore, estimated that the number of people left in the boat besides himself was twenty-six. If the identification of this place was correctly near the Mottes d'Angel, he calculated that those sixty-three unfortunates had some eighty or ninety leagues of desert shore to traverse before they could get to St. Louis. He was glad when Espiaux again headed for open sea.

An hour later they sighted four of the five other boats—the Governor's barge, the Captain's barge, Lapeyrère's pinnace and the yawl. Espiaux had the sails lowered and lay-to, in order to wait for them. When he said that he intended to take in a few people from the more overloaded of these boats, there were shouts of protest. But the Lieutenant was adamant. "They have refused to take any people from us. Let us do better, now we are lightened. Let's offer to take some from them."

He hailed Lieutenant Lapeyrère in the pinnace, calling out that he now had room in the longboat for more people. Did the Picard family want to come aboard? Did anyone want to be ferried ashore? Lapeyrère shouted back that his pinnace was all right, although it was obviously far more crowded than the two barges. Then the amazed men in the longboat saw the pinnace abruptly turn away from them, using her oars the quicker to get clear of the stationary longboat. The other boats also hauled off in concert, as though they too dreaded to come near the longboat, which indeed they did. Espiaux could see that there was some sort of conference going on, for the little yawl was going from one boat to another, as if carrying messages or instructions.

What they did not know was that morale had broken down in the other boats. The men had been betrayed from the top so many times that everybody now suspected everybody else of the worst motives for anything proposed. And there had been an incipient mutiny in the pinnace that morning. Less than an hour before, a group of sailors, some of them armed had demanded to be set on shore. When Lapeyrère refused they threatened to commandeer the boat, using their firearms. The officer had leapt at one man who was menacing him with a musket, and in the struggle they both nearly went overboard and M. Picard, hanging on to Lapeyrère's clothes in order to save him, lost his hat. In the blazing sun that could have been fatal and he immediately let go of Lapeyrère in order to pick the hat out of the water.

It was in these rather ruffled circumstances that the encounter with the longboat had taken place. Also, all the boat commanders had tender memories of how yesterday the army officers with Espiaux had threatened to fire on them for cowardice when they had abandoned the raft and how a quartermaster had actually levelled a musket at de Chaumareys. They did not know that it was Espiaux who had prevented the man from firing and looked upon the Lieutenant as an enemy of the worst sort. Some also suspected that the longboat's unruly crew had mutinied and were out to save themselves at the expense of the luckier people in the better boats. And all were convinced that the offer to take passengers from them was nothing but a trick. Even the Picards were brought to believe this. They were sure that the longboat was only apparently two-thirds empty, sure that she was still packed with men, sure that they were crouching low behind the gunwales ready to leap into the other boats as soon as they came near enough.

One keen look at the way the longboat, lightened that morning of the weight of sixty-three people, was riding much higher in the water should have dispersed their suspicions. But it took more than that, it took near-disaster to do it. An hour after the boats had shunned Espiaux's craft the wind got up and soon the frail yawl was in difficulties. It was the smallest by far of all the boats, yet carried fifteen men. From the Governor, from the Captain, from Lieutenant Lapeyrère there was no assistance to be had. At last, in despair, the crew took the sinking yawl down to Espiaux's longboat, lagging far behind them.

As it came alongside, Bredif gave a shout of joy. He recognised in the yawl his friend de Chasteluz, safe and sound. He called out to him and, the two boats pitching and tossing wildly alongside each other, de Chasteluz made a leap for the longboat, tottered uncertainly for a moment on its side, was grabbed by Bredif and dragged down to safety. One by one the other fourteen men chose their moment and jumped the gap between the two hulls. One of them was M. Richefort, part-author of their misfortunes.

It really was a fortunate sequence of unplanned events, thought Bredif. If the sixty-three men and women from the longboat had not absolutely insisted on going ashore, against Espiaux's advice, then the overloaded craft could not possibly have saved anyone. They would have had to watch the yawl and its crew go down in front of their eyes, for the better-found boats had abandoned it as they had abandoned the raft. Virtue had brought a reward, too, he realised. Only minutes before, soaked through from bailing out the leaking longboat, he had taken off his clothes to dry them in the hot sun; and in so doing had lost the purse containing four hundred francs in gold, which represented half his wealth. The other four hundred francs he had given previously to de Chasteluz for safe-keeping; and only moments after the loss, by the wildest of coincidences, he had helped to pluck de Chasteluz from the sea.

It was now about nine o'clock in the morning. By noon the heat was becoming intolerable. The sun

struck them like a blow. Some were almost unconscious and Charlotte Picard felt that death was near.
The sky was covered with a hot mist which was really
sand from the desert; it collected on the boats, it was
sucked into their lungs as they tried to breathe.
Through the mist the sun glowed like an ominous red
disc and the surface of the sea shimmered and danced
around them. There was no horizon. Although the
boats lapped slowly through the water, they seemed
becalmed in some limbo where the only relief from
torment was to chew on something, a lead musket ball
or a fragment of leather, so as to get at least the
illusion of moisture in their mouths.

The same sun glowered redly down on the idly rolling raft, the same fine rain of dust fell upon the sea-
drenched castaways around noon. But it had been a
very different dawn, as the fury of the nightly gale
spent itself and a thin bar of light streaked the horizon. As the shadows dissolved and men could look
into each other's faces again, they saw that during the
night the raft had become an abode of death. About
a dozen corpses lolled grotesquely in the water, their
legs caught in the gaps between the timbers of the raft
under their feet. Hopelessly trapped amid the swaying,
shoving crowd of men buffeted by the seas which
swept over them, they had become too weak to struggle free and had choked and gasped their lives away
in the darkness.

There was a sudden cry of distress and a swirl of
movement where two young men had recognised a
motionless body as that of their father. They began to
weep with pity until a more objective onlooker noticed
that this "corpse" was still breathing, although faintly.
Savigny the doctor applied first aid at once and by
degrees the unconscious man was made to breathe
more deeply. When he finally opened his eyes, his sons
helped him up and held on to him desperately so that
he would not fall again.

The number of men dead or lost during the night

was conjectural. At ration time, fresh serial numbers were given out to all the survivors, but Corréard and Savigny were sure that some of the soldiers had cheated by calling out more than once in order to obtain an extra ration or two. The survivors were still so crammed together that it was hard to prevent this abuse. Further, the number of people actually on the raft to begin with was known only in round figures. Roughly, it had been 150. The number of rations claimed on this morning was about 130 and if this figure had been correct it would have meant that twenty men had gone. But it was not correct, for an unknown number of men had claimed two, perhaps even three rations instead of one. The raft had been lightened of more than twenty men, in the most sinister manner. The sea must have taken most of them, the fury of the gale sweeping them bodily off the raft and out into the black wilderness of tossing water.

There was no general loss of morale, hope was still high. The hulk of the *Medusa* was no longer in view and there was no sign of land, but among the packed, suffering mass of people there was the certainty that the boats could not really have abandoned them and that, as the officers said, as soon as they had landed their passengers on the shore opposite the *Medusa,* they would come back again in search of the raft. The oppressive suffocating heat which was so tormenting the people in the boats had the opposite effect on men standing to their belts in the waves. For the calm, almost dreamy isolation of their existence as they drifted in the mist was soothing after the black fury of the gale. If only this would continue, they could endure.

The weak, however, were already giving up. Not the physically weak, but the immature or emotionally unstable. Already, the previous day, a gentleman called Griffon (the Governor's secretary) had tried to drown himself in despair. Savigny had brought him back to the raft, where his talk was vague and disconnected. Shortly afterwards, he again threw himself into the sea, but then caught one of the far-projecting crosspieces of the raft and clung on to it. And so he was saved again. Perhaps these were gestures.

On this, the second day, however, there were no gestures. Three men gave up. Two were youngsters, the third a baker. They said goodbye to their friends and companions, then there was a splash and they were gone. In others, the breakdown on this day was less dramatic but was increasingly to affect everyone on the raft (and some people in the boats as well). Here and there a happy cry would break out, as some castaway sighted land. But only he could see it. A little later a man would point wildly to the boats approaching them, or a ship. But there were no boats, there was no ship. These men, having lost hope of external aid, had withdrawn inwards to a dream world of their own, rejecting the unspoken horror which inwardly must have lurked in all. That they would drift and drift under the scorching sun until long torment at last brought them peace.

At four in the afternoon the terrible and extraordinary heat of that molten day was lightened by the freshening onshore breeze from the north-west. In the pinnace, going south for Senegal in company with the other boats, Charlotte Picard noted how the fresh sea air revived them all. The dust-laden mist from the land vanished and the sky became wonderfully calm and clear, an indication of a good night, she hoped. For the second time that day, rations were issued by Lieutenant Lapeyrère: a small glass of water and one-eighth of a biscuit. Everyone, she thought, appeared reasonably content now. Conditions were more bearable, all the boats were speeding through the water purposefully and some time next day, after a good night's sailing, they should be in sight of the mouth of the Senegal River, a short distance from the town. They would have a tale of adventure to tell, but nothing really unbearable would have happened.

At half past seven the sky clouded over with ominous swiftness. A strange gloom came over the sea and the waves began to rise. Over the coast of Africa the clouds were visibly boiling as the cool winds from the sea were sucked in towards the superheated air of the desert. These clouds looked like a hideous chain of mountains piled on top of one another, their summits vomiting fire and smoke. Bluish clouds, streaked with dark copper tints, detached themselves from the billowing activity above the land and were sucked individually out to sea where they merged with the overcast.

Miles away on the raft, the effect was shocking. The demonstration of their helplessness, of their idle, uncontrolled drift to nowhere was plain. The horror of the oncoming night seized them. They shouted that they had been deceived. There were no boats, the boats would never come for them. There was no hope. The efforts of some twenty determined men, mostly officers, who had managed to instill a measure of calm and purpose evaporated in an instant. There were shrill cries of terror, hoarse shouts of fury. And then the gale broke on them with sudden and appalling violence, sweeping across the sea. The waves rose mountainously around them, half blotting out the sky.

The raft, drifting far from land, became an oasis of white and broken water in the darkness. The boats, fleeing to the south, half-swamped by the seas, were caught dangerously inshore and tried to claw their way seaward, the thunder of breakers bursting in the coastal shallows sounding continually like a distant, growling bombardment. Somewhere in the howling sandstorms ashore, the sixty-three men and women who had landed from the longboat were hiding in the dunes, the first night of their long desert march spent in cowering before the fury which raged on sea and land alike.

Far out in the Atlantic, somewhere on the driven wastes of the Arguin Bank, the storm pounded at the stranded *Medusa*, spray hailing as high as her strangely lopped masts. The whole hollow structure shuddered and groaned; loose timbers banged and thundered incessantly; water rolled, surged, sucked, and cascaded noisily through her submerged hold and lower deck. The very plank seams began to work and open under the crouching bodies of the seventeen men left marooned inside her, each one huddled into an individual refuge of his own choosing.

What could have been a simple accident of the sea, had the original situation been met with firmness and determination, was now about to turn into the most terrible shipwreck of the century.

6

TERRIBLE DARKNESS

Night of July 6 to 7

SOMETHING very strange had begun to happen to the castaways even before the gale overwhelmed them. Savigny the doctor felt lethargic; he knew he should keep awake, but his eyes closed and he could do nothing about it. He drifted away into dreams and visions. He was wandering through a splendid countryside where everything was a delight to the senses. A small spark of reason still remained, which told him that it was a trance, that he must stay awake. He started nervously, was able to ask for some wine, and gradually recovered a little.

In some men the symptoms were furious and impatient shouting. In others they were the reverse. One man turned to his comrades and in a calm and matter-of-fact manner said, "Don't worry, I'm off to fetch help. See you soon." Then he walked off the raft into the sea and disappeared.

Another man was calling, "I want my hammock, I want my hammock! I'm going for a sleep down below. Only for a minute, mates, but I must get a bit of shut-eye."

Then the gale swept upon them. The seas rose mountainously and as the submerged timbers of the raft tripped the waves, so they broke in foam over the heads of the castaways. More than half floating, lacking the full force of gravity to pin them down, the mass of men (among whom was one woman) were driven irresistibly from the back of the raft to the front. Flexing and trembling in the surge, the projecting timbers and spars at the sides gave but slight footing now. Only around the mast in the centre was there a semblance of solidity. Those men who were on the outside struggled briefly for a footing or a hold of some sort or floundered desperately towards the mast. But in a moment scores of them were swept away, their heads bobbing in the waves, arms flailing. The crush in the centre, where the officers stood around the base of the mast, was terrible. Men slipped and disappeared under the water, other men lurched and fell on them. The waves stifled them or plucked them away.

The fury of the seas would inevitably have destroyed them all but for the direction of the wind, which was behind the sail they had rigged to the mast. The advance of the mountains of water appeared to be slowing down. Really, the raft was beginning to give way before the wind, moving obliquely shorewards. And it was lighter now, much lighter. More than half its original load of humanity had now been shed.

The rolling combers pursued the raft, slowly heaving it up on their bulging crests and then sending it sliding down the incline of their backs. One moment, one side of the raft was tilted up to the sky, then a few moments later it was the other. The officers, trying to keep a footing in the centre round the mast, began to call out for the men around them to rush first this way, then that, in order to balance the structure. But this attempt to control their destiny did not last.

Sure they would all be drowned long before daybreak, many of the soldiers and sailors felt like having a last fling. They knocked a hole in a wine cask which was in the centre of the raft and as each man still had the tin drinking cup he had been issued with, all made merry. Sea water soon spoiled the wine through the hole they had made, and curses of disgust rent the air. They drank on empty stomachs. But worse, most were suffering from the tropic heat to which they were not accustomed, from the dehydration and lack of salt which accompanies exposure in such conditions, from

almost total exhaustion after two days without sleep
or rest of any kind, and from the hysterical excitement
which danger and the prospect of imminent death can
create. And perhaps there was something more. Afterwards, Savigny thought so, although he could not decide what it might have been.

Nothing the officers could say or do could stop this
last, desperate orgy. All their efforts achieved was to
spark resistance, an uncoordinated revolt of individuals. Among the soldiers recruited from the jails of
Toulon, Brest and Rochefort were Spaniards, Italians,
Portuguese and Negroes, as well as Frenchmen. They
did not yet combine as such or even as simply soldiers,
for not all were yet suicidally affected. But it was a
giant Asiatic, a soldier from a colonial regiment, who
made the move which turned drunken grumbling into
an insane action. When shouts of "Get rid of the officers!" were bellowed, he strode into the middle of the
raft waving a boarding-axe above his head. Towering
over every other man there, he gave an impression of
hideous power and determination. His curly hair was
short-cropped, his sallow-skinned face dominated by
an enormous gash of a mouth and a large nose. His
physical strength was enormous. With a single blow of
his fist he felled man after man who stood in his way.
He waved high the axe at an officer who tried to stop
him. For long minutes he dominated the raft, while
behind him lesser individuals cried out to him to cut
the rope-bindings and let the raft go to pieces.

No real blood had been shed. So far there had been
only gestures. The critical change came when the colos-
sal and crazed Asiatic leapt from the middle of the raft
to the edge and with crashing blows of the boarding-
axe began to sever the cords which held the timbers
of the raft together. Restraint vanished in an instant.
The curved blade of a sabre rose and fell and the
demented giant sank to his knees and collapsed, the
first victim.

Shouts of fury from his friends and cries of alarm
from those still in part-possession of their senses

formed the castaways into two opposing factions
within the instant. Soldiers, but not all the soldiers,
formed the largest part of the suicidal faction. The
officers, passengers and engineering workmen, but not
all the workmen, formed the basis of the survival faction. The soldiers among the mutineers drew sabres
or bayonets, other men flashed out their knives. Like
a moving hedge edged with sharp steel points, they
advanced on the officers grouped at the foot of the
mast. The points were presented, not raised to strike.
But as the crowd closed on the officers one frantic
mutineer lifted his sabre for a deadly stroke—and was
at once cut down, pierced by many wounds. The
crowd stopped unbelievingly, shocked by the swiftness
of the retribution, and retreated, still screaming with
rage.

Now they used cunning. While the mass confronted
the officers' party with the bristling steel blade points,
blocking their view of the back of the raft, some of
the mutineers started to slash unseen at the ropes.
One man pretended to slump against the low railing
at the side, as if exhausted, while stealthily he began
to cut the cords with a knife. A servant who saw this
told the officers what he was doing and a concerted
rush was made at the man. The first officer to reach
him was at once attacked from behind by a soldier,
but the wild stab of the knifeblade only pierced the
officer's coat. Swinging round, he threw the soldier
into the sea and a moment later, his saboteur comrade
after him! Instead of further cowing the mutineers, it
had the opposite effect.

What up to now had been a wary confrontation of
the respective masses encouraging individual champions, at once became a general combat. "Lower the
sail!" yelled someone, and a tide of raging humanity
surged forward and swarmed around the mast, slash-
ing at the yards and shrouds, cutting the stays. The
mast fell, pinning a captain of infantry, knocking him
unconscious and nearly breaking his thigh. He was
plucked up and thrown into the sea. His friends saved

him and placed him on a barrel so that his head would be above water. The mutineers swarmed upon him and were going to cut out his eyes with a penknife. The officers' party lost all restraint. Their heavy sabres flashing, they cut and slashed their way through the ragged lines into which the mutineers had drawn themselves. Men screamed in agony, clasping sudden gaping wounds gushing blood, and collapsed into the water. Some of the civilian passengers joined the officers in the merciless struggle. All had momentarily forgotten how completely outnumbered they were.

Alexander Corréard thought he was in Italy, a tourist with all the time in the world. That seemed a fine thing, he was so tired. Somewhere far off he could hear shouting, screams, curses. That was strange, but he was too weary to bother. Then, near at hand, there was a shout like a trumpet blast. "To arms! To arms!" He stirred and shook at the remembered command. "To arms! Or we're finished! Help us, comrades!"

Shakily, he staggered to his feet. The trance was leaving him, but only because he willed it to go, and that was a hard fight. Armed with his sabre, which was but poor defence against the dreadful lethargy which only slowly drained away from him, Corréard got his engineering workmen together in a group at the front of the raft. Many were ex-soldiers and one was a former sergeant of the Old Guard. But this was not war, these were deluded fellow countrymen who had lost their internal struggle against whatever malaise it was that plagued the wretched castaways. Corréard told his men not to hurt anyone if they could help it. That was easier said than done, for the mutineers who were pushed overboard from the struggle at the back of the raft were carried by the waves to the other end, where they climbed aboard again.

Mutineers came at them from the back and from the front. The sharp steel of knives, sabres and bayonets threatened them from two sides; and also a new weapon, for many of the rioters had picked up empty muskets to use as clubs. The workmen stood stolidly in line, presenting the points of their sabres calmly, as a withheld menace. Reluctant though they were to fight their fellow countrymen in earnest, they soon had no choice. Groups of demented but armed mutineers rushed on them. The hoarse, sharp breathing of men in combat with cutting and clubbing weapons requiring great physical energy to use showed how deadly the fight was. Man after man was slashed and torn, many repeatedly. Corréard had his flesh opened by a blade several times, but hardly felt it at first.

He heard a voice crying out from the sea for help, was told that it was one of his own men by the name of Dominique, who had fought on the side of the mutineers, and immediately Corréard jumped in after him. Seizing him by the hair, he dragged Dominique back to the raft. It was still fairly dark, but they were able to find the wound and, judging it extensive, his comrades bound it up for him with a handkerchief, for he was losing a great deal of blood.

While Dominique still appeared half-drowned and half-dead, another tumult arose and there were more cries out of the heart of the dark sea. Some of the madmen had thrown the canteen "girl" and her husband overboard. She was actually a middle-aged woman, having served the Napoleonic Armies in many campaigns. The despairing calls of the drowning woman aroused Corréard again, in spite of loss of blood from his wounds. Sensing his growing weakness, this time he tied a rope round his waist before jumping into the gale-lashed sea. Then the pair were hauled back to the raft, the woman invoking the aid of her favourite saint. Meanwhile the head foreman of engineers, the ex-Guards sergeant Lavillette, rescued the woman's husband. To keep them from collapsing into the water which swept over the raft, the man and his wife were placed in a seated position upon some dead bodies, with their backs supported by a barrel. Neither was fully conscious yet.

*   *   *

Almost as suddenly as it had begun, the fighting died. The mutineers, although they utterly outnumbered the officers' party, retreated to the back of the raft and were quiet. Some fell at the feet of the officers and begged pardon, which was instantly granted for all were aware of the mysterious malaise. Those who still had some control over themselves achieved this only by immense internal effort. Now the moon came out and lightened the narrow space which had been a battlefield and was still strewn with dead and wounded, while the storm still howled and raged around them.

The canteen manageress and her husband recovered very quickly. Finding themselves in each other's arms, instead of in the raging surf where they had been driven by swords and bayonets, they cried with happiness. The woman's first rational thought was to find out who had saved her, and then to pour thanks upon Corréard. Finding that insufficient to express her feelings, she searched her pockets for the only possession she still had left, a little box of snuff, and gave it to him. Seated on a corpse, she handed him the magnificent present which Corréard, who did not use snuff, had to accept.

Feeling at a loss for conversation, but immensely moved by the gesture, Corréard ventured to observe, "Didn't I hear you mention our good Lady of Laux just now? There's a Department of that name in the Upper Alps. Do you come from there?"

"Indeed, yes, sir. But I left there twenty-four years ago and ever since I've run a canteen. I was in the campaign in Italy, and many others. You see, it's a useful woman whose life you've saved!

"Often, I've risked death on the battlefield to help those brave men. I always let them have my goods, too, whether they had money or not. Sometimes, my debtors never came back, poor fellows. But after a victory, why, then others would pay me more than they owed. So you see, I too had a share in the victory!"

She positively glowed at the thought that her life had been saved by a Frenchman. But Corréard was drifting away again. He was in Italy, travelling across a splendid plain. He started drowsily from his trance-like state when an officer nudged him and stated gravely, "I know we've been deserted by the boats, old chap, but don't worry. I've just written to the governor and he'll be here in a few hours."

"That's good," murmured Corréard drowsily. "I suppose you had a pigeon, or the letter wouldn't have got there so quickly."

They were all lost in these private dreams. Some were back in the *Medusa*, in their own quarters. Others called out to passing ships for help. One man saw them approaching a harbour with a splendid city built on the heights above it. Others again dreamed that their dreams were of hand-to-hand combat ringing with cries of despair. When they woke, they thought it had all been a dream. Illusion changed places with reality. They asked had anyone else heard those disturbing sounds and other men would reply yes, they had, but it was just a vision, merely the effect of exhaustion.

Savigny the doctor recognised a delirium, like a burning fever where a thousand visions pass through the mind but few can be recollected when the patient wakes up. It was a fever of the night, he noted. The night brought a natural terror much enhanced by the brutal situation they were in. With daylight, people became calmer. But dawn was many hours away. It was not yet midnight.

Although they thought the crisis was over, the officers' party grouped themselves in the middle of the raft and kept their weapons close. For an hour they all lay quiet, hopelessly outnumbered for there seemed less than two dozen of them. Afterwards, they wondered how they had survived so long against so many. The truth was, the tradition of the Napoleonic armies lay with them, whereas most of the men who wore the uniforms of soldiers were the rejects of society, degraded by the newly re-established practice of branding. In the mass conscript armies of France which had dominated Europe for twenty years there had been a revulsion against flogging and branding. It was argued that such treatment broke a man's spirit and that he was never any good afterwards. Napoleon's conscripts went to war no more willingly than anyone else: they missed their homes and families: they found military life both harsh and boring. But they did not feel misused or degraded, that they were outcasts rejected by society. The jailbirds whom the Royalists had formed into a regiment had had the mark of society's rejection permanently and brutally imprinted on their bodies by the branding iron, like cattle. Small wonder, thought the officers, that in the delirium which affected all on the raft most of these men lacked the inner strength to retain some spark of sanity. Further, they had mixed wine with their fever.

Just before midnight, they rose again. They were now without restraint, beyond all reason. Those who had lost their bayonets or knives clawed and bit. They surged at the officers like a wave. The officers' group held together, then drove back the yelling madmen. Wild blows cut cloth and sometimes flesh. With clothes rent to tatters the officers fought on. Savigny's right hand was slashed by a knife, rendering two fingers useless. He was bitten in the leg and in the shoulder. Four mutineers seized one of Corréard's workmen. One held him by the right leg and began biting into the sinew above the heel, while the others belaboured the man with the flat of a sabre or the butts of their carbines. His screams reached Lavillette, ex-sergeant of the Guard, who led the rush to free him.

No sooner had they saved this man than the mutineers seized another, a junior army officer called Lozach, shouting that they were going to be revenged on Lieutenant d'Anglas. In vain, Lozach protested that he was not d'Anglas. "You bastard, now you'll pay

for what you did to us in garrison! Remember the Ile
de Ré? We haven't forgotten!" The terrified Lozach,
who had seen as little service as the man they took
him for and who it appears was almost equally dis-
liked, gave a last shout of despair as the mutineers
were hurling him over the side. That told the hard-
pressed officers that there was still a chance to save
his life, and they rushed to his rescue in small groups,
aided by some of the workmen. Savigny, Corréard,
even the disabled Coudein struggled forward, as well
as Lieutenants L'Heureux and Clairet and the indomi-
table ex-sergeant Lavillette.

In the struggle the workman Dominique, who had
deserted them earlier for the mutineers, whom they
had saved and helped nevertheless, was seen fighting
again on the side of the madmen; and this time he
was killed. Lozach was rescued and dragged back to
the middle of the raft, and this caused them more
trouble than almost anything else. The mutineers
bayed around the group like vicious dogs, demanding
that d'Anglas be given up to them. In vain the officers
shouted back that d'Anglas wasn't on the raft at all.
He had gone back to the frigate before they had been
cast off. They had seen it for themselves. Still they
howled for d'Anglas. Somewhere in their disordered
minds they perhaps remembered that Lozach, an officer who had seen service only with the Vendean bands
of Saint Pol de Leon, and was not popular with the
officers either, had also imposed harsh punishments
for trifles. Perhaps it was just that they remembered
a hated face.

Momentarily cheated of their chance to avenge dim
barrack square memories, the mutineers turned on an
easier victim. Midshipman Coudein, the nominal commander of the raft, who had been injured aboard the
frigate weeks before, had now been wounded in his
effort to save Lozach. Exhausted, bleeding and totally
incapable of further fighting, he was hunched out of
the water on a barrel, and trying to protect Leon, a
young sailor boy only twelve years old, from the mad-

dened rushes of the struggling men to and fro across
the submerged timbers of the raft. He and the lad
were easy prey. Coudein, boy and barrel all together
were hurled off the raft into the stormy darkness. Not
quite done, and still holding on to the boy, Coudein
flung out his other arm and grasped one of the projecting spars of the raft. Eventually he was able to get
the youth back on board again.

There was one thing and one thing only which could
be said in favour of the raft—that, as a design, it was
far better fitted than any boat to survive a gale. Its
openwork construction guaranteed that. Literally, it
would not hold water. The waves rose and fell through
the gaps as if through a grid. And it was almost impossible to overturn.

Even in the best-found of the six boats morale
reached breaking point that night. They were all running before heavy, following seas with deep hollow
troughs and immensely high crests. They were being
pursued by these waves and could not travel fast
enough to outrun them. This is one of the most dangerous situations possible. It is almost like surfing, the
rudder having little or no effect. But, nevertheless, if
the boat swings slightly so that a following wave
strikes at an angle, she is likely to overturn. And even
if she can be kept straight at the critical moments, a
breaking sea can roar right in over the stern regardless, filling the boat and probably sweeping the helmsman from the tiller. A fair amount of luck and
extreme skill is required to survive.

Midshipman Charles Lèonard Rang was one of the
two men holding the tiller of the Captain's barge, the
other being the sailing master. Rang was the son of
an emigré but had joined the Navy in 1809, immediately after a successful incendiary raid by the British
on the French fleet at Rochefort. Possibly his motive
had been revenge. In any event, apart from a cool,
detached intelligence, he had both youth and experi-

ence on his side. In a quiet way, he was to describe the
silent horror of the pursuit of the boats by the waves.

"That night was terrible and deprived most of the
men of the small amount of courage still left in them.
It was very dark at first, but when the strength of the
wind finally cleared away the thick cloud which was
hiding the land, then the moonbeams lit the huge
waves which were breaking around us and allowed us
to realise fully the horror of the position we were in.
The master and I were steering and everyone else was
simply staring at the waves running after us, while we
were trying to avoid the next one astern."

The situation was the same in all the other boats,
but some men were so exhausted with the continuous
roaring and pounding, the lack of food and drink, the
impossibility of proper rest, that they just dozed off
where they were.

M. Bredif, the mining engineer, was climbing in the
Alps. The splendid scenery entranced him. Best of all
he enjoyed the shade, as he walked out of the sun
under the trees. How much better things were now
than during the war! There was that terrible time, in
a forest just like this, when he and his sister had hidden from the Cossacks who were over-running Kaiser-
slautern. Surely there must be a waterfall near here?
There was the sound of a torrent running through a
gorge, and why, he must be hanging over it. his face
was wet with spray!

The engineer's body jerked with the mental effort
of preventing himself from falling into the swift river,
and his eyes opened. He was indeed suspended over
water, from the side of Lieutenant Espiaux's longboat,
and the roar of the torrent in his dream had been the
lashing of the waves against the side, in reality.

The awakening was not pleasant. His head was stiff,
his neck wracked with pain. He opened his ulcerated
lips, but his parched tongue licked only at a bitter
crust of salt which had formed in his mouth from the
spray. The terrible shock of disillusion made him de-

spair, and for a moment he thought of ending it all with a quick leap over the side. Then the weakness passed and he determined to endure.

At least the longboat was still afloat and the helmsman himself had doubted that she would survive long in the confused and raging seas that had sprung up with the storm. He had thought it impossible to dodge every giant wave and if they shipped only one over the stern, he had said, it would be a quick death. No one had laughed.

The silent horror they all felt was increased by a hollow, booming thunder sounding far off in the night, but becoming more audible and menacing as the hours went by. Believing that they had covered a much greater distance than was really the case, they took the sound to be that of the waves breaking on the bar of the Senegal River. The thought that they were nearly opposite St. Louis was heartening and sail was shortened and the boat almost hove-to, in order not to over-run their destination during the hours of darkness.

This was an error which was to have serious consequences, as they later realised. The booming was indeed the sound of breakers, but merely of those tremendous rollers typical of West Africa. Lieutenant Espiaux's longboat was still more than sixty leagues north of the Senegal in fact.

The fretful crying of the children mingled with the howling of the wind and the hissing roar of the waves which buffeted Sub-Lieutenant Lapeyrère's pinnace. Tears streamed down the young Madame Picard's face at the helpless, shuddering cries of the suffering child in her arms. The little boy was aflame with thirst. But she had bared her breast and found she had nothing to give.

The agony of her parents was beyond Charlotte Picard's powers to describe. The young children, too young to understand, were racked by thirst and hunger, and every moment tossed violently this way and that as the brute waves smashed at the timbers of the pinnace in never-ceasing vicious motion. M. Picard and his wife had brought their large family to this and yet were powerless to help, let alone protect them from the dangers of the sea.

The wind howled and screamed over their heads like some live beast, increasing in force and power every minute. The driven waves climbed higher still until one great monster rose up at them like a mountain and swept the boat from end to end. The torrent of water dove the women and the children from their seats in an instant, carried overboard the little luggage they had brought with them, ripped a sail from the mast and plucked it away. Only the father, clinging on with both hands, still kept his place, while his wife and the six children were washed and thrown about the boat, screaming.

Miraculously, the pinnace recovered. But M. Picard was more affected than his family were. He was in despair. The financial loss he had suffered from the wreck of the *Medusa* spelt ruin to his family if they should survive it all. And there was nothing he could do to help them survive. Even if there had been only a single person looking to him for help, he was powerless to give it. His family at once flocked around him, but it seemed to make matters worse. He clasped and hugged them all, tears streaming down his face. Inwardly, he was saying goodbye to his loved ones and blaming himself for their fate.

The shock the family had had from the terrible power manifested by that giant wave, they shared with every other soul in the boat. But the reactions showed in different ways. Many of the sailors became quiet and still, shaken and bewildered; others cheered and encouraged one another. The children clung tightly to their parents, sobbing without pause; some through their tears gulped out pleas for a drink, while they vomited up the sea water they had just swallowed. Others asked for nothing, just sobbed their hearts out, wanting only to stay with their parents until the seas closed over them.

Thunder growled and thumped out over the water and the lightning flashes showed an indescribable wilderness of black waves streaked with white foam. Almost everyone in the boat was helping to bail out the water which continually burst over the sides, but still the floorboards were covered with it. They soon found the reason—a large hole in the side where a plank had been literally stove in by the power of the sea. Instantly, they began to stuff it with anything to hand—old clothes, sleeves of shirts, shreds of coats, shawls, useless bonnets—and hoped that the plug would hold.

About the middle of the night the winds died as abruptly as they had risen and the waves began to flatten out and lose their force. When the sky lightened, with the sun still hidden, they did not know which way to go, for the compass had been smashed in the storm and there was no land in sight anywhere.

As the same sky lightened over the raft, now driven far, far to the south, the miasma of the night evaporated with the darkness. Weakened, but no longer feverish, the survivors could take in the full horror of the scene. There seemed only about sixty of them left. Their numbers had been more than halved during the wild fury of that night.

Of those who had been lost, Savigny estimated that no more than a quarter had been swept off the timbers by the gale or had simply committed suicide by allowing themselves to be carried away. The majority had died by being cut down or battered to death in the desperate hand-to-hand conflicts which had swept back and forth across the half-submerged structure. He based this guess on the fact that many of their bodies still littered the raft. Only two were from the officers' party and neither of these was an officer, but the wounds among the survivors were too many to count or to compare.

On every face was the deepest despondency, as they realised what they had done to each other.

When, slowly, they began to take stock of the situation the numbing truth came home. In the madness of the night, the mutineers had thrown into the sea the bulk of their drinking supplies. Both barrels of water and one of the wine barrels had gone. Only a single barrel of wine now remained. That would not last sixty men very long, even on half rations.

7

INTOLERABLE PRESSURES

July 7 and 8

THE 7th of July was their third day adrift for the
castaways on the raft. The third day of close confinement. The third day of helplessness. The third day
of exposure to extreme heat and burning sun with
insufficient drink and food. The third day of a malaise
about which Savigny was to speculate later and to dis-
pose of some previous theories by the evidence he was
collecting, but without being able to reach a satisfactory conclusion.

The third day was notable for a reduction in the
sense of irritation felt by the castaways. With so many
gone overboard or sprawled dead on the raft, there
was more space; their sense of confinement and re-
striction was eased. There was also a faint sense of
hope once more, of at least going in the right direction, of doing something to aid themselves.

Soon after dawn the sea became calm and this enabled them to set up the mast again. The coast was
not in sight but all thought that they could perceive
the distant shimmer of heated air from the burning
desert. Having seen so many illusions, they were not
entirely convinced now; but it seemed logical that land
was only just over the horizon. All night the gale had
been blowing them inshore at an angle to the coast.
That much was sure.

All the same, they had undoubtedly reached a wa-
tershed and half had passed over the other side. Some
thirty men were far gone and, thought Savigny, clearly
dying. "The half of our men were very weak, and
bore on all their features the stamp of approaching

dissolution." For them, rescue would have to come this day or it would be too late.

Unless they could find food. They dreamed of food. Men had even fought for food during the night, attacking other men and demanding that they be given a wing of chicken or a loaf of bread. Although the water had gone overboard, there was still a little wine left. But not a man had touched food of any sort for two days. Their last "meal" had been a little sea-soaked biscuit on the day they were abandoned. Proper food had not passed their lips since the evening of July 4, nearly three days ago.

They thought of fish and despite their exhaustion set about devising ways and means to catch some of the live meat that was so prolific in the sea around them. They made hooks out of the identity tags carried by the soldiers, but the raft was such a crazy mass of timbers that the lines became entangled and useless. These were meant to catch little fish. But a shark would feed them all. They bent a bayonet into a curve to make a shark-hook, and saw one of the streamlined monsters make a dash at it. The shark bit but was not hooked. Instead, the bayonet was straightened out.

They were still standing to their knees in water. For three days no one had been able to lie down. A shark could have swum over the raft to feed on them, but they were beyond fearing the great fish. They thought only of catching a shark in order to eat it. But the task was beyond them. They were now too weak to attempt any form of food gathering which required great mental or physical effort.

There was fresh meat on the raft, a great deal of meat. The bodies of their companions who had been killed during the night. Some of the castaways began to cut the corpses with their knives, stuffing the bits of flesh into their mouths and devouring them with desperate urgency. Many men abstained, including almost all the officers; but it was soon clear that the men who had eaten felt better for it and might live a little longer. Hope of being found by the boats or a ship from the squadron was still with them. More men decided to try to save themselves in this way, but shuddering at the thought of uncooked human flesh soaked in seawater, tried to dry it before eating.

Many could not overcome their repugnance. The spectacle of other men eating made them desperate, however. They tried to consume bits of leather hacked off their swordbelts or cartridge pouches, washing the morsels down with a little wine. Some men gnawed at pieces of clothing, others chewed at pieces of leather from their hat-bands, the grease and dirt giving an impression of food. One sailor tried to eat excrement, but could not force himself to swallow.

Midshipman Coudein later reported briefly: "Among the unfortunate people spared by death, the most starved ones rushed onto the remnants of one of their brothers, tore flesh off the corpse and fed themselves with this horrible meal. At that moment, a great number of us did not touch it. Only a short while later, we were forced to do so."

The long day of July 7 was calm and so was the night which succeeded it. For once the onshore gale did not blow, but they were now beyond all attempts to trim the sail to a favourable wind. They were resigned to letting the raft drift wherever the winds and currents happened to take it. When darkness fell they tried to sleep, swaying together in a dense mass with the waves washing about their knees. From long exposure to the sun their skins were dry and blackened and their legs, from immersion in salt water, were puffy and sore. Added to the torments of hunger and thirst, these agonies caused men to cry out in pain, continually waking those who were asleep on their feet.

When the sun rose on the morning of July 8, the fourth day of their ordeal, they could see that another ten or a dozen men had failed to survive the night. The effect was salutary. Even the fastidious man came to know that he was under sentence of death and that execution could not be delayed for more than a few hours if he did not eat. The bodies were rolled off the raft to lighten it.

All bar one. That single exception was reserved as a meat ration. The previous day the object had been a man. To some of them more than that—a friend. They had even shaken hands with him, hands trembling with fatigue and fever, and vowed to survive together or die together.

This day also was calm and fine and a little flicker of hope returned. At about four o'clock in the afternoon a shoal of flying fish passed under the raft and found the spaces between the projecting side timbers a trap. They were tiny fish, smaller than a small herring, but the castaways flung themselves on the struggling creatures and scooped them up. Nearly two hundred were caught and put in a barrel and, eaten raw, this food seemed delicious.

In the morning an ounce of damp gunpowder had been found and by afternoon the organizing group had managed to dry it in the hot sun, so that it would burn. In the same parcel there had been wrapped also a steel, some flints and tinder. A fireplace was constructed by cutting a large hole in a wooden cask and putting damp material underneath. The cask was placed on a barrel to keep it well above the waves which still washed over the raft, and inside the cask a fire was lighted, the principal fuel being dry linen. Some of the fish were cooked in this way and were hungrily devoured. The entire catch would not really have sufficed to satisfy one man, so some human flesh was added as well. The mixture of fresh fish with the meat made it less loathsome to eat. For the first time all the officers ate some human flesh and from now on continued to eat it.

However, this was the last hot meal they were to have. The wooden fireplace caught fire and in putting out the flames the essential materials were lost. There was neither powder nor tinder left. But they felt better, definitely better.

*   *   *

The castaways on the raft suffered predominantly from hunger and the pressures turned them all by degrees to cannibalism during the two-day period of July 7th to 8th. In the three ill-found boats it was otherwise. Thirst was their principal torment and this also grew to be intolerable during the same two-day period of July 7th to 8th. There was little to eat, mostly biscuit, in these three boats, but whereas there was a tiny water ration in the longboat and the pinnace, the men in the Senegal port-boat had nothing at all to drink for two days.

The gale had separated all the boats and the morning of July 7 found each one alone. The pinnace commanded by Sub-Lieutenant Lapeyrère was out of sight of land when the darkness lightened before dawn. With a broken compass, it was steering erratically until the sun rose. Then it was sailed towards the sun and the sand dunes of the Sahara.

Some of the sailors had been sufficiently desperate to drink seawater, which had increased their thirst. They urged Lapeyrère to land on the coast and look for water, but most of the passengers were too afraid of the Arabs. In any case, they all expected to reach the Senegal River next day, not knowing how wrong the Sub-Lieutenant had been in his calculations. Nevertheless, the sailors demanded to be set on shore at once, so Lapeyrère agreed to take them in as close to the breakers as he could and let them swim to the beach from there. Eleven men agreed to risk this but when the boat was near enough to see the actual height and fury of the surf through which they would have to swim, they changed their minds. They went back quietly to their oars.

The day's ration was distributed shortly after and when it had been given out what remained for the future was four pints of water and six biscuits to be shared amongst more than forty people. As the pinnace coasted southwards everyone looked anxiously for some gap in the breakers through which the boat might be safely steered, but all they saw was a party of Arabs. They headed out to sea again, still believing that they would sight the river mouth tomorrow. One more day of pitiless sun blazing down on their heads from directly above. Almost all of them, including Charlotte Picard, now drank salt water. To her shame, she also observed that some of the sailors drank urine. But it hardly mattered. Laura, her little step-sister, aged only six, lay dying at her mother's feet. Her cries for water were so pitiful that her father conceived the idea of opening one of his own veins, so that she might drink his blood. He was prevented by a man who observed that not all the blood in his body would prolong for one moment the life of his child.

The coming of the on-shore wind in the evening was a blessing. It gave some relief from the heat and glare but was not so strong as to endanger the boat. They were able to anchor fairly near the shore and everyone was able to sleep peacefully.

On the morning of July 8 the sails were hoisted again but the wind soon fell away to a dead calm. They began to row but the men were too exhausted to make much progress and a halt was called for the distribution among forty-two people of the final ration: six biscuits, four pints of water. When this had been consumed, which did not take long, there were no more supplies of food and drink whatever in the boat.

The very finality of it emphasised that they now had to make a choice between two alternatives: to risk a slow death from the sun by continuing to row towards the Senegal: to risk rapid death from the sea by attempting to get through the breakers and reach the shore of the Sahara. The majority favoured the latter, although death by drowning appeared to be more of a certainty than a risk. But then, if the calm continued and they were forced to row, all must be dead long before they could reach the mouth of the Senegal. With her crew slowly and painfully pulling at the oars, the pinnace crept in towards the coast. Dunes of white and burning sand could soon be made out, and then a few small trees. The prospect did not look very promising, even if they survived the passage of the breakers, and only the splashing of the oars broke the mournful silence into which they had sunk. Then a sailor started up, and pointed:

"Look, the Moors!"

Petrified with terror, Charlotte Picard saw what he was pointing at—a number of men walking very quickly along the crest of one of the dunes. The pinnace turned out to sea immediately, to get away from the beach. Even in spite of the breakers, they all feared that the Arabs might somehow swim out to the pinnace and capture them. This was the slave coast of Africa and to the Moors human beings were as valuable as animals.

After several hours the pinnace again approached the coast, when several figures were seen standing on top of a very high dune. The Arabs were everywhere! . . . Waiting for the ship-wrecked men and women to be cast upon the shore. . . .

Lieutenant Espiaux gave M. Bredif the engineer of mines the task of making out a new list of the men in the longboat and of distributing the water ration to them from a central point. The passengers had changed considerably since the previous day, July 6, when sixty-three men and women had insisted on going ashore and fifteen men had soon after been saved from the sinking yawl. There were now only about forty people in the longboat, less than half the number embarked directly from the *Medusa*. Even so, they had little water left. As each man came to him for his meager ration, Bredif poured it out from a tin cup while he held the actual list underneath its lip, so that if any tiny droplet of moisture spilt it would fall on the paper and could still be used for moistening his lips. Only a few men drank seawater and Bredif observed that this seemed to worsen their condition.

The longboat with its forty passengers was alone until about midday on July 8, when another boat was sighted, lying still in the water. This proved to be the

Senegal port-boat commanded by Ensign Maudet, with its crew and passengers in a state of mutiny. The twenty-five men in it had suffered more severely than those in the longboat. All were determined to go ashore and seek water, as they had now had nothing to drink for two days. The angry debate then raging was whether to coast along until a safe approach to the beach could be seen or whether they should turn into the breakers immediately and take their chance of drowning. The sailors demanded to be landed at once, emphasising their wishes by waving their sabers. The officers opposed the plan, and had pistols. For a moment, it seemed that the kind of butchery which had taken place upon the raft would be enacted also in this boat, but the officers capitulated. The boat's two sails were hoisted and with oars beating the water the Senegal boat gained speed for the attempt to surf through the breakers. For long minutes the passengers in the longboat watched its progress.

When they saw that the boat survived the passage of the breakers, although it filled with water on the far side, and that the men were able to wade through the shallows to safety, the sailors in the longboat were encouraged. They recklessly demanded a chance to do the same. Espiaux said that he would land them if he could but would not risk the longboat itself because he for one thought they had a better chance to make St. Louis by sea. Those who agreed with him grouped themselves round the water supplies and drew their swords to defend it. Espiaux put out an anchor so that the longboat could be drifted close to the breakers on a line but could still be hauled off to safety. The sailors, however, cut or untied the line and the longboat was heaved by the swell into the broken water. The first breaker went right over their heads, leaving the boat three-quarters filled with water but still afloat. A sail was hoisted which took the water-logged craft straight in towards the beach.

Bredif was virtually naked as he had been drying out his clothes at the time the decision had been taken; he did not put them on again because they might hamper his swimming. His friend de Chasteluz could not swim, so as the floundering boat was flung shorewards by the breakers, Bredif took the end of a rope which de Chasteluz was fastening round himself. Bredif planned to swim to shore with the rope, then pull in his nonswimming friend like a hooked fish. The last breaker filled the boat entirely and it sank. Bredif threw himself overboard and was surprised, and relieved, when he found that his feet touched the sand. He was standing only chest-deep in the sea.

Relieved of anxiety about his comrade in the water, Bredif got back into the sunken boat and started to look for his clothes and his sword. Some of them had already been stolen by quick-witted sailors and he could find only his coat and a spare pair of pantaloons. He had no shoes, and a negro at once offered to sell him an old pair for eight francs.

The sailors had also saved the barrel of water which represented the total of their drinking supplies. Once they had it safe on the beach they fought among themselves for a drink. This was much too much for the half-naked and infuriated Bredif. He burst into the crowd, hurling them aside, snatched the barrel from the man who was gulping down the liquid, and swallowed two good mouthfuls before losing the barrel to someone else. They did him as much good as two bottles, he reckoned; without them he could not have lived more than a few hours longer. As it was, he was wet through, stripped of most of his clothes and all his possessions; with no water to drink and a few soaked biscuits for a food ration. And, like all the rest, he was afraid of the Moors whose ferocity was legendary.

The forty men of the longboat waited until they were joined by the twenty-five men from the Senegal boat which had been wrecked a short distance to the north. Then they set off to march along the beach because the sea breeze made the edge of the sea a little cooler than the interior of the Sahara and the damp sand was easier to walk on than the fine, shifting sand of the dunes inland. They had been tramping southwards for only half an hour when they saw yet another boat, the third to be wrecked that day, coming in towards the beach under full sail. As it drove violently on shore, to be stranded in the shallows, Bredif tore off his clothes again and dashed into the water to help, for he could see that there were women and children aboard.

The pinnace was also driven to shore by the thirst of all the occupants, but by common consent. There was no dispute in their case as to the wisest course to take. What had prevented them from landing until now was the belief that the people they had first seen ashore were Moors. After several hours slow progress they again saw on a dune several people whom they took to be Arabs. But when the distant figures began waving at them, they looked more attentively. As soon as they realized that these men also were castaways from the *Medusa*, they replied to their signals by hoisting a white handkerchief to the mast top and set about looking for a way through the breakers. The sea itself was calm, it was the Atlantic swell spending itself on the shores of Africa which made the last lap perilous.

The helmsman was directed to the right, where the waves seemed deceptively lower. Almost at once they saw another group of people ashore, a large group this time, and close enough to recognise individuals. Charlotte Picard was terrified, for they were now into the breakers. Each wave that swept in from seaward, sensing resistance from the shelving beach after its 3,000 miles uninterrupted passage across the Atlantic, swelled up suddenly and monstrously under the boat. The bow of the pinnace rose high in the air, then dropped shudderingly down the face of the wave, throwing the occupants backwards and forwards alternately. The helm was now given to the old seamen whose skill had saved them during the gale, for at all costs the boat must not swing sideways to the rollers.

The pinnace came safely through two lines of breakers, when they saw ahead a third and final range. Beyond it was the beach and the men from the other boats. They were all trying to signal warnings. Then some turned away as if not wanting to witness what was to happen, while others dashed forward into the shallows to be able to help the sooner. The water in front of them heaved itself up to a prodigious height, then fell upon the sand with a hollow clap of thunder that seemed to shake the coast.

That third range took the pinnace as though it were a straw. Picked it up, slewed it sideways, flung the occupants around like peas. The next wave of the series broke actually upon the floundering pinnace in a vast explosion of water, the groaning of strained timbers, the splintering of oars. All the occupants were suddenly engulfed in boiling foam. As the water drew back again, the pinnace reappeared, immovable, actually stranded on the beach. There was no time for more than a few gasping breaths before the next roller was rearing up. It broke just to seaward of them and a hissing torrent of water came rushing up the beach like a striking snake, covered with white foam.

Charlotte Picard was up to her neck in water and she was a full-grown girl. The four young children were all under the age of six years, and quite helpless. Confronted with an emergency they understood and could handle, the sailors who had seemed so mutinous and selfish produced an astounding burst of energy under the spur of real danger. In a flash, the grapnel was flung out to hold the boat high up the beach and prevent it being dragged back out to sea, under the bursting rollers. Then they plunged overboard, scooped up the small children in their arms and ran them up the beach to safety. Returning, they picked up the older females, put them on their shoulders, and carried them also up the beach. Charlotte found herself sitting on the sand beside her stepmother, her brothers and her sisters, who seemed half dead. Only her father was missing.

M. Bredif plunged into the surf too late to save any of the children, which had been his intention. The sailors had acted instantly. But he was able to help them get M. Picard from the wreck and up the beach to join his family. Then he went to look for his clothes and once again discovered that they had been stolen. This time his rage was violent and his language uncontrolled. He bellowed out what he thought of petty thieving in these circumstances. Possibly the robber may have felt remorse, for shortly afterwards Bredif found his coat and pantaloons lying further along the beach.

Four out of the six boats had now gone: the yawl, the port-boat, the longboat and the pinnace. The bulk of their occupants amounting to about 110 men, women and children were now ashore in one place, with little food and no water at all. The sixty-three men and women who had voluntarily landed from the longboat earlier, somewhere to the north, with some eighty to ninety leagues to march across the desert, had suffered severely until they found a freshwater lake. Several people died during their march, including a gardener and a soldier's wife. They had no reliable chronicler among them, so little is known. On the evening of July 8, therefore, more than 170 of the *Medusa*'s people were ashore from the boats and in desperate circumstances.

The two seaworthy and well-provisioned craft, the barges of Captain de Chaumareys and Governor Schmaltz, were still afloat and far to the south. By sunset they had sighted Grieuse Wood, a landmark not far from the mouth of the Senegal River, their destination. Since the morning of July 7 they had been keeping company on an otherwise empty sea. Neither of these two men had appeared concerned about the fate of the longboat or the pinnace or any of the other boats; they certainly did not search for them, but carried on southward. Their crews also had suffered from the overpowering torment of the days. Men had become so thirsty that some had drunk seawater, others had satisfied themselves by sucking on lead shot from the pistols and muskets.

In the Captain's barge there had been a demand from some of the men to be set ashore in order to find water, but it was not strongly pressed until next day, when their total supplies were found to consist of three bottles of Teneriffe wine. The gentlemanly and perhaps politic gesture was made of presenting one of the three bottles to Madame Schmaltz, the Governor's lady, in the accompanying boat.

The sailor's reaction was marked. They demanded that a vote be democratically taken as to whether or not the Captain's barge should run ashore to search for water. When it seemed that the vote would go in favor of a landing, Governor Schmaltz made a graceful reciprocal gesture. He kindly offered a place in his barge to Captain de Chaumareys and his two officers, Sub-Lieutenant Chaudiere and Midshipman Rang. However, the men did not go through with their intention when repeatedly assured that the boats must reach the Senegal within a few hours.

At ten o'clock that night, shortly after sighting the approach marks to St. Louis, the shapes of two vessels were seen. They proved to be Captain de Vénancourt's corvette *Echo* and Lieutenant de Paranajon's brig *Argus*.

The corvette, as the senior vessel, hailed the approaching craft, asking who they were.

"Two boats from the *Medusa*."

There was a pause. Then the corvette hailed again. "Who are you?"

"Two boats from the *Medusa*."

There was no reply until the barge carrying de Chaumareys had come alongside the corvette. Then a rope was thrown to them and an officer asked them to come on board at once. Leaning over the side, he called down:

"Where is the *Medusa*?"

For long seconds, no one replied. Not a man spoke, de Chaumareys was silent.

Then Rang said, quietly: "Her captain will tell you in a moment."

These two boats and the raft were all that was left. Of the 150 who had embarked on the raft, still drifting somewhere out at sea, the majority were already dead. Another night of butchery was about to begin and by morning only one woman and twenty-nine men would be left alive.

8

TIME RUNNING OUT

July 9 to 13

BY nightfall on July 8 fragmentation was complete among the castaways on the raft. Earlier, there had been a tendency for the people to reject their identity as part of a suffering mass because they rejected the unfair sufferings inflicted on them for no fault of their own. Then they coalesced into subgroups grumbling among themselves and consoling each other; and showing hostility to other sub-groups. To begin with, the lines were not firmly drawn. Most of the soldiers were on one side, but not all. Some people were on nobody's side; they were neutral.

Now, however, the jumbled mass of humanity shook down into its basic ingredients and coalesced at that level. The negroes among the soldiers became negroes first and soldiers a long way second. Their sense of basic identity was reinforced by the nearness of their own continent, Africa. They felt, from signs obvious to them but not to the Europeans, that the raft was close in to the coast; and that, once ashore, they at least could survive. Their actions were soon to show that they had been much less oppressed physically by the suffocating heat and burning sun than the Europeans, whose bodies were seriously depleted of both water and salt. Confidence in their own powers of survival in these conditions enabled them to concoct a plan by which they would survive at the expense of the others. Because they needed greater numbers than they at present amounted to, the negroes approached another newly-formed sub-group for an alliance.

Led by a Piedmontese sergeant, these men were all

Italians or Spaniards and most had been neutral or
had actually supported the French officers. But the
offer of the negroes to guide them across the desert,
once they were ashore, gave them hope of being able
to reach ultimate safety. That in turn led their
thoughts towards money, without which they might be
little better off. The valuables and cash belonging to
everyone and amounting to 1,500 francs had been put
in a bag which had been tied to the top of the mast
for safety and was temptingly in view all the time. The
sergeant had already stolen some of the wine for his
people, an easy task because the officers had put him
in charge of it, and seems to have conceived the details
of the plan to drive the officers off the raft.

An attempt was made to subvert some of the
French sailors. This proved to be fatal to the success
of the plot because these men had formed a separate
sub-group. The seamen had a basic psychological advantage matching that of the negroes' confidence in
their desert-survival capabilities. A factor behind the
despair, resentment and irritation which had afflicted
so many and had led in part to the suicidal butcheries,
was the sheer unexpectedness of being one moment
safe on board a ship and the next cast away and apparently doomed to die. Many had been maddened with
rage at this abrupt and unfair transition. For an experienced seaman, however, the prospect of shipwreck
and possibly death in the sea was an accepted occupa-
tional hazard. Not to be welcomed, but part of the
world as it was. Their attitude was professional,
calmer; and this bound them together. To them, the
plot was crazy; it ignored the difficulty of actually getting ashore on a coast that was not even visible on
the horizon.

They told the officers of what was afoot and pointed
out to them those men whom they knew definitely to
be in the plot, but they did not know them all. The
signal for revolt was given by a Spaniard moving towards the mast. Once there, he drew a knife and with
his other hand made the sign of the cross. The sailors

overpowered the man and threw him into the sea. An Italian soldier did not wait to be disposed of in the same fashion. Still holding the axe with which he had armed himself, he jumped overboard. The plot had gone wrong from the outset, the advantage of a surprise rush lost.

Nevertheless, the negroes and the remaining Italians and Spaniards launched their attack. They were gibbering with rage and crying out for Lieutenant d'Anglas to be handed over to them. This had become a kind of rallying cry and it was impossible to reason with them. In the vicious fighting which raged in the darkness the canteen manageress was again thrown into the sea; she was rescued by the injured Courdein and some of the engineering workmen who remained an organized body led by their foreman, the redoubtable ex-sergeant Lavillette. Savigny and Corréard cited his courage and effectiveness in close-quarter fighting as a main factor, once again, in the survival of their party. The brief burst of energy which had fueled both the revolt and its repulse was succeeded by exhaustion, nervous as well as physical. The survivors were drained of all feeling and emotion and lay supine until the sun rose.

They could now count the living and see that some twenty men had died during the night, including four or five loyal sailors. Of the thirty people left, many were seriously injured. The canteen manageress had suffered a broken thigh from being thrown between the timbers of the raft, while her husband's skull had been cut open by a slash from a saber. Only about twenty men were still capable of standing upright. And they, like the badly injured, were in agony from long immersion in sea water. The skin had almost all been stripped off their legs while their bruises and cuts burned with the salt water irritant. They could not keep silent, but cried out with pain continually.

An additional torment was the derangement of the young sailor lad, Leon, who ran about the raft as if demented, calling out for his mother, for water, for food. When he stumbled over the feet and legs of the men, their agony was terrible. They screamed at him not to do it, but without real reproach. They pardoned him everything, for it was hard to see a child dying before he had had a chance to live. Besides, the boy had been very brave and was half a veteran for he had been on campaign in the East Indies the previous year. He was given more than his share of the little wine they had left, but clearly his life was flickering out like the flame of a lamp when the fuel runs low.

The 9th of July was their fifth day afloat for the castaways. The only food they had left were a dozen small fish. The wine might last the thirty of them four days more. After that, death would come swiftly for them all. They calculated over and over again the simple arithmetic of rescue and always the answer came out the same. The boats had not come back for them. Therefore, they had either been wrecked in the surf in trying to land on the coast, or they had gone on to St. Louis to get help. If—if—they had gone on to St. Louis, they could not reach there in less than three or four days. They might have got to the Senegal yesterday, perhaps. But then a search and rescue operation would have to be organised, ships would have to be prepared and stored, and then they would have to find the raft, which, as far as they knew, might have drifted anywhere. Working out how long that search might take was an unrewarding exercise, for they themselves did not know where they were. But all could see that they had not enough time. They began to think of ways to prolong their existence just a day or two more beyond the four days which was still their final horizon.

The feverishly impatient hopes of the castaways, that with luck the boats might already have arrived at St. Louis, had not been far off the mark. But they were not the whole truth. One boat had been sunk, three driven ashore and wrecked because the occupants were dying of thirst. All these people were themselves now in need of rescue. Although the Captain and the Governor had sailed into the roads off St. Louis late on July 8, the situation was so chaotic that they felt they could not cope with it until next day. Therefore, although Lieutenant de Parnajon was ready and eager to sail at once in the *Argus,* a full council had to be held before he could be given his orders.

These were from Governor Schmaltz, dated July 9. "You will proceed along the coast of the desert and search for the shipwrecked persons in the most likely places, excluding St. John's Creek, where they could not penetrate, and you will supply them with such provisions and ammunition as they may want. After having assured yourself of the fate of these unfortunate persons, you will sail along the coast up to the point where the frigate lies, because there is a possibility that the men on the raft may have sheltered there, if helped by favourable tides. You will then continue your course towards the *Medusa* and you will do everything in your power to find the three barrels containing 90,000 francs in gold belonging to the King. These three barrels will be found in the storeroom, as they could not be taken away when we left the ship. . . ."

Of course, it was proper for the Governor to think of the money belonging to his treasury; but it might have been better if he had ordered a search to seaward for the raft. In effect, instead of the boats bringing a ship to aid the people on the raft, a single vessel only was to be sent out—to the aid of the people from the boats. And to save the treasure of the *Medusa.*

The truth, which the thirty tormented survivors on the raft could not guess, was that they had already been given up for dead. When the news of the shipwreck was discussed in St. Louis, it was bringing the stoic comment: "It's a pity the raft was abandoned, for there were many brave fellows on board. But their sufferings are over now. They may be happier than we are, for who knows how all this will end?"

The arrival of the French Royal squadron in such disarray, with its flagship and many of its passengers lost in circumstances of obvious incompetence, made the English governor, Colonel Brereton, unwilling to hand over the colony of Senegal to the new French governor, Colonel Schmaltz. It was this serious situation which was now the prime concern of the senior French officials.

Lieutenant Espiaux had taken command of the combined crews of the three boats which had stranded at intervals, more or less in the same area, during the morning and afternoon of July 8. Charlotte Picard recalled that he had reproached them for their suspicions and explained how he had earlier landed sixty-three people and so had room for the Picard family. That party was now somewhere to the north, too far away to make contact, but sufficiently numerous to hold off small bands of Moors. Espiaux led his group of more than one hundred people southwards, sometimes along the beach, sometimes trending inland in hope of finding water. Very often they marched during the night or through a part of the night, and although the sequence of events they record is the same, the actual days blurred in their memory. Either Mlle. Picard gained a day, or M. Bredif lost one!

The first event was a decision to march inland in search of water which they found by digging holes in the sand. The water under the dunes contained more salt than did the sea itself, so they trudged on to an inland plain where Bredif noticed little clumps of tall, hard grass growing. When they had dug here to a depth of three or four feet, they uncovered water which was white in appearance and smelt of sulphur. Bredif risked taking a mouthful, found it delicious and cried out: "We're saved!"

They drank their fill, rested, tried to eat a little of the soaked biscuit they had with them, then trudged back to the firmer sand of the beach to continue their march southwards. This event took place on the eve-

ning of July 8 according to Bredif, on the morning of
July 9 according to Charlotte Picard. These times, the
evenings and early mornings, were the most favorable
for walking; in the full heat of the days it was so
suffocatingly hot that they could do little more than
lie down and try to rest. Both accounts make clear
how the presence of the young children of the Picard
family was a constant hindrance to the progress of the
march party and the underlying fear of everyone in it
that even a small delay during a trek across the Sahara
might involve the deaths of all.

The Picard family's clothes were in tatters and they
had lost their shoes in the wreck of the pinnace. It
was painful for them to walk on hot sand, let alone
over areas strewn with sharp-edged sea shells. Madame Picard and two of the older girls gratefully accepted items of men's clothing from the officers, who
also took turns to carry the children. The sailors followed their example. The family were set at the head
of the party so that they should not be left behind if
they straggled. Even so, the women and children had
a hard time and Bredif recalled a moment when M.
Picard could stand no more and for the sake of his
family demanded that everyone halt. His position was
peculiarly unfortunate, as the head of a group which
was keeping everyone back and risking the lives of all;
and yet there was little he himself could do. The poor
man could hardly carry four children simultaneously
and help his wife and grown-up daughters at the
same time.

On July 9, according to Charlotte, the conflict came
to a head. Two naval officers complained of the inability even of the adult females in the family to keep up.
There was a proposal to abandon them. M. Picard
replied bitterly with accusations of selfishness and bru-
tality. These officers and their few supporters put their
hands on their swords. M. Picard seized the hilt of the
poniard with which he had armed himself aboard the
frigate. The females flung themselves in front of M.
Picard and loudly implored him to stay in the desert

with them, rather than ask for help from Frenchmen who were clearly worse than Moors. This touched an infantry officer, Captain Bégnère, who persuaded his soldiers to stay with the family; and their decision shamed the others into acceptance. Soon afterwards, however, two members of the party left it individually and strode off inland on their own. They were the naturalist, M. Kummer, and M. Rogéry, a member of the Philanthropic Society of Cape Verde. They thought, doubtless, that their specialized knowledge and experience would give them a higher survival value alone than when tied to a party marching at the pace of the slowest female.

To Charlotte, Africa was a terrible place. That night, she was awakened by the roaring of leopards and the camp was alarmed by the sight of a lion, which proved to be a bush moving with the night breeze. Marching on at sunrise, their scouts sighted two Moorish tents just inland, the homes of shepherds. They were occupied only by Moorish women and children, virtually naked, who struck Bredif as being as "ugly and frightful" as the desert they inhabited. However, they were able to buy or barter food from them, including two goats. They rested here during the worst heat of the day until startled by a cry of "To arms, to arms!"

The alarm was caused by the approach of a small party of Moors and Negroes armed with lances. The French armed themselves against attack and nearly came to blows with the intruders, whom they greatly outnumbered, until by means of sign language the Moors seemed to indicate that they came as guides. Bredif thought them fine-looking men and their well-dressed Negro slave a proud and handsome man. This Negro could not contain his mirth at the evident fear of some of the Negro soldiers with the French party, who still had their swords drawn in alarm. He stepped into the middle of them, placed the points of their sabres to his chest, and threw his arms wide in a gesture to show that he was not afraid of them, they ought not to be fearful of him.

Their guides led them to a large Moorish camp some distance away. By the time they reached there Charlotte's dress was further torn and her legs streaming blood from walking through the prickly shrubs which grew in abundance. The women, children and dogs of the tribe thought the tattered French party as outlandish as the Mooresses had appeared to Bredif. They swarmed round to examine the strangers, pinched them, snatched at their hair, threw sand at them. The dogs bit at their legs, while the old crones, delighted, cut the buttons off the officers' coats or snatched away pieces of lace. At length, the guides drove this crowd away and they were taken to the chiefs, who had a good supper prepared for them, gave them water without limit, and charged either nothing or only a low price. Suddenly a Moor approached her father with a shout of recognition: "Tiens toi, Picard! ni a pas connaître moi Amet?"

Astounded at finding himself addressed in French by a Moor, M. Picard at last realised that the man was Amet, a young goldsmith whom he had employed long ago during his previous time in Senegal. To him at least he could tell the full story of the shipwreck and its aftermath, which reduced Amet to tears. The Musulman instantly distributed free a large amount of milk and water to the Christians and had a tent raised just for the Picards. His religion would not allow him to sleep under the same roof with them. They only got a little sleep, however, for the cries of the night watchmen guarding the cattle alarmed some in the French party who had always thought they had been led to the camp merely to be plundered, and they urged everyone else to be well away before daylight. One man, an old naval officer who had been appointed Captain of the Port of Senegal, had somehow managed to retain 3,000 francs, but most of the French party possessed little worth plundering.

Seeing that their guests were determined to leave,

the Moors appointed guides and offered to hire asses
to carry those who were too weak to walk. M. Bredif
noted that the men most often overcome with fatigue
were those who looked the strongest. He concluded,
complacently, that it was mental strength that
counted in a crisis. He was happily astonished at his
own revealed capacity to endure privations at least
as well as the next man. His normally weak stomach
had not troubled him at all. He congratulated himself too soon. After only a few hours walking he fell
asleep literally on his feet and would have been left
behind had not a straggler found him. At the halts,
the inevitable cry of: "On your feet! March!" was the
sound he dreaded most.

M. Picard had managed to hire two asses which
carried the young children, while he and the rest of
his family walked trying to keep up with the soldiers.
When Captain Bégnère saw this, he lent the ass which
he had hired for himself to the grown-up girls. He
also was no longer a young man, so it was no mere
gallant gesture.

Very early on the morning of July 11 the march
party again reached the beach to continue their trudge
along the shoreline. For those riding the asses, it was
a momentous event. The poor beasts, weary of the
weights they had been carrying for five hours, broke
into a run and lay down amid the breakers, reveling
in the cool water. Some of the riders fell off. Charlotte
was pinned underneath her animal for a moment and
took an involuntary bath. One of her young brothers
was nearly swept out to sea, but she managed to grab
him. Then they all burst into laughter and continued
the march, happy except for the asses which had been
pressed into use again.

At about ten o'clock a sail was sighted. Shortly
after, the well-remembered silhouette of the brig
Argus came into sight. A handkerchief was tied to the
barrel of a musket and waved in the air. Keeping out
beyond the area of broken water, the *Argus* lowered
her sails and hoisted out a boat. But this could not

get through the breakers, so five of the Moors plunged
into the sea and swam out through the rollers towards
it. After half an hour they came back, swimming between them three small barrels of provisions. Charlotte
felt ashamed of the suspicions they had all had of the
Moors, at this demonstration of their willingness to help.

The provisions consisted of wine, brandy, biscuit
and a Dutch cheese. With them was a note from Lieutenant de Parnajon to Lieutenant Espiaux, telling him
that convoys of camels loaded with provisions were
being sent out by the governor and that the Moors
had been asked to give every assistance. The effect of
water, wine and brandy mixed with good news, after
so long under the fierce heat of a vertical sun and fear
constantly with them, produced an extraordinary joy.
Life, which had been a burden to endure, now became
precious, noted Charlotte. Lowering and sulky faces
became split into wide grins. Enemies became friends.
The greedy forgot their cupidity for a moment. The
children smiled for the first time since the *Medusa* had
been wrecked. "Everyone seemed to be born again,"
she wrote, adding archly, "I even believe the sailors
sung the praises of their mistresses." Perhaps she was
implying that the suffering men had had until now no
thoughts of women, even when they were as naked as
the shepherds' wives had been, or clothed in revealing
tatters as she and her sisters were.

At about six o'clock that evening it was her father
who was physically worn out, for he had thus far
walked all the way. He wanted to stop for a moment
and sit down. His wife and Charlotte stayed with him.
The children and the other older girls jogged on behind the caravan, riding on the asses. The halt was a
mistake, for all three instantly fell asleep. When they
awoke, it was late, the sun was sinking in the west,
and there was no sign of the march party. Instead, a
small group of bearded Moors was riding towards
them on camels. The Picards' instinctive uneasiness
returned, but they were in no condition to run away.

The Arab chieftain alighted from his camel and con-

fronted the ladies. For the second time they heard a
Moor speak an unexpected language. This time it was
English. He introduced himself as Mr. Carnet. He
asked them not to mistake him for an Arab, in spite
of his headdress and robes. He was, however, friendly
with some of the desert chieftains and hearing that
there had been a shipwreck on the coast, had hurried
forward to help. Their main party was only two
leagues away and he could give them a lift there on
his camels.

M. Picard accepted the offer with alacrity and was
soon perched on a British camel. The two ladies were
sure they would fall off the hairy haunches of the animals and preferred to walk. They spent the night at
the main camp and next day Mr. Carnet went off to
get provisions. He would bring them to their next halt-
ing point, some hours' walk ahead. By noon, however,
the heat had become intolerable, even the Moors had
difficulty in enduring it, and they searched about for
any sort of shade. All they could find were some mi-
mosa and ground plants. But they were better than
nothing at all.

Charlotte compared the heat reflected from the
sand to the blast from an oven door as it opened. She
felt literally suffocated and about to die. A man called
Borner, a smith, saw her plight and offered her a drink
of muddy water from his reserve container—an old
boot. She seized the boot and drank the awful contents in frantic gulps and with such evident pleasure
that others wanted to share. But the remnants were
so disgusting that they spat it out.

M. Bredif found the sand so hot to the touch that
he could not endure putting his bare hands to the
ground. He gathered some stalks and leaves of a
creeping plant and made a little shade for his head,
which he laid on his coat. But the rest of his body felt
as if it were in a furnace, roasting.

Mr. Carnet returned with a small caravan of supplies which included drinking water as well as rice and
dried fish. It appears that he was part of a rescue

operation set up by the English Governor of Senegal, who had not handed over to M. Schmaltz and was still in control of the colony. The French Governor-designate had contented himself simply with sending out a single ship, the *Argus*.

Charlotte is very coy about the incident which followed the meal. Driven by the heat, the whole party marched for an hour towards the beach in order to plunge themselves in the sea. The Picard girls stayed in the water a long time and then took themselves off to a secluded spot among the dunes, where, she says, they "shaded" themselves with some old clothes they happened to have. Her cousin had an officer's tunic with gold lace and this, she says, attracted the attention of a Moor who, thinking the two girls were asleep, tried to steal the tunic for the sake of the lace. But as soon as he saw they were really awake, he stopped and merely looked at them very "steadfastly." Charlotte was much concerned later to deny a story that she was the one covered by a tunic, that she had nothing on underneath it, and that the Moor had lifted up the covering and had been both astonished and delighted by what he saw, which he had related with gusto to his companions.

At three o'clock next morning, the 13th of July according to Charlotte, they began their final day's march. Mr. Carnet went on ahead to get an ox. M. Bredif, whose dates do not agree, says that when they rendezvoused with the animal it was "small, but tolerably fat," and a negro killed it for them by twisting its neck like a chicken. They lit a fire and sat round it, roasting the beef on the point of a bayonet, or a sabre, or just a pointed stick. It was many hours to dawn and the darkness accentuated the bearded, sunburned faces of the men, while the constant thunder of the breakers on the coast of Africa and the roaring of wild beasts out in the dark desert made a picture which, thought Charlotte, David or Girodet would have loved to paint. It could be hung in the Louvre and be titled "Cannibals Feasting." And no one in

Paris would guess that some of the cannibals had been born beside the Seine or imagine the pleasure to be derived from eating wild plants, drinking muddy water out of a dirty boot, or gulping down a delicious roast cooked in smoke. It was a sensation the fashionable, worldly-wise youth of Paris would never know.

Late that morning they were led inland to the top of a dune and saw that the desert had ended. The last part of their march was among green trees haunted with humming birds and parrots. Shortly after, they reached the banks of the Senegal, a freshwater river, and their perils were over. At two o'clock a small boat appeared, being rowed slowly against the current. Two Europeans got out and asked for M. Picard. They said they had been sent by his old friends, M. Artigue and M. Lambouré, with a hamper of provisions just for himself and his family. This was a personal gift. Two much larger boats, full of provisions provided by the English Governor of Senegal for all the castaways, were on their way from St. Louis and would arrive within an hour or so.

In the evening the boats took them all down river to St. Louis, where a great crowd was assembled to greet them. As Charlotte tartly remarked, everyone in the town seemed to be there with the exception of their late commanders, Captain de Chaumareys and Governor Schmaltz. The English Governor rode up with his staff, which included Mr. Carnet, to make them welcome and seemed to be distressed particularly by the plight of the children and the young women.

The most sickly members of the march party were taken to hospital, the rest were distributed among private householders, for St. Louis was only a small trading post. But everyone was glad to help, the English officers appearing particularly eager to have the pleasure, as they put it, of caring for some of the castaways. M. Artigue had no room to put up the entire Picard family, so Charlotte and her grown-up sister

Caroline gratefully accepted the offer of an English couple, Mr. and Mrs. Kingsley, to stay with them.

After they had been combed, cleansed and dressed by the domestic negresses, the two girls were given white dresses which contrasted strangely with their sunburnt, almost blackened faces. Charlotte felt faint at the change in her fortunes, which seemed unbelievable, and she was shy when invited downstairs to join their hosts and some English officers at a meal. She could eat little and understood nothing of the language.

A young Frenchman who knew some English was able to ask questions and translate her brief replies. Everyone seemed astonished at the way in which children and young girls had endured such misfortunes. To Charlotte it was all quite unreal, the pleasant room, the kindly, interested people. The miles of burning sand were still underfoot and the walls of the house heaved with the motions of the waves. She asked to be excused and once in bed fell into a restoring sleep of total exhaustion.

The young engineer Bredif and some of his companions were taken into the house of two merchants of Bordeaux, Potin and Durecur, who were lavish with their resources. The castaways were completely outfitted and given feather beds or good mattresses to sleep on. But M. Bredif slept badly. The bed seemed to rise and fall underneath him as if on a stormy sea, or else he was trudging from nowhere to nowhere across burning sands.

There was still no news in St. Louis of the two men, Rogéry and Kummer, who had struck off on their own from the main party which had escaped the shipwrecked boats and who had gone inland some days before. Nor was there any sign of the party of sixty-three who had landed earlier from the overloaded longboat at a point still further north, believed to be near the Mottes d'Angel.

But the British were not too worried. They had a standing agreement with the local Moors that any lost or shipwrecked Europeans would be cared for and a reward paid to those who brought them to St. Louis. This was why most of the Moors had been helpful rather than hostile to the passengers from the stranded boats.

The raft was a different matter. The search for survivors still at sea was not a British concern, but that of the French officials who possessed ships but no belief that anyone could still be alive either on the raft or in the wreck of the *Medusa*.

9

"The Eyes of Argus"

The castaways, July 9 to 19

THE same high sun which burned and suffocated the marchers ashore blazed down on the raft as it drifted idly with the current, out of sight of land. For the castaways there were no waterholes to dig, no Moorish goats to be milked. They could only wait, for rescue or for death, whichever came the sooner. On July 9 they had worked out that the remaining wine might last them for four days more, until the 13th. And they had calculated that although rescue was possible by that date, it might be delayed by many days, in which case the rescue vessel would discover only a raft covered with blackened, sun-dried corpses.

They watched the wine barrel most carefully and on the 11th detected two soldiers secretly drinking from it. They were lying down, apparently innocent, but were sipping by putting a reed through a hole which they had bored in the wood. The men had already determined what the punishment for this should be, and it was carried out. The two soldiers were thrown overboard.

The boy sailor, Leon, died shortly afterwards. There were now twenty-six men and one woman remaining, a dozen of them badly wounded, delirious and unlikely to last more than a day or two. This judgement was certainly that of Savigny the surgeon, who gave the best of them not more than forty-eight hours. The logical course which followed from it was debated by the fifteen men who were still fully conscious. The rations of the twelve if given to the fifteen might keep the fifteen alive for six more days. A moderate course of merely reducing the rations of the sick would be cowardice; the sick would die by inches, the fifteen would not last so long. The debate was on a note of despair because although death had been with them every day for a week, it had been inflicted upon others of their number as if by fate. Both the canteen woman and her injured husband would have to die. What a way to repay her for twenty years of service to the French armies—slaughtered by Frenchmen while she lay unconscious with a broken thigh. Could any of them actually do such a thing?

Eventually self-preservation prevailed, the decision was made, and four volunteers said they were ready to take on the task of execution. Three were sailors, one was a soldier. The remainder turned away while the things were done. Some wept.

The instruments of execution were thrown overboard in an outburst of horror; but one sabre was kept in case it might be needed to cut rope or wood. A sour mood set in and during sleep the images of their dead companions returned.

On July 13 an unimaginable event occurred. A white butterfly fluttered over the raft and after darting about, at length settled down on the sail and folded its wings. It appeared a visitor from another world, for the universe of the castaways was restricted to a few metres of wave-washed timbers floating over unknown depths and drifted at random by winds and tides. All took the appearance to be quite literally a message that land was near. Some men were so desperate that they thought of munching the creature, but others swore the butterfly was a sign from heaven for them and banded together to protect it.

On succeeding days more butterflies came and fluttered above the heads of the castaways and occasionally a large seabird came near. The butterflies had given them hope and they found an energy they had not thought they possessed. They again tried to catch fish but without success, and also tried to lure one of the birds to settle on the raft, which it seemed almost about to do. This attempt failed also.

The waves which in all but the calmest weather rolled across the raft stung the sores with which their bodies were covered, so that they could not sleep. A low moaning and crying usually marked the position of the raft in the darkness. Several times schools of stinging jellyfish were carried against them by the waves, intensifying their agony.

They found the strength to dismantle some of the timbers at the ends of the raft and from them construct in the center a kind of raised platform. It did not keep the sea off them entirely, but it was better. There were holes between the planks of the platform, through which the waves slopped upwards and wet them. So they covered it with what old clothing and other effects they could find, which made it less hard also. This resulted in a few chance finds among the effects: a lemon, which the finder was forced to share; thirty cloves of garlic; and two little bottles of a liquid designed for cleaning the teeth. The latter proved delightful. A tiny drop held on the tongue removed for a few moments the terrible thirst which racked them all.

Each of these discoveries produced rage immediately and a demand for a share, which was agreed to; very nearly, there was on each occasion a return to the violence which had swept the raft of all but fifteen of the 150 people who had embarked on it. But in every case the emotion died without result. It seems that they now had what they needed above all else, even water-space.

They lay all together on the raised platform and took turns to tell yarns of personal experience, the more sharp-witted egging the others on. The twenty-eight-year-old Clairet had served in Spain and fought at Waterloo. Ex-sergeant Lavillette in particular had many good stories of his campaigns, both by land and by sea. He was fond of recalling Lutzen, Bautzen, Dresden, Leipzig, Hanau, Montmirail, Champaubert, Montereau and other scenes of battles, forced marches and privations of all kinds. "And none of them," he would declare, "were anything at all in comparison to what I have to endure on this frightful machine. To start with, I had to be afraid only during the battle, but here I am in danger all the time and, most dreadful, I have to fight Frenchmen, my own comrades. Then I have other enemies—hunger, thirst, the stormy sea and its monsters, the terrible sun. And on this battle-field, although I have fresh wounds among the old scars, they are not tended; I have no means of dressing them. I can do nothing whatever to save myself and, unassisted, I would put my survival at no more than a day or two longer."

Then the conversation would turn to the plight of France, and anger would keep them alive. Military occupation by the armies of Russia, Prussia, Austria, England—armies they had often defeated in the field—was hard to bear. Their resentment could momentarily make their own fates seem in comparison of little importance when measured against the national disaster.

In the suffocating, searing heat of midday nothing could banish the torment of their thirst, not even the routine of moistening their parched lips with urine. They kept this in small tin cups which they placed in little pools of sea water to cool. One man never could bring himself to swallow it. Savigny, who kept himself sane and his mind active by continual observation and thought, observed that some men's urine was more agreeable than that of others. Really, it did not taste too disgusting, but in some men, it was true, the liquid had become thick and very acrid. In all men, the drinking of it made him want to urinate again almost instantly. They also drank sea water, but not very much. Although their thirst was quenched for a deli-cious instant, a moment later it had returned and was even more severe. M. Griffon du Bellay, the gover-nor's secretary, was the exception; he would drink ten or twelve cups of sea water in succession.

They devised a series of tricks to relieve their thirst

or to give themselves the impression that they had relieved it; and perhaps also to break the monotony or manufacture a luxury. Some found that pieces of pewter held in the mouth produced a kind of coolness. Washing their faces in sea water could produce relief; so could soaking their hair, or holding their hands in the sea. The most prized sensation was that produced by a single empty perfume bottle. When it was sniffed, the perfume of roses could still be sensed and inhaled and proved extremely soothing. The tiny bottle was passed from hand to hand like a pipe of peace. There were some who did not drink their ration of wine straight off but put it in a tin cup and using a quill sucked at the liquid gradually. They found this very beneficial.

Although the wine ration was minute, nevertheless Savigny observed that it could now produce a state verging on intoxication which resulted in discord. The worst occurrence was on July 14, when three normally rational and responsible men suddenly agreed between themselves to, first, drink all the wine remaining in the barrel, and, second, commit suicide. They were Jean Coudein, the naval officer and nominal commander of the raft, Sub-Lieutenant Clairet, and Sergeant-Major Charlot. No combat had actually ensued, and the other men were still arguing with them, when everyone's attention was diverted by the appearance of a crowd of sharks around the raft. These were no ordinary sharks but monsters nearly thirty feet long cruising on the surface with their backs high out of the water. They swam to within inches of the raft, so near that ex-sergeant Lavillette was able to strike several of them with a sabre. When struck by the steel blade, the monsters would submerge but then reappear only seconds later quite unperturbed. Probably they were harmless basking sharks which feed on plankton.

The sight of ordinary sharks was commonplace, for they often surrounded the raft. No one cared about them any more. Some of the castaways would immerse themselves completely in the water which continually submerged the front part of the raft; they found this relieved their burning thirst a little. Others jumped over the side for a swim, which had the same cooling, soothing effect. Nothing counted now except relief from heat and thirst.

The sharks did not attack. Almost certainly, the raft had begun to collect marine organisms and probably small and not so small fish in some numbers, as it offered food, protection from predators, and shade. The sharks may have been attracted by the fish but have been discouraged by the difficulty of getting in among the crevices between the timbers in which their prey could hide. The body of a fish contains a great deal of water—fresh water—and much of the nourishment which the castaways required lay all around and even underneath their feet. But all their attempts at fishing had failed for want of the proper equipment.

Some could still joke. One wag thought of the phrase, "If they send the brig out looking for us, pray God she'll have the eyes of Argus." This was thought very witty and became a catch-phrase in the final days.

On July 16 they thought the land must be very near and eight men were still strong enough and sufficiently determined to make an attempt to sail and row there. They made a primitive canoe of solid wood from a single timber some twelve metres long with crossboards fixed and a little mast. The sail was a hammock and for oars they were going to use barrel staves. Fortunately a sailor who was walking on it had to put his weight a little off-center in order to get round the mast, and that was sufficient to capsize the "canoe" and throw the sailor into the water. They decided to give up the attempt and to let death come to them where they were.

Their thoughts that night were very gloomy. It was hard to tell exactly how much wine was left in the barrel, but certainly they were coming to the end of their meager rations. The human flesh which they kept with them for their meals was beginning to stink, and the fact that it was human reminded them of their own mortality. They could not look at it now without feeling oppressed by terror. Daybreak on July 17 brought a cloudless sky, without any shield against the coming blaze of the sun. As the heat began to be felt, they said prayers and the wine ration was given out. They began to savour the momentary delight of drops of liquid in their mouths before submitting to the thirteenth day of torment.

The castaways had assumed the *Argus* would be chosen to undertake any search because of her small size and shallow draft. They had also assumed that everyone would be thinking of them. Their plight had been so much more desperate than that of those in the boats and their ability to survive for any length of time clearly limited. It seemed obvious that to find them would be the main object of any search.

The captain of the *Argus* had received other orders, however. His main task was to cruise along the beaches north of the Senegal River as far as the Arguin Bank in order to look for survivors from the boats who had been cast ashore and to get supplies to them from seaward. This order, while it showed that the French authorities had an accurate idea of how small a chance most of the boats had of making the Senegal on their own, was also unnecessary. The English had an established rescue system based on contact with the local tribes and it was this system which brought most of the boats' survivors without further loss to St. Louis. The *Argus,* kept offshore by the breakers, was through no fault of her captain able to contribute little—three small barrels of supplies, to be precise. She should have been directed primarily towards an estimated track of the drift of the raft from the *Medusa.* Her involvement in shore operations may have been mainly a "prestige" operation to show the English that the new French administration was not without resources, initial impressions to the contrary.

Obeying his instructions, Lieutenant de Parnajon, captain of the *Argus,* had cruised northwards along the coast inshore of where the raft actually was and although his lookouts also searched to seaward they saw no sign of the castaways. On the morning of July 17 he had given up the search and was returning to St. Louis with a favorable wind which had brought him to within forty leagues of his destination, with failure to report.

Then the wind veered round from north-west to south-west, which was foul for the Senegal, but ideal for making an attempt to locate the wreck of the *Medusa* somewhere on the Arguin Bank, a task which was also included in his orders. On an impulse, Parnajon ordered the ship put about and the *Argus* began to move northwards and out to sea. After two hours on the north-west tack, the lookout at the masthead reported another vessel in sight. It was still too distant to make out what kind of craft it was.

The *Argus* was sighted by the castaways many hours before her lookout saw the raft, because the brig's tall masts were visible for a great distance. A captain of infantry was the first to look up from sipping at his wine, which had just been issued, and catch sight of three topmasts above the horizon. He gave a shout of joy and everyone was infected with his delight for a moment, feeling that deliverance was certain. Then fear entered, a frantic fear of not being seen. The metal hoops were torn off casks and made into a tall flagstaff, colored handkerchiefs were tied to the end, and a man was shinned up the mast by their united efforts, so that he could cling to the top and wave his bundle of flags.

For half an hour hope alternated with fear. There were those who saw the topmasts grow larger, others who thought they were disappearing. Both were correct, for the brig was steering a southerly course parallel to the raft, on her way back to St. Louis. When first seen, she would have been coming slightly nearer, but after half an hour would have been moving away.

They could not be sure even that it was the *Argus,* for they never saw her hull.

When the unknown brig had disappeared, they shut themselves in and gave up. They made a tent out of a spare sail and all crowded inside it to escape the burning sun; they closed all entrances and tried to console themselves with sleep. But sleep was not what they wanted. Their minds were alight with irritation and despair, they wanted to hit out. A proposition was made, that they write a brief account of what had happened to them on a wooden board, which all would sign, and then as a final gesture they would fasten that message to the top of the mast. It would tell the government and their families how and why they had died and by whose hand.

For two hours they lay in the semi-darkness, wracked by a torment worse than the violence of the noon sun. At length M. Courtade, who had been master gunner of the *Medusa,* had to leave the tent to relieve himself. But he was only halfway out into the sunshine when they saw his face take on a look of awesome joy, both hands stretched out towards the sea, his breathing so shallow that he could only whisper, "Saved! The brig—it's close, close!"

There was a convulsive scramble to get out of the tent. Even those whose feet and legs were in such a state that they had been unable to move for the last two days somehow crawled on their bellies out to where they could lie down and see deliverance approaching. Tears ran down their faces; those who could, embraced each other, or waved handkerchiefs at the brig which, half a league distant, was bearing down on them under all press of sail.

As it came closer they could make out a large white flag at the head of the foremast, which showed she was a ship of the Royal Navy of France. And shortly after, they could see that this was indeed the *Argus,* and their joy redoubled. When two musket shot distant, they saw her sails lowered, which took the way off her, and the brig coasted slowly past the raft, her bulwarks and shrouds crowded with men waving hats or handkerchiefs. A boat was hoisted out and lowered to the water, then began to pull across the waves towards them.

The boat was commanded by an officer, M. Lemaigre, and what he saw as he ran alongside the raft must have astounded him. Fifteen men, almost naked, faces and bodies blotched and disfigured by the scorching sun; the skin almost stripped from their legs and feet; covered with sores and wounds. Fifteen hollow faces with staring eyes from which tears ran down; and long unkempt beards to make their appearance more wild and frightful. Only about five could even attempt to stagger across the raft to the boat. The others crawled or simply lay helpless. One of the latter was Alexander Corréard. He had not expected to last out this last day, yet had a foreboding that rescue would come. Dimly, he had felt that a series of events so extraordinary could not be destined for oblivion. Some of them at least would survive to tell the story.

Lemaigre boarded the raft and helped or carried the more helpless castaways to the boat. As, man by man, the wasted figures were brought on board the *Argus*, the crew were silent, but pity and compassion could be read in every face. They were given light food, a broth, with some wine, and their wounds were dressed. The little ship was turned into a hospital. But the fever lingered. Some became delirious once more. An army officer got up and tried to throw himself into the sea, to search for his pocket book; and had to be forcibly prevented. Others showed equally strange signs of continuing derangement.

The winds being unfavourable much of the time, the final stage of their journey to Senegal took two more days. The position at which they had been found was many miles from the coast; their belief that land was near had been illusion, perhaps a fortunate one. The only time they can have been really close to land was soon after their towrope to the boats had been loosed, for just south of this position the coast of Africa juts out seaward for some distance. A little more determination, some spark of courage in the leaders, might have brought the raft to shore after a day or two. Lieutenant de Parnajon did not know this, for the wreck of the *Medusa* had not been located and the original start-position of the raft could not yet be calculated. All he knew was that his discovery of the raft was luck, a fortunate chance inspired by a feeling, as the wind changed, that somehow he ought to search again for the *Medusa*. Now, as he told one of the castaways, "If they made me captain of a frigate, I couldn't feel any more pleasure than I did when I sighted your raft."

On July 19 the *Argus* anchored in the roads off St. Louis and the fifteen survivors of the 150 were transferred to a small, decked vessel for the passage over the river bar and up to the town itself, where Governor Schmaltz and a crowd of brilliantly dressed officers, French and British, were waiting to greet them. The moment of confrontation was near.

The men they were expecting to greet consisted of four Army officers, Captain Dupont, Lieutenant L'Heureux, and Sub-Lieutenants Clairet and Lozach, plus Sergeant Major Charlot and Jean Charles, a negro soldier. The Navy was represented by a single officer, Midshipman Coudein, Savigny the ship's surgeon, Courtade the master gunner, a sailor called Coste and a pilot named Thomas. The geographical engineering party were represented by their leader, Corréard, and the foreman, ex-sergeant Lavillette. The list was completed by Griffon du Bellay, the Governor's secretary, and a hospital administrator named François. These were the men who were expected to step ashore at the official, multi-national reception arranged on the quayside.

What the brilliant crowd actually saw were fifteen shrunken scarecrows, a little more presentable than they had been forty-eight hours before, but a still-living accusation. Five were so far gone that they would never recover and were to die at St. Louis within the next weeks. They included the two Army officers, Clairet and Lozach, the master gunner and the black soldier. Some of the others were to be hospital cases for months.

The castaways saw horror and compassion mingled on every side, a genuine surge of feeling which contained also admiration, for these men, had, as it were, come back from the dead. It should have been a heartening welcome, overflowing with joy; but it was not. For among those who had come to greet them were people who should have been ashamed and were not; and one of the hands extended to them in welcome was that which, two weeks before, had cast off the towrope linking them to the boats and had loosed the raft upon its fatal journey.

10

THE SPECTRE AT THE WINDOW

In Senegal, July and August, 1816

SAINT LOUIS was built on a sandbank about two leagues up the Senegal River. The island was 4,000 yards long by 600 yards wide. Originally, the site had been chosen for nothing more grand than a trading post, with an eye to defense. But it was now the center of government administration and had a population of 10,000. Only 500 were Europeans. Two thousand were negroes or free mulattos, 7,500 were slaves. The wide streets, unpaved and covered with banked Sahara sand, were flanked by 150 European houses. The rest of the dwellings consisted of straw huts. It was the poor capital of a poor colony.

Although founded by the French in 1621, Saint Louis tended to change hands when there was a war. It had now been French twice and British twice, and was about to become French for the third time. Some of the settlements on the coast had been founded by the Dutch even earlier than Saint Louis, but had fallen to the French later on. These also tended to become British during a war. Consequently the European hold on the area was fragmented and tenuous, confined virtually to a few places on the coast. The interior was largely unknown and generally hostile, both in its population and because of its diseases.

On July 22 the two men, Kummer and Rogéry, who had gone off on their own into the interior sixteen days before were brought in to St. Louis by a Moorish chieftain, Prince Muhammed, who claimed the reward. They had news of the party of sixty-three who had lightened Espiaux's longboat on July 6 by going ashore at what was thought to be the Mottes d'Angel but may have been Cape Mirik (modern Cape Timiris) still further north. If so, they had marched 400 kilometres through the desert in seventeen days, for by the afternoon of the 22nd they had reached the banks of the Senegal. They staggered into St. Louis the following day, minus five of their number—four soldiers and a soldier's wife. Among the survivors was the Army officer Lieutenant d'Anglas.

Most of the men who had preferred the land to the sea two and a half weeks before had been soldiers. D'Anglas recalled distinctly that the first two days in the desert had been harsh but bearable. On the third day hunger and thirst began to torture them. "Our skin is dried up, our lips are cracked, our tongues are black and have retreated into our mouths. . . . The wife of a corporal, Elisabeth Delus, collapses onto the sand, dead. The sight of this corpse troubles our imagination; it predicts our own fate. But we have neither the courage nor the strength of will to dig a grave for her."

The story which was now beginning to go round in St. Louis was that the corporal had buried his wife's body by the sea shore, after first cutting off her head. That he then put the head in a beggar's sack and would not be parted from it until he was taken to the hospital at St. Louis, where he died of his privations a few days later.

The sequence of the long trek blurred in d'Anglas' recollections after the first few days, as indeed did the memories of everyone else, whether in the desert, with the boats, or on the raft. This was inevitable. But particular incidents remained vivid. D'Anglas recalled the first meeting with Moors, perhaps on July 11, at which they exchanged firearms and gunpowder for foul-tasting food. Then they were seized by another tribe and made to work for them, unloading camels and digging up roots for a fire. "We change masters without changing our bad luck" was the way he put it, adding that the Arab women were particularly cruel. They threw sand into his still festering wounds.

One day they saw the brig *Argus* out to sea, but were not seen by Parnajon. This event, which may have happened on July 13, depressed them greatly. Two days later, perhaps, they met the English (or Irish) political officer, Carnet, wearing his usual Moorish robes and turban which the French assumed was a disguise. More probably it was comfortable, convenient and a subtle compliment to the Arab chiefs who really ruled most of the colony. Much later, another British intelligence officer, T. E. Lawrence ("of Arabia") was to dress exactly in the same way for much the same reasons. Carnet had brought a supply of rice and beef for them, but so hungry were some of the marchers that they ate the rice uncooked and devoured vast portions of beef. One soldier, an Italian, gorged himself so much that next day he lay on the ground with distended stomach and could not get up. Ignoring his cries and contortions, his comrades pulled him to his feet and helped him forward.

On July 18 the *Argus* was seen again, coasting along the shore, and this time the brig's lookouts sighted them. But de Parnajon could do little more than send encouragement. They were still some twenty leagues from St. Louis. Arriving at the banks of the Senegal on July 22, some distance north of the town, they met Kummer the naturalist and Rogéry the explorer being taken in by another party of Arabs for ransom. These gentlemen's local expertise had not done them much good, but they were able to direct the marchers to the best route.

The march of the sixty-three had been an epic, although only fifty-eight lived to tell of it. All the desert groups had been peculiarly ill-dressed for such a trek, particularly the soldiers in shako-topped uniforms and the scientists in their formal clothes. Rang described meeting the naturalist Leschenaux immediately after he had come in. "He had just covered a hundred leagues in the desert, clad as a scientist who is going to the

Academy. The black silk stockings had been so ill-treated that they only covered the upper part of his leg. He showed his usual good humour in all the tales he told us."

Now, all those who had abandoned the frigate on July 5 were accounted for—alive, half-dead, dying, drowned, butchered or lying dehydrated in the desert. So far there were about 140 known to be dead out of some 380. This left only the seventeen men left aboard the *Medusa* unaccounted for. They were presumed to be dead, although the wreck had not been found by the *Argus*. Lieutenant Reynaud was preparing a salvage vessel to go out to search for the frigate and recover the 90,000 francs in gold. There was no thought of saving life and no urgency in these preparations.

The story told by Kummer and Rogéry at some length illustrated the real situation of the colony and the actual role of St. Louis. The desert to the north was controlled by the Moors under King Zaide, whom they had met. He also had been interested in salvage, but only as regards the wrecks of the boats on the shore, and the two Frenchmen had been used as his guides to the wreck sites. The Moors were basically of two races, the most numerous impressing the French with the austere nobility of their features. A minority were ugly and savage-looking. The Moors were quite well-informed concerning European events, including the French Revolution and the almost continual wars which had followed, particularly the campaign in Egypt. Almost their only misconception was their impression that Napoleon and Bonaparte were the names of two different French generals. The Moorish King and his aristocratic Princes were astonished that, in Europe, it was possible for a mere general to become an Emperor; they found this faintly shocking. Their principal wealth consisted of cattle and slaves, but they did have some commerce and manufacture. Rogéry could not have been very comfortable in their encampments, being an early zealot for the abolition of slavery.

The slaves were negroes basically friendly to the French and more open and amiable than the Moors, whom the Europeans always mistrusted in some degree. Apart from its frequently poor soil, it was the well-organised slave trade which prevented Senegal from being fully cultivated, for the negro plantations and villages were often raided by the Moors and life was insecure. Some of the victims were shipped to America from St. Louis, where the slave market was. The basic clash of interests between Europeans who wanted to cultivate or mine the land and Arabs who wished to raid the villages for the pick of the black population had not been resolved when Europe was convulsed by war. M. Picard had been one of the earlier colonists and owned the nearby island of Safal where in 1807 he put down about 100,000 cotton plants. When the English finally captured Senegal in 1809 he had had to abandon the project and return to France.

The English had expected a full French convoy to arrive in 1816, bringing a French governor, a garrison of soldiers, and a host of specialists and administrators as well as supplies of all kinds. What happened was the arrival of three French ships not as a fleet but at varying intervals and without their flagship. Then the new Governor turned up as a fugitive from the wreck of the most important ship, lost in ridiculous circumstances which soon appeared as something worse when, between July 13 and 23, other survivors straggled in with tales of abandonment and cannibalism. More than a third of the people from the flagship were dead and most of the others were haggard castaways clad in rags and tatters, some needing lengthy hospital treatment.

If the local English had wanted an excuse to delay the handing over of the colony, this was it. The French suspected that they did, for two reason. Firstly, the year's crop of Gum Arabic, one of the more profitable exports, was ready to be harvested as a result of the work of the English merchants and planters; naturally, they did not want the benefits of their work to go to the incoming French. Secondly, part of the English administration and garrison would have to leave St. Louis for the nearest English settlements, which were in Gambia, then justly known as the "white man's grave"; and the very season of the year which normally proved mortal to two-thirds of any unacclimatised newcomers was just about to begin. Some of the French suspected that the English intended to hang on to the colony forever, but in fact it was to be handed over after a delay of six months, in January, 1817.

The day after they had staggered out of the desert into St. Louis, the Picards were told that the English Governor had instructed the French Governor to withdraw the bulk of the French contingent to the Cape Verde peninsula, as he had not received orders from his home government to hand over the colony. The French camp was to be set up opposite the Island of Goree which, because of its favorable climate, was used as a convalescent depot for the sick. Goree itself was still in English hands but the locality opposite, then called Daccard (now Dakar) was to be French. The French Governor, Schmaltz, then gave detailed instructions as to who was to go and who was to stay. The Picards were to go.

The English family, the Kingsleys, with whom the Picards were staying were indignant and went straight to the English Governor. He sent back a message by his aide-de-camp that, considering the wretched condition the family were in, they might remain; and all the officers of the *Medusa* likewise. After twenty days with the Kingsleys, the Picards moved out to a hired apartment in St. Louis, but they were very poor. As there was no French administration, M. Picard was not receiving his salary as the public notary; his money and possessions had been mostly lost in the *Medusa*; and his cotton plantations on the Island of Safal had been

uprooted and destroyed by wild animals during the
years since he had been forced to leave in 1809. He
was not even receiving rations from the French stores
and the family were soon reduced to living on a cheap
native diet. They could not afford bread or wine.

In the middle of one such meal an English officer
visited them, and could not conceal his astonishment,
although it was shaming to the Picards. This officer
was Major Peddy, a veteran of the Peninsula War.
The very next day the Picards were put on the English
ration strength, receiving an officer's allowance of
bread, wine, meat, sugar and coffee. This cannot have
improved their relations with the French Governor,
whose meanness towards the family may have been
connected with the fact that M. Picard had been a
voluble critic of the way in which the *Medusa* had
been carelessly stranded and then precipitately abandoned. Indeed, underlying the entire chaotic situation,
particularly those in authority, was a time bomb. The
knowledge that it was there must have nagged away
at them constantly.

Savigny and Coudein were fortunate, for they were
housed and cared for by a French merchant, M. La-
salle. The worst treatment and conditions were reserved for those too ill to be put in private care and
instead were taken to the hospital, which was poorly
equipped and badly staffed. They were laid on truck
beds, without mattresses, and with sheets disgusting-
ly dirty.

The sailors and soldiers were put into one room,
close-packed. Corréard was put into another, together
with the four surviving Army officers from the raft,
Dupont, L'Heureux, Lozach and Clairet. The food
consisted of ordinary rations, unsuited to the recovery
of men brought nearly to death by their ordeals on
the raft or in the desert. On the evening of their arrival, Colonel Schmaltz and Captain de Chaumareys,
accompanied by a numerous suite, visited them with
a grave air of compassion; they were promised money,
new clothes, and wine to restore their strength. The

Governor-designate said that he was about to go to the Camp of Daccard, but that he had given orders that they should want for nothing in his absence. His wife and daughter were not among their compassionate visitors that day or any other day. The point of this, indeed at first even the fact that it had a meaning, was not grasped by Corréard or his comrades.

The sick men asked the English doctor of the hospital for more suitable food. He replied that he had no authority to change the ration scale. They passed their complaints to the English Governor, Lieutenant-Colonel Brereton, without result. Eventually the same Major Peddy who had helped the Picards arrived at the hospital to offer assistance. Apparently he came on behalf of the British garrison officers rather than the British administration, which was bound most probably by inflexible rules. The French were begged to accept this aid because of the generous treatment which Major Peddy and his comrades had received from the French Army during the war. The Major's intervention came too late to save some of the men and on August 24 Sub-Lieutenant Clairet died in the next bed to Corréard.

A few days later Corréard was woken by the bugles and drums. Covering himself in a sheet, for he had no clothing, he struggled to a hospital window. They were burying Clairet. Two French officers and two British carried the coffin, draped inappropriately with the old lily flag of France. British soldiers and French soldiers and sailors formed the procession, Major Peddy being the senior British officer. This at least was fitting for he also had fought in the Peninsula, although against the army in which Clairet had served. The procession marched out through the gates of the hospital and then Clairet, at twenty-eight a veteran of Talavera de la Reina, Sierra Morena, Saragossa, Montmirail, Champaubert, Montereau, Waterloo, and the raft of the *Medusa,* was gone.

Corréard, unutterably depressed, felt sure that he himself would follow soon to the same graveyard, but without such ceremony. Haggard, clad in a white sheet, he must have seemed to those who saw him at the window a spectre welcoming a companion.

It was just as well that he could not know then the contents of a letter which Mademoiselle Schmaltz, daughter of the Governor-designate, had written to friends in Paris and which was being circulated in the capital. She had avoided visiting the hospital, she said, out of horror at what the men on the raft had done. She could not have endured seeing them without showing some of the indignation she felt at their conduct.

On 25 August, the day after Clairet died, the wreck of the *Medusa* was at last found by the salvage vessel, at the third attempt. The little schooner, commanded by Lieutenant Reynaud, had first sailed on July 26 with insufficient provisions; contrary winds had forced Reynaud to return. The second time she was driven back because a gale tore her poor-quality sails to shreds. Some other ship could easily have been sent, but this was not done and the schooner went out of St. Louis for the third time late in August, reaching the wreck fifty-two days after the frigate had been abandoned by her captain and the commander-in-chief. Reynaud's principal task was to recover the three barrels containing the 90,000 francs in gold.

Reynaud reported the *Medusa* as now lying entirely on her larboard side, with only the starboard side showing and even this swept almost completely by high waves. She was therefore a difficult structure to enter, even for his native divers, which he gave as the reason why he was unable to find the gold. However, by cutting a large hole through the planks and framing of her starboard side, his men were able to recover forty barrels of supplies, several sails, some tools, furniture and personal luggage.

The most shocking discovery, however, was of the bodies of three men, gunner Coutant and two seamen, Dalestre and Lescouet. It was not that they were dead, but that they were still alive, although only just. They were the sole survivors of the seventeen men who had been left behind or had preferred the wreck to the raft as a means of survival. In fact, only one of the fourteen missing men had actually died of privation. The other thirteen had perished in attempts to escape when, after forty-two days on board the wreck, provisions began to run out. In despair, a dozen of the most determined had constructed a raft of their own on which they hoped to drift ashore. This raft did eventually reach the coast, where it was found by Moors owing allegiance to King Zaide, who reported the matter. There was no trace of the men and no one knows their fate. A few days later, another man had attempted to drift to shore, this time by launching himself on a chicken-coop. He was seen to drown after covering only a few hundred yards.

By now, the four men left on board were very weak and half-crazed. Each had his separate den, which he never left except in search of something to eat, and then only with knife in hand. As long as the wine had lasted, all had been tolerably well, but during the last days there was only brandy to drink. For food there was only tallow and salt pork. One man died only hours before Reynaud's schooner arrived at the wreck. The *Medusa* had not broken up, but bedded down in the sand, and although the salvors failed to find the gold they returned highly pleased with their booty. Coutant, Dalestre and Lescouet were weak and incoherent, but they all recovered in due course to testify to the fact of abandonment. The number of known dead now totalled approximately 155, without counting those who were not to recover from their privations.

The day after Reynaud's schooner returned to St. Louis the area of the town became a public fair for the sale of the salvaged goods. These included the personal possessions of both the dead and the living. The national flag worn by the *Medusa*, hoisted at the last by Lieutenant Espiaux, was also auctioned and cut up to make table-cloths and napkins. The affair was so successful and the frigate so far from being gutted, that the merchants of St. Louis were permitted to send out a salvage fleet of four vessels on the understanding that the proceeds should be evenly divided between the French authorities (owners of the frigate) and the salvors (who would do the work and take the risks).

The arrangement and the terms were not unusual under British precedent at the time; were indeed fair as regards Government property. Modern salvage laws operate on the same principles.* What irritated, even infuriated, the wretched survivors was the refusal of Reynaud's party to return their own personal property, particularly clothing, of which they were destitute. They were laughingly brushed off with a remark that these were now a "good prize." Strictly speaking, this may have been correct, except that the proceeds from their sale should have been equally divided between the salvors and the owners, in this case the survivors. But Reynaud, the Government salvor, returned nothing and paid nothing. An amusing sidelight was that Governor-designate Schmaltz received as a present from Reynaud some vases he had recovered from the wreck which were shortly afterwards recognised by Captain de Chaumareys as belonging to himself.

There was no compulsion upon the commercial salvors to restore personal effects, if found, but a few books and other items were in fact returned to the original owners, without any payment being demanded. This second salvage operation lasted for nearly three weeks. Corréard strongly suspected, from the strange fact that the salvaged goods were disposed of through a commercial firm and not a Government agent, that Schmaltz had benefited. Not directly, not in a way which could be shown to be illegal, because that was not his method, but linked to it by a business

---

*See the British Merchant Shipping Act, 1894, designed to regularise existing procedures.

friend who was deeply involved in the commercial salvage operation.

It is interesting that at this time Reynaud who, it was felt, should have kept very quiet because it was his hand that loosed the raft, was in fact in the best of spirits and intimate with the Governor-designate's daughter. "Well, would you believe it!" wrote a survivor. "This officer would play the fashionable around Mademoiselle Schmaltz, affecting airs of carelessness and coquetry."

Indeed, considering the salvage fleet which worked for weeks on the wreck, one begins to wonder about those 90,000 francs in gold. The type of container was known exactly, the location of these containers was known exactly, and the layout of the ship was known exactly. Theoretically, their recovery should not have presented undue difficulties to the native divers, although Reynaud mentions that the interior of the hull was cluttered with displaced wreckage and rubbish. Had they been recovered, they would simply have been barrels as far as the divers were concerned; just three more barrels among many brought up. Disposing of them ashore would present few problems, provided that the salvaged goods were not inspected by a Government agent. Those goods recovered by the commercial salvors were not so inspected but were delivered instead to M. Potin, a director of the firm with which Schmaltz had close connections. Nor does this exhaust the possibilities of illegal disposal. It may be that the *Medusa* did not remain a "treasure ship" for very long after her stranding.

These are only speculations. But what was fact, and a fact obvious to all at the time, was that three men had survived for 52 days aboard the *Medusa* after she had been abandoned as in danger of breaking up. And that great prizes in the way of stores and supplies were being taken from her intact hull two months afterwards. Without a doubt, there had been time enough for Schmaltz and de Chaumareys to have everyone aboard ferried ashore in relays by the boats, granted that they were very nervous and thought this necessary. Without a doubt, an able and resolute commander would have never abandoned the ship at all, but dispatched the two best boats to St. Louis for help. The raft need never have been used, let alone filled up with men and then cast adrift. There was not the shadow of an excuse for the loss of a single life.

Less than a week after the rescue of the last three survivors of the unnecessary tragedy, the time bomb reached France. Not the feeble, spluttering squib to be ignited by Mademoiselle Schmaltz's letter to her Parisian friends but earth-shaking firsthand material. The means of transport had been provided by her father.

On July 29 the corvette *Echo* had sailed for France. She was taking home fifty-five survivors of the shipwreck, many of them invalids, but this was not her main task. The loss of the frigate and so many men, together with the large amount of supplies she had aboard which were destined for the colony, required replacing. The difficulties being made by the British Governor also necessitated new orders for Colonel Schmaltz. The fact was, the whole expedition had been wrecked, not just the *Medusa*. The dispatches she carried were therefore vital and would be closely studied. They included two reports, both dated July 29, written by de Chaumareys to gloss over or obscure the size of the disaster and his own responsibility for it.

"My Lord, it is with the saddest spirit that I have the unfortunate honor of informing you about the wreck of the *Medusa* on the sand bank of Arguin.

"Every possible means was undertaken to save His Majesty's Frigate. I would have had the satisfaction of doing so, if a strong north-west wind had not been blowing, which destroyed in a short while the efforts that the zeal and enthusiasm of the crew and officers had happily produced.

"The Arguin bank is much more to the west than the navigational information suggested and it covers a greater distance to the south-west. The sands are continually on the move according to the strength of the current. Therefore the depths vary very much.

"It is with the greatest satisfaction that I let your excellency know that, out of the 280 men who were on board the *Medusa,* including the 63 men landed at Portendick, the number present now totals 220."

In his second report, de Chaumareys described the finding of the raft by the *Argus* but failed to mention that only fifteen out of some 150 men put on it were still alive.

The figure of 380 appears to omit the seventeen men abandoned in the *Medusa* by de Chaumareys, a deadly fact which he would not be anxious to publicise because it would make him guilty of a capital offence. Putting together the various estimates, of those carried by the boats and raft, not altogether accurate and sometimes conflicting slightly, the total number of persons aboard the *Medusa* appears to have been approximately 405. When finally corrected to include the deaths of those left aboard the stranded hulk of the frigate (not known until a month later) the number of immediately fatal casualties rose to a total of 155. There were therefore to be some 250 survivors in all.

Fifty-five of them were now homeward-bound with de Vénancourt in the *Echo.* Three were boat commanders—Lieutenant Espiaux of the longboat, Ensign Maudet of the Senegal port-boat, Ensign Lapeyrère of the pinnace. Others had been executive officers in the boats—Midshipman Poutier of the longboat, Midshipman Barbotin of the Governor's barge. Paymaster Clanet had been an active passenger in the Governor's barge and had opposed the casting loose of the raft. There was also the senior surgeon, Follet, a rather old-fashioned and unimaginative medical man.

In the minority, naturally, were the survivors from the raft. There were only two officers—Midshipman Coudein, the raft commander, and Junior Surgeon Savigny, who had led the organising group.

When assembled together these witnesses could testify to almost everything that had happened. All were in fact required to submit reports, with the single exception of Surgeon Savigny. This did not stop Savigny. He spent the month-long voyage writing his own narrative of the extraordinary events on the raft. Undoubtedly, he felt that these were so incredible that they ought to be fully detailed; and that, as a doctor, he was peculiarly fitted to deal properly with the psychological and physical phenomena which he had not merely witnessed but experienced as a participant.

On the second day of September, 1816, the corvette arrived at Brest and Savigny took ashore the explosive pages which were shortly to rend France and echo round the world.

11

"THERE'S ONE WHO'LL NEVER GET TO FRANCE"

In Paris and St. Louis, September to December, 1816

WHEN Surgeon Savigny reported to the naval authorities at Brest, he was advised to go to Paris and present his report in person. He was told that his misfortunes should procure a sympathetic hearing at the Ministry of Marine, headed by Vicompte Du Bouchage. Not all his wounds had healed and he still wore one arm in a sling. Merely by surviving in such circumstances, he had done something extraordinary.

The report he carried, which concerned the raft only, was clear, frank, and surprisingly objective in the circumstances. Of course, no mere words could actually describe the experience, but the means by which he and his fourteen companions had lasted long enough to be rescued were detailed without evasion. That is, by consuming the bodies of the slain and by a series of "mercy killings" of those too weak to last much longer.

When Savigny reached Paris on September 11 the news of the loss of the *Medusa* had been public property for less than twenty-four hours. The official *Moniteur Universel* of September 10 had carried one small paragraph placed in an inconspicuous position which read:

> On 2 July, at three o'clock in the afternoon, the frigate *Medusa* was lost, in good weather, on the shoals of Arguin twenty leagues distant from Cape Blanc (in Africa, between the Canaries and Cape Verde). The *Medusa*'s six launches and lifeboats were able to save a large part of the crew and passengers, but of 150

men who attempted to save themselves on a raft, 135 have perished.

Savigny's reception at the Ministry on September 12 was noncommittal. Although his report was accepted for the files, the events recounted in it could be damaging, if widely circulated. Savigny was therefore not only astounded but alarmed to read next day in the pages of the popular opposition newspaper *Journal des Débats* extensive quotations from his own report, beginning with the hasty and chaotic abandonment of the *Medusa* and detailing the sufferings of the 150 people on the raft. Although soberly and tightly written, the facts of cannibalism and butchery were in themselves sensational. Nor had he concealed the fact that the towrope of the raft had been deliberately cast off by the First Lieutenant of the *Medusa,* amid cries of "Let's abandon them!" No feelings of delicacy had restrained him from making clear that the tragedy was not the result of some natural, inescapable force. It had been man-made.

Nor was the strange story given as from an anonymous source, which might have weakened its authority, for the newspaper stated that the material had been written and signed by Savigny "on board the corvette Echo" on August 22, 1816. The Editor had blandly pressed on an exposed nerve by inserting a note to his introductory paragraph which read: "The writer, we suppose, leaves it to the captain and other marine officers, if alive, to explain how the shipwreck took place." The two deadly words "if alive" suggests that the editor may have known very well that the senior officers of the frigate had reversed the established traditions of the sea.

On the day this article was published, Savigny was sent for by the Ministry of Marine and there was an ugly scene in the office. He was accused of leaking confidential information to the press and when he denied it, was not believed. How had a complete copy of his report reached the offices of an opposition

newspaper? Savigny did not know. He recalled letting
only one copy go out of his hands. He had given that
one to Frigate-Captain de Vénancourt at Brest, partly
as a matter of interest, partly because de Vénancourt
had promised to have it sent on to an official of the
Ministry of Marine in Paris. This had suited Savigny
at the time, as he had intended originally to go directly
home without visiting the capital. As it turned out, de
Vénancourt had indeed sent the report to a senior
official in Du Bouchage's Ministry.

The surgeon was now told that it was up to him to
prove his innocence of all complicity in the affair,
which had greatly annoyed the Minister. At the same
time he was berated, not merely for publishing what
he had written but for actually writing it. The astonished Savigny found that the world was upside down.
Now he was being forced to defend himself for his
sufferings on the raft. That he had been put there by
the actions of others was a forbidden thought. He was
so enraged that he threatened to resign his commission as a naval surgeon, but was persuaded not to by
some people in the office who suspected the real
meaning of the affair.

Unaware apparently of the tangled web of politics
into which he had blundered, and believing that truth
would be a complete defense, the surgeon rushed
round to the offices of the newspaper which had
printed his report. The editor of the *Journal des Débats* was perfectly willing to give him proof of innocence and with this document in his pocket Savigny
returned to the Ministry. Triumphantly, he produced
the note, which read:

"I certify that it is not from M. Savigny that I have
the details of the shipwreck of the *Medusa* inserted in
the Journal of 13 September, 1816."

While Savigny waited, the note was taken away and
shown to the Minister, Vicompte Du Bouchage. It
came back with the reply that His Excellency was not

satisfied. While the document appeared to establish the innocence of Savigny, it was not conclusive because it failed to reveal who had passed the doctor's manuscript to the editor of the leading Opposition newspaper.

In an effort to clear himself with authority, Savigny sat down that same day to write an open letter to the official newspaper, *Le Moniteur Universel*. In this he denied having given a copy of his confidential report on the shipwreck, intended only for the Ministry, to any journalist. Further, he denied having any knowledge at all of how the "leak" had occurred. Explaining that the affair had put him in a dangerously embarrassing position, Savigny implored the editor, in the name of justice, to publish his denial officially as soon as possible.

The editor did so two days later, on September 15. But this was too late, for already, on September 14, the *Moniteur* had printed a letter from the Minister himself, bitterly and brutally attacking Savigny.

"When the first news of the wreck of the *Medusa* was received, many newspapers attempted with sound and fury to exploit this cruel event for their own purposes," His Excellency had declared. "The very diversity of these reports, which departed from the truth to an extent varying with the veracity or otherwise of their sources, together with the manifold contradictions which they exhibited, caused great confusion in the minds of the public. But how can one describe the emotions one feels when reading in the *Journal des Débats* of 13th September an article actually signed by one of the doctors of the expedition, in which one cannot help but notice a certain note of malignant insinuation and inexactitude regarding the facts in dispute. The author of this article should have remembered above all that he may be held accountable for his opinions to a Court Martial which will possess thorough knowledge of the affair. And could the evidence of this witness possibly be accepted, when he has already exposed himself publicly as a biased ac-

cuser? That would be stretching the imagination too
far."

This letter, with its official reproaches holding a hint
of menace, frightened Savigny. It angered him also.
The moment he read it, he hurried directly to the
offices of the *Journal de Débats* and demanded that
the editor supply him with the name of the person
who had actually handed over a copy of Savigny's own
report. This the editor refused to do. But, under pressure, while still not naming any individual, he con-
sented to identify the organisation for which that
person worked and wrote out another note, with a
sting in the tail:

> "I certify that it is not from M. Savigny that I have
> the details inserted in the Issue of 13 September, but
> from the office of the Minister of the Police."

What on earth did the Police have to do with it?
When Savigny took this second note to the Ministry
of Marine, they understood well enough. It was admitted that he had been the innocent victim of an indis-
cretion and not a member of a plot. No action would
be taken against him.

To find the informant who had passed on the report,
they must now look within their own Ministry, that of
the Navy. He was in fact that senior official, Forestier,
to whom Frigate-Captain de Vénancourt had passed
a spare copy of the surgeon's unsolicited report regarding the raft. And Forestier was an informant for
Élie Decazes, the powerful Prefect of Police, an ambi-
tious politician who was then intriguing against the
Minister of Marine, with the approval of the King.

Oddly, but only at first sight, Du Bouchage the Navy
Minister, opposed by the king, was an ultra-royalist. His
strict policy was to give officers' commissions only to
members of the nobility and to returned émigrés in
particular. His choice of de Chaumareys as captain of
the *Medusa* and commander of the Senegal squadron
was an example of this policy, and also of its dangers.
It was untrue that the Bourbons had learned nothing

and forgotten nothing. Louis XVIII could see very clearly the unwisdom of excluding from both the army and the navy the experienced officers who had risen to command under Napoleon, in favor of unskilful and inexperienced aristocrats. In this view he was supported by the Prefect of Police.

The fate of the *Medusa* under an aristocratic émigré appeared an excellent weapon to use against the Navy Minister and Du Bouchage had rightly scented political machinations behind the printing of Savigny's report. His deadly—and also unscrupulous—denial in the *Moniteur* had been designed primarily to bring about a showdown. To make the intriguer show his face. And secondly to brand the author of the report as a suspect, malignant and mendacious person. For if the report was accepted as true, it could be argued that all the émigrés, such as de Chaumareys, were dangerously incapable. And that made the position of the Minister, who had appointed them, untenable.

But one aspect of the tragedy, the apparently cowardly abandonment of his men by their aristocratic captain, while possibly not typical, could be made to seem so and therefore tended to undermine, not merely Du Bouchage, but the monarchy itself. Political opponents did not lose the chance to draw the obvious parallel—the carelessly shipwrecked *Medusa* and her wretched crew were France and the French under the Bourbons.

The Minister's intervention in the *Moniteur* and Savigny's denial published in the same paper the next day increased the controversy and inflamed the scandal still further. In less than a week it had attained international proportions. The *Times,* London's equivalent of the *Moniteur,* carried a free translation of Savigny's report lifted from the *Journal des Débats.* The rest of the world's press duly copied and a month or so later the appalled Governor, Captain and First Lieutenant of the *Medusa* were reading in Senegal, in an English newspaper, an English account which was less oblique than the original French.

Captain de Chaumareys, the only one of them who
stood to lose his life as a result of the affair, was the
least affected. Still complacently cocksure, he was
heard loudly declaiming that the loss of the *Medusa*
was a mere "bagatelle." Lieutenant Reynaud, playing
the gallant to Mademoiselle Schmaltz and babbling
away as if he had not a care in the world, while the
survivors of the raft glowered silently, was merely dis-
guising his uneasiness. Colonel Schmaltz was fully
aware of the dangers looming in Savigny's report. He
was also in a position to act, and without scruple. Reynaud was as fully implicated in the abandonment of
the raft as he was, and must therefore cooperate. Two
to one. Then his own secretary, Griffon du Bellay,
who was dependent upon him, was also a survivor of
the raft. There were other survivors, still in Senegal,
many of them physically weak and mentally exhausted
from their ordeal.

With Reynaud, he prepared the draft of a letter to
be written by du Bellay and signed by other raft survivors which would satisfactorily explain the casting off
of the raft, refute the charge of abandonment, and cut
down Savigny with the deadly charge of "murderer."

The letter, addressed to the Minister of Marine and
finally dated November 13, 1816, was a long one. It
began by relating how they had read with horror, in
the English newspapers, a translation of an article by
Savigny in the *Journal des Débats*. They admitted the
terrible atrocities which had occurred on the raft but
stated that in these excesses Surgeon Savigny himself
"had always been the promotor and principal executor." They affirmed that the waves and the currents
had combined to cause a break in the towrope; they
denied that it had been deliberately cast off. They
described as a barbarous libel any suggestion that the
First Lieutenant had ever cried out: "We abandon
them!" And finally they accused Savigny of base ingratitude towards the officers of the frigate who had
done everything in their power to save him and had
in fact succeeded by sending out the brig *Argus*.

If many survivors of the raft could be persuaded to sign this document, then Savigny would be exposed as a lone troublemaker peddling reckless stories to the discredit of others, while he himself was guilty of criminal acts. The campaign was conducted with great care and much trouble was taken. Some of the castaways were ill or dying, racked by fever, troubled by still vivid memories of the heaving sea and the horrors on the raft.

One of these was the former Sergeant Tousche-Lavillette, master carpenter and foreman of Corréard's party of engineers. Bredif visited him in the Saint Louis hospital on July 23, soon after his rescue. Confidentially, he noted that the sick man was babbling about Doctor Savigny and two or three Lieutenants behaving like thugs, committing murder, organising a horrible system of destruction, so that the unfortunate men on the raft kept on killing one another. He kept on talking about how the number of men decreased every night, how two men came to murder him, and how instead he murdered them, the one by a cutlass slash to the head, the other by holding his face under water until he drowned. And then how he himself was asked to help in the slaughtering of ten or a dozen men the officers had decided must die; that he would not do it, and that because he kept a gun by him, he was respected. In a final moment of lucidity, he added that: "After each slaughter, they would kiss, thanking God; after the last one, all the guns were thrown overboard."

In all the feverish babbling there was some truth and in that final sentence set down by Bredif, although it rings oddly, there was absolute truth. But that it was true, why it was true, and what it really meant, was not to be known for more than one and a half centuries. There were undercurrents in the story of the raft of the *Medusa* which were to be endlessly debated ever after and were not even capable of resolution until recently.

Tousche-Lavillette signed the documents presented

to him by du Bellay on behalf of Schmaltz, probably without knowing even what was on it, for not only was he certifying that Savigny had been "the promotor and principal executor" of the killings on the raft, but that the towrope had broken accidentally and that there had been no deliberate abandonment. This was the important point, for whatever happened on the raft afterwards was the direct result of its abandonment. Whether Savigny was guilty or not guilty, or only part-guilty, was of lesser importance because, like all the other castaways, he was merely reacting to the pressures of an intolerable situation created for him by others.

Another easy signature was that of the poor, dying negro soldier Jean Charles. No one could know then the strange way in which his ordeal on the raft was to become immortal. The signatures of the soldiers Captain Dupont, Lieutenant L'Heureaux and Sergeant-Major Charlot were also obtained. Naturally Griffon du Bellay, the Governor's secretary, also signed; he had very little option, unless he wanted to wreck his career.

None of the living castaways were at all normal at this time. A distinguished visitor to the hospital, the Prince de Joinville, aptly described it as being like an "anti-chamber to the morgue." Even those who were not destined to make that final journey took many months, and in some cases years, to recover; some never really recovered. One of the latter was Alexander Corréard, the engineer and republican. Even so, his signature to the document was not obtained. It was not for want of effort, and Corréard, because he survived, was able to record the sort of pressures which must have been applied to all the others.

Although still a very sick man, he was slowly getting better, largely as a result of the help given by Major Peddy and Captain Campbell of the British garrison of St. Louis. When the Governor's version of affairs was brought to him for signature, he noted that it had already been signed as correct by Griffon du Bellay, who owed his life directly to Savigny on at least one occasion. This, he thought, showed ingratitude, because the statement attacked Savigny personally for directing the slaughter from first to last, not just the "mercy killings" during the last days. But what enraged Corréard and decided him to resist were the plain untruths regarding the real authors of what eventually happened on the raft.

He commented bitterly, "One paragraph was employed to prove that the towrope had *broken*. Could I certify to that, when I was myself an eyewitness and had been told by more than twenty persons that it had been *cast loose*. Besides this falsehood, it was stated in one passage that when the raft was left, the words *we abandon them* were not pronounced." Corrérd returned the document, unsigned.

Then the pressure came on. "The Governor's secretary came several times to the hospital to urge me to give my signature, but I persisted in my refusal. The Governor himself pressed me most earnestly one day when I went to him to ask permission to quit Senegal, but I answered that I would never sign a letter quite at variance with the truth, and went back to the hospital. The day after my friend, M. Kummer, visited me and pleaded with me to go to the Governor and sign this paper because, he had been told, if I continued to refuse, I would not be permitted to leave Senegal. These gentlemen must have indeed been deeply interested in the matter, if they employed such measures towards an unfortunate man, exhausted by a long illness, whose recovery depended on his return to Europe; for this they would not grant him, except on condition of his signing a false narrative contrary to everything he had himself seen."

Of those who did sign, Corréard commented: "They were suffering from that terrible fever which was then carrying off the French so rapidly, when they were invited by the Governor to sign this narrative. Some yielded to the fear of displeasing His Excellency the Governor; others conceived hopes of obtaining his protection which, in the colonies, is no trifling advantage; others again were so weak that they were not even able to make themselves acquainted with the paper to which they were asked to put their names."

Corréard persisted in his refusal and Schmaltz had to be content with only six signatures. That of course was in addition to his own testimony and that of Lieutenant Reynaud regarding their own innocence of any desire or intention to cast off or abandon the castaways on the raft. Hopefully, that would be sufficient to clear Schmaltz of all blame for the tragedy. The document, which was addressed to Du Bouchage, Minister of Marine, was to be dispatched in the transport *Loire* commanded by Lieutenant Gicquel des Touches, due to sail for Rochefort on the first of December, 1816. The reasons for this sailing may not have been known to Corréard, but the Governor must have been well aware of them; indeed, they made most urgent the matter of obtaining as many signatures as possible to the document.

A swift passage home in the *Loire* seemed to Corréard his only chance to survive. He sought and found allies among the British. Their doctors wrote out a certificate to the effect that, as his health was not improving, but on the contrary declining, it was imperative that he be repatriated immediately. When Schmaltz received this certificate from what was still the reigning authority in Senegal, with whom he was having most difficult negotiations, he had little option but to allow Corréard to return to France.

In the last days of November, Major Peddy and Captain Campbell called on the sick man to say goodbye. They were about to leave St. Louis with an expedition consisting of 130 soldiers and 400 pack animals which was to explore the interior, for at that time only the coasts of Africa were known to Europeans. The interior was a mystery which might or might not contain minerals of far greater importance to Europe than the Arab-controlled slave trade. From this expedition they did not return, both dying of fever. But before he left, Major Peddy had a warning for Corréard. They were both in the same line of business, for the Frenchman's original task had been exploration, and this may account for the friendship.

"Since you intend to return to France," warned Peddy, "I hope you won't mind if I give you some advice. Men are all pretty much the same and though I can't predict exactly how your Navy Minister will treat you, it's safe to assume that you'll obtain no redress from him. Remember, a politician who has made a mistake doesn't like to be reminded of it. Believe me, my friend, don't take the road to Paris. Go to London. You'll find people ready to help you, when they learn what you have suffered. I have with me three hundred francs, which will cover your expenses, either to Paris or to London, whichever you choose. Think about it, and if you decide to go to London, let me know. I'll give you letters of introduction."

Corréard was deeply grateful but also distressed. He found it hard to admit that he would not, sooner or later, receive justice in France. He accepted the money and said that he hoped to be able to repay the debt, and with interest, in terms of assistance some time in the future to an Englishman in trouble. They then parted, Major Peddy to his death in the interior of West Africa, Corréard to what he always regarded as a very narrow escape indeed from the same fate.

On November 28 he was put on a small coasting vessel which was to take him and other passengers out over the bar of the river to where the storeship *Loire* was lying in the deeper water of the roadstead. Corréard had hardly stepped on board the coaster when he began to shake with a fit of fever. These fits came on him almost every day at about the same time, but on this occasion the direct blaze of the noon sun made his condition even worse than usual. Then the wind fell away to a dead calm so that the vessel was motionless and the sick man, who had been resting against some ropes coiled on deck, began to drift off to sleep. Just before he drowsed off, Corréard heard a voice say, "There's one who'll never get to France." When he awoke, five hours had passed and he was in a desperate condition, having been left all this time out in the sun. He felt just as he had during the last days on the raft, when he was not far from death. Yet all the other passengers had been taken off nearly five hours before by a boat sent in from the *Loire* to collect them. Only Corréard had been left behind to suffer from the sun on the exposed deck of the coaster; no one had even bothered to wake him. He felt sure that this was no oversight but a final attempt by Schmaltz to silence him forever. Whether or not there was any truth in his suspicions, the *Loire* was still lying out off the bar and as a breeze had now sprung up, the sailors had no excuse not to take him out to her.

The storeship made a good passage home, faster in fact than the *Echo*. Twenty-seven days from St. Louis to Rochefort, as compared to de Vénancourt's thirty-six days from Goree roads to Brest. This in spite of the fact that the Dockyard Superintendent at Rochefort had doubts about her hull and had authorised her voyage to Senegal only on condition that she returned home for a refit before the advent of the hurricane season. However, Schmaltz had ignored this and kept her in Senegal because of his difficulties with the British. It was now the period of the winter gales in the North Atlantic, which follows the hurricane season in the South Atlantic, so the *Loire* had been at risk from either the one or the other from July to Christmas. Schmaltz was luckier with the *Loire* than he had been with the *Medusa*.

The *Echo* had carried home fifty-five *Medusa* survivors, including almost all the junior officers and boat commanders as well as the commander of the raft, Coudein, and surgeon Savigny. The *Loire* rounded off the list of critical witnesses by bringing home among further *Medusa* survivors her Captain, de Chaumareys, and his First Lieutenant, Reynaud, as well as a sick and vengeful Corréard and the letter originated by Schmaltz and signed by Griffon du Bellay which accused Savigny and exonerated Schmaltz and Reynaud from any complicity in the tragedy of the raft. Corréard was determined to warn Savigny of his dangers and wrote out an account of the pressures which had been brought to bear on him to sign the Schmaltz document.

The ineffably conceited de Chaumareys, perhaps because he had leaned on Schmaltz as the real leader and decision-taker of the expedition, had no apprehension of danger whatever; although he must have known that a Court Martial must inevitably follow the loss of a King's Ship.

Lieutenant Gicquel des Touches, the *Loire's* captain, was to recall that de Chaumareys "was very upset by the loss of his ship but happy to have come out of the affair so well. He spoke in a very free way of this catastrophe. I think I did right in telling him to prepare his defense. I did not hide from him that the impending Courts Martial would find, without doubt, that there was no excuse for his conduct: and that this was in fact my own opinion. But he did not seem to understand what he had done. When I saw that we were not speaking the same language, I gave up; but for some reason the poor man pursued me for a long time afterwards with his letters, hoping to find in me a very indulgent judge of his conduct. He was without a doubt truly guilty, but shouldn't a large part of the responsibility have been shouldered by the Government which had entrusted such men with tasks they were incapable of fulfilling?"

When the *Loire* anchored in the roads off Rochefort from where the *Medusa* had sailed just over six months before, de Chaumareys sat down importantly to write a report for the Minister of Marine regarding the situation in Senegal and in particular his own part in organising the emergency camp at Daccard. At the same time, he demanded absence of leave to visit his estates. Six months before it had been high summer, now it was after Christmas and bitter winter; and the reply he got from the Port Admiral was just as bitter.

On that Admiral's desk there had been lying for more than two months a letter from Du Bouchage, the Minister of Marine. It instructed that officer to report immediately to Paris the arrival of the ex-captain of the *Medusa* and to ensure that "For no reason or pretext whatever" would he be given the home leave which the other officer and under-officer survivors of the frigate might naturally expect. Instead of a leave pass, the Port Admiral signed an order for the arrest of Frigate-Captain de Chaumareys, Chevalier of the Royal Order of St. Louis and Henry IV.

12

DUE PROCESS OF LAW

At Brest and Rochefort, 1816–1817

ALTHOUGH the result might be death for an individual, there was nothing dramatic in the way the French legal system went to work. It was entirely cool, objective, thorough and confined at first largely to documentation. There were no theatricals. Nor did anyone concerned with it wear blinkers. However, the antennae were extremely sensitive and warnings went up to the Ministry early that this was no ordinary shipwreck case. On the contrary, it held all the makings of a most dangerous scandal.

Consequently, the public utterances of some individuals were mostly at variance with the facts. It was not that they did not know the truth, but that they did not wish the truth to be known.

The legal proceedings lasted in one form or another for more than six months—from September, 1816 to March, 1817. The official record of them was to total no less than 650 pages, an almost unprecedented length. But they were not made public. They were secret, a secrecy enforced by the authority of the state.

Essentially, they were enquiries into facts divided into two main phases, that of the *Echo* and that of the *Loire*. The first stage began with the arrival of the *Echo* at Brest on September 2, 1816. She carried fifty-five witnesses from the *Medusa* as well as the all-important log of the *Echo* herself. By September 18 the Minister had decided that Frigate-Captain de Chaumareys must be recalled to explain his conduct before a Court Martial. In the meantime the matter was transferred to

Rochefort and a Commission of Enquiry was held there during most of November.

Then there was a delay, caused by Schmaltz, until the arrival of the *Loire* at Rochefort on December 27 with the two principal officers of the *Medusa*, de Chaumareys and Reynaud. The transport also brought home a vengeful Corréard and a defensive document from Schmaltz. The Courts Martial proper was held intermittently on various dates between January 22 and March 3, 1817, and included a thorough and careful examination of de Chaumareys which lasted four days.

The basic documentation provided on September 2, 1816, by de Vénancourt's *Echo* consisted of the official reports of eight officers of the *Medusa* who had travelled in her, plus de Vénancourt's own official report. The captain of the *Echo* could take the story only to the night of July 1st/2nd when his corvette parted company with the frigate. He stressed that the ships had separated several times before this and that in no case had he received any signal from the *Medusa* as to the course he was to take. However, there was a standing instruction that in case of separation the ships were to sail directly to St. Louis. That more or less covered him, being true so far as it went. De Vénancourt was careful to add that Bellin's chart was extremely inaccurate and that the Hydrographer of the Navy should be informed. This could be read as providing an excuse for de Chaumareys, but it justified first and foremost the action taken by de Vénancourt to steer a night course which would take him well clear of the vaguely-defined danger zone.

De Vénancourt's suggestion was acted on and two ships were sent out later that year to re-survey the cost of West Africa, with results that, although they were received too late to influence the Courts Martial, did have a distinct bearing on the conduct of de Chaumareys and his advisers.

The critical documents, however, were the official reports of the *Medusa*'s officers. They affirmed that the course of the frigate during daylight on July 2 was south-

south-east—directly towards the Arguin Bank: that at 2
p.m. on that day, sixty minutes before the stranding,
de Chaumareys had refused to take a sounding because it would cause a delay; that a number of men
had volunteered to remain on board the frigate, and
did so; and that the towrope had been cast off because
it was found impossible to tow the raft.

Point one meant that de Chaumareys had made a
major error in his navigation. Point two meant that
he had proceeded with extreme carelessness in waters
known to be dangerous. Point three meant that he had
not been the last to leave his ship and was therefore
technically guilty of a fault punishable by death. Point
four, abandoning the raft, might well carry the same
penalty. This latter admission by the officers rendered
useless at a single stroke all the intricate and industri-
ous work then being undertaken in Senegal by
Schmaltz to conceal his vital role in the ghastly tragedy of the raft. However, as Schmaltz had no naval
responsibilities, he could not be tried for it: it was de
Chaumareys who would have to answer for him.

The report by the raft commander, Midshipman
Jean Coudein, was not entirely damning. He stated
that although the wind was blowing directly towards
the shore and was therefore favourable, the tidal
stream proved the stronger force and took the raft to
seaward of the *Medusa*. He did not state, because it
was a law of nature known to everyone, that the current was bound to reverse its direction and join with
the wind to take the raft inshore. Nor did he state,
what seems obvious also, that had the boats anchored
during the periods when the tidal stream ran offshore,
no ground would have been lost. Coudein neither criticised nor made suggestions, but stated merely: "I do
not know what were the reasons that caused the boats
to cast off the life-raft at the time they did. But the
fact is that they abandoned us, crowding on all sail,
holding the wind as closely as possible, until, in the
most awful despair, we saw them disappear."

By September 18 all the facts as so far known were

on the Minister's desk and he had considered them thoroughly. On this day he himself reported to the king. He did not minimise or conceal anything. The affair involved not only the loss of a valuable ship with valuable stores and the death of 132 Frenchmen as so far known, but would mean the mounting of a new expedition with all the expense that involved. There was considerable evidence to show that the ship was lost through faulty calculations, lack of foresight and a lack of elementary precautions. An absolute opinion could not be pronounced, however, until the Captain and those of his officers who still remained in Senegal had returned and been heard at a Court Martial. This should be done as soon as possible.

The Minister did not consider that the Captain alone had been to blame for abandoning the raft; all those in the boats must have been responsible to some degree. Midshipman Coudein had told simply and bluntly what had happened on the raft afterwards, but here the Minister did not go into detail. Instead, he wrote: "I spare your Majesty the narration of the terrible scenes that took place on the raft, resulting from hunger and despair, and of those horrors which were committed during the thirteen days of desolation. I still bemoan the fact that journalists have revealed events that should never have been placed before the eyes of mankind."

The newspaper controversy of the previous week, in which Du Bouchage had thrown official doubt on Savigny's narrative, imputing untruthfulness and malign motives to him, had been no more than a paper battle for the public, after all. The Minister had been only too well aware of the truth.

Du Bouchage also wrote to Vice-Admiral Rosily, who had issued the navigational orders to be followed by de Chaumareys, asking him to comment on his own "fragmentary" first impressions. The two reports written by de Chaumareys on 29 July had also arrived with the *Echo*; even to a layman, there were great contradictions apparent, when compared to the re-

ports of the officers. De Chaumareys had declared that
he had been steering south-south-west away from the
bank when the frigate struck, while the officers gave
the course at that time as south-south-east, directly
onto the bank. Du Bouchage asked Rosily for a confidential technical report on the conduct of de Chaumareys, adding that there seemed to him to be
imprecisions in the captain's narrative which made it
appear that his statements were not firmly based on
the log of the frigate.

Rosily reported on September 25, a week later, noting that he had been compelled to use as his primary
document the log of the *Echo* which had been sailing
in company with the *Medusa* up to the night of July
1st/2nd. There was no log available for the *Medusa*,
only the two reports by de Chaumareys in which Cape
Blanc, the shoremark for the first "leg" of the dogleg,
was stated to have been sighted on the evening of July
1. The log of the *Echo* did not corroborate this. On
the contrary, even at midnight, de Vénancourt had put
the position of his ship, then a little ahead of the *Medusa*, as north of Cape Blanc. It was obvious that neither ship had actually sighted Cape Blanc, so that the
start of the seaward turn was from an imperfectly
known position. Rosily found it inexplicable that the
two vessels had in fact separated during the night
when they were both supposedly following the course
stated in the reports by de Chaumareys.

But two points were clear. Firstly, de Chaumareys
had not obeyed the Ministry instruction to head for
open sea as soon as the lead showed shallow water
and to keep on out to sea until he had passed safely
round and was to the south of the Arguin Bank. Secondly, de Chaumareys had not obeyed the Ministry
instruction to take proper soundings at regular intervals in order to stay in safe water and avoid the shallows. These were elementary precautions, given the
hazardous "coasting" route laid down by the instructions. Rosily concluded by stressing that if, as the officers said, a course of south-south-east was being

followed, the noon sight on July 2 should have made clear that the frigate was heading directly towards the Arguin Bank. "With such conflicting evidence," he wrote, "it is impossible to judge without either having the ship's log in front of one or reassembling all the witnesses."

The ordinary seamen were already being questioned at Brest by Rear-Admiral de Saint-Haouen. The only matter of navigational importance was the testimony of apprentice Bernard Benjamin Chassériau as to a change of course during the early hours of July 2, when the *Medusa* and the *Echo* parted company. The time, he thought, was about 2 a.m., when the soundings began to give depths of only sixteen to eighteen fathoms. Lieutenant Reynaud, who was on watch, hurriedly ordered a change of course westward. The captain, of course, was asleep and did not know what his First Lieutenant was doing or what course he had actually steered up to that point.

Seaman Quévélec Mathurin gave confirmatory evidence of the conduct of Lieutenant Espiaux. When all the other boats had abandoned the raft, Espiaux had made a lone attempt to take up the tow, but had been prevented by his men: they had argued that the occupants of the raft, "who had water up to their belts, would rush the longboat and all would perish uselessly." Mathurin also revealed that he had been sleeping in the maintop at the moment the frigate stranded and had not felt the impact; he had had to be woken up by friends telling him he was shipwrecked.

When the evidence of the seamen had been obtained by questioning and added to the written reports of the officers, yet another commission of enquiry was set up. Under Rear-Admiral Maurville, this body was based on Rochefort and worked from November 7 to December 2, 1816. They rationalised the matter by producing a twenty-five-point questionnaire to be answered by the officers, principally regarding the navigation, starting with the hour at which Cape Blanc was seen, followed by an estimate of the distance away at the moment of sighting.

The six deck officers (no-one asked the surgeon or the paymaster, but they might just as well have done) gave six different times for the sighting, varying from as early as nine p.m. to as late as half-an-hour before midnight on July 1. Their estimates of distance varied, but not by so much. This was very odd, because the log of the *Echo* made clear that Cape Blanc had not been sighted and never was seen. The deck officers were also at variance in their recollections of the position indicated by the noon sight three hours before the stranding. But on one thing they were completely agreed. De Chaumareys had ordered a change of course at 7:30 on the fatal morning of July 2, and that course was south-south-east. This was the really vital point: the time and heading of the second "leg" of the dogleg, the course which would take the *Medusa* back towards the coast of Africa.

The commission noted a curious air of reserve among the officers, which was repeated among the petty officers and other experienced seamen. The missing key to their attitude consisted of one word which was never employed during these proceedings. That word was "Richefort." The captain had rejected his officers and a "vile impostor" of a civilian had in fact been navigating the ship. And the policy decisions, also rightly the captain's, had been usurped by Honorary Colonel Schmaltz. In these circumstances, these officers had ceased to take an interest in anything except the work of their own departments, although they had noted with melancholy resignation the steady march to destruction which began at 7:30 on the morning of 2 July. There was little else they could have done, short of mutiny, and that could not succeed because of the number of soldiers on board, all at the orders of Governor Schmaltz.

The commission reported to the Minister that there was a clear case against de Chaumareys and that they had formed a poor opinion of the courage and zeal of his officers, with the exception of Lieutenant Espiaux. Now, there was nothing to do but wait for the arrival of the *Loire*, which was, inconveniently, during Christmas.

The next stage of the de Chaumareys Case began at Rochefort on January 22, 1817. The president of the court was Rear-Admiral de Tullaye, flanked by the obligatory seven Ship-Captains. The recording-attorney was Ship-Captain Le Carlier d'Herlye and the proceedings consisted of the taking of more statements. The documents placed before the court included the minutes of the two previous commissions of enquiry, the written reports of the officers, and the log of the *Echo* from June 16 to September 2, 1816.

First Lieutenant Reynaud's examination did not produce a favourable impression on the court. Apart from being wordy, he was vague. He thought that Cape Blanc had been sighted at 8 p.m. on July 1 about four or five leagues away, but was not sure. He admitted that he had had the course changed at two in the morning of July 2, but was unable to explain why. He claimed complete ignorance of the change of course ordered by de Chaumareys at 7:30 in the morning of July 2, because, he said, he was too busily engaged with the running of the ship. He could not recall the position of the frigate at noon on July 2, three hours before the stranding.

But Reynaud did admit that he had cast off the tow-rope to the raft at the direct order of Governor Schmaltz. Of the other officers examined, Sub-Lieutenant Lapey-rère was especially firm in his insistence that it was Schmaltz who had been the prime mover in having the raft cast adrift and abandoned. Midshipman Coud-ein, the raft commander, found the fact of abandonment by men who had been his comrades and were present in court so painful, that he begged to be excused answering questions about this episode and asked the recording-attorney to refer to his original report (in which he had written that, for reasons not known to him, the boats had cast off the tow and fled). It was not Schmaltz who was on trial, however, and indeed the Navy had no jurisdiction over His Excellency the Governor of Senegal.

Having received little enlightenment from the officers, Le Carlier d'Herlye turned to the petty officers and seamen, of whom he cross-examined thirteen. Again, he met that wall of prudent reserve which masked the real situation in the *Medusa* prior to the disaster. It was only when he questioned three of the petty officers, Granche, Dejoie and Griffon (not to be confused with Griffon du Bellay) that he broke through to the effect which that demoralising situation had had on the ordinary routine of the frigate.

Both Granche and Dejoie stated that the first sounding they could recall being taken on July 2 was at 2:30 in the afternoon, half an hour before the *Medusa* struck; and that, furthermore, the result was not reliable because the cast had been poorly carried out by the leadsman, and he had had to do it again. This necessarily took some time and the delay was fatal. Griffon, master mariner, testified: "Because of the clumsiness of the leadsman, the sounding was not correct. He cast again and, finding only six fathoms of water, went over to starboard to take a sounding on the other side." Recovering and recoiling a long length of wet rope is not done in an instant, but it would be unfair to blame the sailor for his error; the captain has to take entire responsibility for the performance of his officers and crew.

It was clear that the *Medusa* had been a very badly-run ship indeed, even if the antagonism between the Captain and his officers is disregarded. Although it did not appear in evidence, almost certainly the fact was known to the court. But none of this was evidence of anything other than unfitness for command, which was a reflection on the Ministry as well as de Chaumareys. The really deadly evidence, potentially fatal to de Chaumareys personally, was contained in the statements of three other members of the crew, master gunner Coutant, seaman Lescouet and seaman Dalestre. They were the three men found by Reynaud still alive on board the *Medusa* nearly two months after she had been abandoned. Just by being alive, they condemned de Chaumareys to death for not being the last to abandon ship.

Their evidence was disarmingly simple and honest.

Coutant stated: "Believing that there would be more risk by going in the ship's boats or on the life-raft than by staying on board, I chose to stay on board."

Lescouet, under cross-examination, admitted to having "taken a little drink," but denied that he had been drunk. He had consciously preferred the wreck to the overfilled longboat or the half-sunken life-raft.

Dalestre stated: "I hid so as not to be forced to leave the ship."

Both in the Revolutionary Navy and the Royal Navy of France the captain, by law, was required to be the last man to leave his ship. It was not just a tradition of the sea, a code of honour, it was a matter of discipline. In no other way could order be preserved in a situation of extreme stress.

The judge-advocate found accordingly. In spite of the conflicting evidence, five main points could be established without doubt:

(1) The shoremark of Cape Blanc was not definitely identified, as by instruction it should have been;
(2) The *Medusa* and the *Echo* parted company, contrary to instruction, without any valid explanation;
(3) De Chaumareys had altered the course to south-south-east without due care and without taking any soundings;
(4) The life-raft had been deliberately abandoned, but the responsibility here was not that of the captain alone;
(5) In violation of the marine code, the captain had not been the last to leave his ship.

Because he was responsible for the loss of the *Medusa*, de Chaumareys had exposed himself to the punishment of being dismissed his ship and suspended from duty; but because he had abandoned the *Medusa* before seeing that every man had got away, he was liable to the death penalty. La Tullaye, in forwarding this report to the Minister, pointed out the extreme peril in which de Chaumareys stood and asked for time in which to question him thoroughly. He also enclosed a pleading letter from de Chaumareys.

Instead of considering the matter a mere "bagatelle," the captain was now thoroughly frightened. He wrote of "a coalition of the Medusa's officers" against him; of "the fears and passions aroused among the families of these officers"; of the fact that he stood alone amid a storm of intrigue, stripped even of the ship's log and his own chart. "I am innocent of the slanders now assembled against me," he wrote. "But I am far from seeing myself as being beyond reproach and, attacked by a mass of enemies who have been preparing their case for five months, I am frightened of not being able to defend myself from them all and on all the points." He talked vaguely of a "route" which he was supposed to have taken and of how he had a declaration by "four officers" (unnamed) as to another (unstated) "route" he claimed to have actually followed. And he posed as a victim of the "party spirit" of the Bonapartist officers, who intended to ruin him because of his association with the heroic (Royalist) affair of Quiberon, more than twenty long years before.

Both this letter and La Tullaye's plea were unnecessary. Du Bouchage had already written to Louis XVIII asking for a stay of execution so that de Chaumareys could be afforded every opportunity of explaining his conduct. He had concluded: "Although Chaumareys is guilty of grave error whose results have been deadly, he has, in other circumstances, given proof of courage and devotion to the Royal cause. He was part of the naval detachment which faced death at Quiberon and was one of the small number of those who escaped the massacre which followed the failure of the enterprise."

13

THE DE CHAUMAREYS CASE

Rochefort, February to March, 1817

THE *Medusa* was a Rochefort ship, as was the *Loire*. The tragedy was a local story. Many people in the town had relatives or friends who had served under de Chaumareys and there were besides many retired naval people living there. No censorship could hold that story and local interest was intense and well-informed. Consequently, de Chaumareys had to be given every chance to explain himself, if he could, and his careful interrogation lasted from 3rd to 6th February, 1817. After that, judgement would be pronounced.

The captain of the *Medusa* made a poor start. Even during the formal procedure of identification he was caught out as having lied about his age at the time of re-enlistment. Le Carlier d'Herlye, acting as prosecutor, sought to establish what sort of a man de Chaumareys was. In particular, was his seeming vagueness concerning matters of fact a deliberate policy designed to blur the truth or was his mind actually as imprecise as it seemed? It was vitally necessary to do this because the mass of evidence already collected from the officers and men was completely at variance on a number of issues with what de Chaumareys had stated in his written reports of July 29, 1816. It was also at variance with the log of the *Echo* kept by Frigate-Captain de Vénancourt, while de Chaumareys could not produce either the log of the *Medusa* or even his own charts. It was merely his word against those of the officers and men of the *Medusa*. Early on, Le Carlier sought to establish the lack of documentation.

Asked to explain what had happened to his chart, de Chaumareys replied: "I gave my chart to a midshipman when I got into my boat and by an inconceivable mishap, it was lost. On this chart were marked all the points on the courses from our departure until noon on the day the frigate was lost."

The next question and answer established that the chart was Bellin's and that it was part of the Ministry's navigational guide, which included recognition drawings of the various prominent headlands to be taken as shoremarks for position identification.

Le Carlier asked: "At what hour did you identify Cape Barbas, at what distance was it, and what was your position at midday on 1 July?"

At this time the *Echo* had been keeping company with the *Medusa*, and Le Carlier had all the answers from de Vénancourt's log. The answer that de Chaumareys gave him revealed that, not only had the *Medusa*'s captain identified the wrong headland as Cape Barbas, but that even now he did not know that he had done so.

Le Carlier then moved to the next shoremark, the most important. "At what hour did you identify Cape Blanc and at what distance was it?"

De Chaumareys replied without hesitation: "At eight in the evening of 1 July, when I expected to. I recognised it perfectly. I estimated we were four leagues west-north-west of it at the time. I estimated the distance we had covered from the average speed of the frigate since leaving Cape Barbas."

As the court had studied the *Echo*'s log, it was obvious to them that the distance the *Medusa* had covered had been "estimated" from one landmark incorrectly identified to another landmark never seen at all.

The questioning then turned to the course held at night, based on the "sighting" of Cape Blanc. De Chaumareys insisted that his orders for the night had been as laid down in his instructions: that is, a course of west-south-west, sounding every two hours, and keeping the *Echo* in sight. He explained: "All I had as a guide for my passage, which neither I nor my officers had navigated before, were the nautical instructions issued to me by the Ministry. These instructions advised me to take a south-westerly course for fourteen leagues after sighting Cape Blanc."

In such circumstances, at the most dangerous part of the passage, a captain would normally be on deck. But further questioning revealed de Chaumareys had been asleep. Indeed, with great indignation, he gave this as his excuse. "To this very day," he declared, "I have been accused of failing to see the corvette *Echo* and to notice that at three in the morning she burned signal flares to draw my attention. I was in my bed. I never had a chance to note the direction of those flares."

By concealing some of the facts, de Chaumareys was making matters worse for himself. The main fact missing from the record was Richefort. The court was not told that, precisely because neither de Chaumareys nor his officers had experience of this coast, the navigation had been entrusted to a man who supposedly did have such knowledge. In effect, de Chaumareys had abdicated in favour of someone who was not even in the navy and had such boundless confidence in him that he could sleep the whole night through during the critical time when the hazardous and only part-known sandbank must be close. Even so, the officer of the watch at that time (Reynaud) should have notified the captain that the *Echo* was signalling.

Le Carlier then reached the time of the fatal decision, 7:30 a.m. on July 2. Here, for once, the testimonies of de Chaumareys and his officers showed no disagreement. De Chaumareys agreed that he had come on deck at 6:00 and at 7:30 that morning and repeated that the leadsman had found no bottom at 120 "brasses" (640 feet). "This gave me such confidence that I thought further sounding unnecessary. I then definitely ordered that the course be changed to south-south-east in order to look for the coast."

In his report of July 29, de Chaumareys had stated

that he had ordered further soundings to be taken, both at 9 a.m. and at 10 a.m. (as indeed he should have done), but faced by the prosecutor he did not repeat this fable.

Nor did his answer to the next critical question chime with his July 29 report, in which he had stated that the sight taken at noon had shown the *Medusa* at 20° 8' North and 19° 30' West, which sounded reasonably professional. Faced by his accusers, de Chaumareys lapsed into imprecision. "At noon the sun was high enough to take an altitude, but I didn't make an observation. In any case, I had little confidence in the latitude taken because the sun was now at the zenith and because the navigational guide told me that one must expect great errors in this area. . . . However, I had every confidence in my reckoning (the distance run from Cape Blanc), although at this moment my memory cannot recall what it was. Indeed, several times during that morning I reflected upon the inconceivable route which the *Echo* was believed to have taken, a route which had taken her away from us to such a great distance that we never saw her at all that day. But with such great confidence in my reckoning, I continued to steer south-south-east."

This does give a clue as to what really happened. If de Chaumareys was relying entirely on an estimate of the distance run since the "sightings" of Cape Barbas and Cape Blanc, and if that estimate had been entirely accurate, it would certainly make him believe that he had completed more of the first "leg" of the dogleg than he had actually done. The *Medusa*'s real start point was problematical, but if it was perhaps ten or twelve leagues north of where it should have been, then the second turn of the dogleg was bound to be made too early. Even so, even if in fact he had managed to correctly identify Cape Blanc and then made his first turn from the right position, he was still cutting things rather fine, particularly in a largely unknown and imprecisely charted area. To add to this recklessness a failure to take frequent soundings to give early warning of approaching danger, could only be explained by his dependence on Richefort. The court was not told that when the officers protested to de Chaumareys of the extreme danger ahead, the captain had had to turn to Richefort, who at once reassured de Chaumareys that he knew his business and that all was well. But the fact that the real navigator had been Richefort was not admissible in court.

This fact being omitted, the next piece of evidence from de Chaumareys bordered on farce. It must be remembered that a sailing ship can rarely be turned quickly; in unfavourable circumstances, it may take up to six miles.

Three hours after the results of the noon sight had alarmed all the officers, the water had changed colour—clearly indicating the imminent approach to a bank—and at last de Chaumareys took action, ineffective as usual. He merely ordered a sounding to be taken. This showed eighteen "brasses" (96 feet). "This caused me extreme surprise," he said. "It made me go over to the starboard side and briefly consult my chart and check my calculations." This, when a thousand tons of frigate was heading inshore with irresistible momentum.

When the inevitable occurred, de Chaumareys was stricken "as much by astonishment as with grief" to find his command heeled right over, hard aground on the Arguin Bank. He could not understand what had happened, except that the bank was in the wrong position.

Le Carlier d'Herlye produced a copy of Bellin's chart, similar to that used by de Chaumareys, and asked the unfortunate captain to show him, on that chart, three critical positions: where the *Medusa* was at 5 p.m. on July 1, at 6 a.m. on July 2, and at 3 p.m. on July 2, the hour of stranding. De Chaumareys indicated the three points with great confidence. But not one was correct. The first one, which de Chaumareys showed as near Cape Blanc, could be proved badly wrong by the log of the *Echo*. The last position, that

of the wreck itself, he had stated in his report of 29
July to be 19° 55' North, 19° 24' West. But he had
declared to the court that his own estimate was now
19° 36' North, 19° 45' West. (A hydrographic mission
sent out a few months later was to establish it as 19°
53' North, 19° 20' West).

Le Carlier asked de Chaumareys to sign the copy of
the chart on which he had just marked the three positions, then he himself counter-signed it: the clerk to
the court, Belanfant, added a final signature.

That ended the navigational questioning. When Le
Carlier turned to the abortive attempts to refloat the
frigate and then the plans to evacuate her and save the
crew and passengers, de Chaumareys again unwittingly
revealed his incompetence, although he could confidently state that "these operations were carried out
with the greatest order." Incompetence is not a crime.
Abandoning men for whom one is responsible most
definitely is. The atmosphere of the courtroom
changed as the shadow of the death penalty began to
loom over de Chaumareys.

The witness stated: "I stayed on board the frigate almost to the last, while I could still see men
manifestly engaged in leaving her. They showed a
pronounced dread and dissatisfaction with the embarkation."

This presumably referred to the brandishing of a
musket by Lieutenant d'Anglas and the threats of the
soldiers to fire on the boats which seemed to be leaving half-empty. Also perhaps to the reluctance of some
seamen to leave the *Medusa* for Lieutenant Espiaux's
desperately overcrowded longboat.

De Chaumareys went on: "I decided, at the request
of several sailors who surrounded me, and to the great
satisfaction of all, to get into my barge. I did so and
very quickly helped by towing the longboat. I remember that at one moment, when the longboat came
alongside the frigate, I positively commanded Lieutenant Espiaux to embark the rest of the men remaining
in the ship. He said: 'Don't worry, captain.' On my

honour, I assure you I was convinced that the longboat was capable of saving them all. At that moment I was not aware of the danger which threatened the raft, but three attempts to tow it failed and it moved away with the currents. I put before you the despair of the men helplessly adrift on it, the fatal consequences which must ensue. From then on, it was obvious that my command was no longer the frigate, but the raft and the boats which were towing it."

The last sentence was a legal nicety, probably suggested to de Chaumareys by his defending counsel, Frigate-Captain Cuvilier, and M. Mesnard, a Rochefort lawyer, who were to invoke a law of 1765 which gave some latitude to officers faced with circumstances unforeseen in their orders or by any regulation. In effect, de Chaumareys was claiming that in leaving the frigate before the last man had gone, he was not abandoning his command, because the bulk of the men under his command were either on the raft or in the boats and his proper place was with them, where he might still be of some use in controlling rescue operations. The raft, he claimed, had not been abandoned; the towrope linking it to the barge carrying the governor and his spouse and their daughter had broken.

When the interrogation of the accused ended on February 6, La Tullaye, the president of the court, sent his own opinions to the Minister in writing. Oddly, he mentioned nothing of the abandonment or even of the abortive attempts to refloat the ship. He gave judgement only on the disputed matter of navigation. He put his finger on the errors made by de Chaumareys. His reliance on an estimate of the distance run along the coast of Africa when his positions were quite erroneous. How a dogleg course begun too far north must bring a ship directly to the Bank of Arguin. He regretted that the only documentary evidence he had in front of him was the log of the *Echo*, so that his opinion was only an opinion. But there was one error committed by Captain de Chaumareys which was indisputable. He had not carried out those frequent soundings which would have revealed the navigational mistakes and averted their fatal consequences.

The critical speeches for the prosecution and the defence lasted from February 24 to March 1, 1817, the vote of the members of the court being taken on Monday, March 3. Tension ebbed and flowed as the prosecutor, Le Carlier d'Herlye, dealt with charge after charge alleged against de Chaumareys and examined the validity or otherwise of the defence he had made.

The first charge was that de Chaumareys had allowed his squadron to become separated off Finisterre, when the *Loire* and the *Argus* were left behind, contrary to instructions. The prosecutor began severely: "This was an entirely voluntary act on the part of M. de Chaumareys. The fault would be very serious, if the reasons which the accused puts forward are not admitted, for the fact of separation has been proved, and it did not occur because of bad weather. But the accused has claimed that the poor sailing of these two ships considerably slowed the *Medusa*, that the governor of Senegal wished to reach his destination as soon as possible, that it was necessary to prepare in advance for the unloading of the troops and stores from the *Loire* and the *Argus*, and that the instructions given to M. de Chaumareys urged him not to delay because of the approach of the bad weather season."

The court waited to hear on which side Le Carlier would weight the scales. The prosecutor went on: "I think that all these reasons, taken together, justified M. de Chaumareys and I conclude that he should be declared 'Not Guilty' of dividing his squadron."

That must have given hope to de Chaumareys, but Le Carlier then turned to the navigation of the frigate and, in great detail and with some irony, tore the captain's defence to shreds. Then he turned to his own conclusions and these were remorseless.

"The sinking of His Majesty's Frigate *Medusa* was

not caused by forced circumstances, because the weather was fine, the sea good, the wind both moderate and favourable. I therefore attribute it to the course taken during the night; to complacency founded on the fact that they could not find bottom at 120 fathoms in the morning; to an over-confidence which led M. de Chaumareys to take the route to the east far too soon and on that course to be taken by the wind further towards the shore than he had expected; and to a feeling of security which made him neglect the indispensable precautions to be taken in dangerous regions and especially when in close proximity to a bank whose area and position are still not well known to this day."

After that broadside, Le Carlier let de Chaumareys breathe for a moment by mentioning his favourite excuse. "I truly believe," said the prosecutor, "that the edges of the Arguin Bank stretch much further to the west than is indicated on Bellin's chart, which is the one M. de Chaumareys was using. If his estimated position had been correct, then he would merely have struck the bank after travelling a further fifteen or sixteen leagues, instead of when he did, but if we take the position given in witnesses' statements, then he would have struck six or seven leagues later than he did."

Le Carlier then stated formally: "I conclude that M. Duroy de Chaumareys should be declared 'Guilty' of the sinking of His Majesty's Frigate *Medusa* through complacency and the taking of insufficient precautions; and, considering the results of this lack of caution, that he should be condemned to be dismissed his ship and declared unfit to serve, in accordance with Article 39 of the penal code."

Le Carlier sharply divided the rest of the story into three phases—the unsuccessful attempts to refloat the frigate and then the final abandonment of first the frigate and then the raft. As regards the failure to get the stranded *Medusa* off the bank, he pointed to three factors beyond the control of de Chaumareys. They were the lack of a heavily-built boat capable of taking out an anchor immediately; the effect of the currents combined with a choppy sea which added to all difficulties and in particular to the taking out of anchors in the desired directions; and, finally, the storm which drove the frigate further aground and stove in her hull. Therefore, he concluded, on the charge of causing the total loss of the *Medusa*, de Chaumareys should be found "Not Guilty."

So far, the balance had swung evenly: for de Chaumareys on the first charge, against de Chaumareys on the second charge, for de Chaumareys on the third charge. If the pattern continued with the fourth charge, that of abandonment, and de Chaumareys was found guilty, he would face death, for this charge alone carried the death penalty. On the face of it, there could be no other finding than that of guilty, for he certainly had not been the last man to leave the *Medusa*. His sole defence had been a rather shaky legal subterfuge.

The prosecutor kept everyone, and not least de Chaumareys, in suspense for a very long time while he meticulously turned over the facts to examine them from all angles, and in the light of various codes and regulations. His opening words must have struck a chill into the heart of the accused.

"The unanimous statements of all the witnesses, and the replies of M. de Chaumareys, leave no doubt that the longboat was no longer alongside the ship when he left her and that there were only a few men still on board after the departure of the longboat." That seemed to mean that de Chaumareys was technically guilty, but Le Carlier went on to consider what did or did not constitute an infringement of Articles 56 of 1763 and 66 of January 1, 1786. "Both of these state that the captain of a sinking ship must not, for any reason whatever, leave the ship until the last moment," he pointed out.

What he was saying could be understood in more than one way. That the captain had waited until the last practical moment, until the longboat had taken on its quota of passengers and left only a few men and himself behind. Or did he mean that, with the departure of the longboat, only the captain's barge remained, and if de Chaumareys got into that without embarking every last man and woman left on board (there were some 60, not "a few"), then he was guilty of abandoning any who remained behind? Or was the fact of the return of Espiaux's longboat, after de Chaumareys had abandoned the *Medusa*, being left out of account? Or was its return the result of an order by the captain? A command which might justify his claim to have left the frigate to control the rescue operations instead?

"I am going to examine with you, gentlemen," continued the prosecutor, "the penalties applicable to that charge which would render the accused liable to capital punishment; that is, if I paid no attention to the circumstances which accompanied the infringement of Articles 56 and 66 previously mentioned, but demanded for him due application of that penalty so liberally stipulated by Article 35 of the penal code for ships of 22 August, 1790." Those were the savage regulations of the Revolutionary Navy.

"In my report I have been guided by a just and severe impartiality regarding the guilt of M. de Chaumareys which, equally, must be the basis of the conclusions which my duty obliges me to take in indicating the penalties which I believe to be applicable to the misconduct alleged by the prosecution.

"You will recall, gentlemen, that in his interrogation and in the debates which followed, M. de Chaumareys alleged, and his defenders have repeated it; that he directed the details of the frigate's evacuation and controlled the disorders that tended to accompany it. M. de Chaumareys and his defenders have invoked in his favour Article 1285 of 1765, by which His Majesty, not being able to foresee all the tasks and orders which may be necessary, orders only that in unforeseen circumstances an officer conduct himself generally for the greatest good of the Service and in

accordance with the laws of honour. Now, it is alleged
further, that he had to directly supervise the em-
barkment of a large part of his crew onto the life-raft
as well as into the boats, and that he saw this as more
important than passively remaining on board his frigate in order to try and make the rest of his men leave
the ship."

The thinness of that excuse must have seemed even
more flimsy when spoken by the prosecutor, in framing a reply to it, than it had done when put forward
as a legal nicety by the defence. The court waited,
and for de Chaumareys this must have been the worst
moment of the long ordeal, for Le Carlier to reject
the plea out of hand. Indeed, several members of the
court expected that the prosecutor would instantly demand the death penalty. For a moment it seemed that
he was going to.

"Even if I try to temper the severity of my Minister,
any indulgence cannot go beyond the bounds of equity,"
declared Le Carlier. "I cannot admit that these extenuating circumstances are sufficient to clear the accused
of all guilt. On the other hand, I cannot entirely refute
the validity of the motives he has given to excuse his
infringement of Articles 56 and 66. Therefore, although I cannot regard them as extenuating circumstances for his grave misconduct, I can put them in
the balance to weigh in favour of the accused when
the question of the death penalty is considered."

The shadow lifted from the room, and from de
Chaumareys, and there was a certain amount of astonishment at this promise of leniency. It was with
lessened tension that the court listened to Le Carlier
continuing to prove why he thought de Chaumareys
was guilty.

"Unlike M. de Chaumareys, I do not see his command at the last divided between the life-raft and the
boats which lay alongside the *Medusa*. I always visu-
alise the frigate as sinking and not completely evacuated when he left her. The regulations foresaw the
case of a sinking vessel. They are very clear and do

not leave the captain the option of making up his own mind where his presence is most necessary. But I am persuaded that it was not through any weakness, which it was the intention of the law to punish severely, that M. de Chaumareys left his ship before the moment laid down by the regulations. I believe it was only an error of judgement which led him to make a false interpretation of the various articles in the regulations.

"Even so, gentlemen, if some doubts do arise concerning the actual intentions which M. de Chaumareys alleges motivated him at this time, can we forget those principles which direct all men called to judge their equals to weigh the doubts in favour of the accused? Can we forget this, above all, when it is a case of capital punishment? Guided by this principle and by my conscience, I would exclude from my conclusions a penalty which the legislative could only have wished to be used for cowardice or for treason."

The prosecutor blandly continued: "But if I do not find in the conduct of M. de Chaumareys any fault specified by the regulations which would warrant capital punishment, I am far from declaring him 'Not Guilty.' The fact that he infringed the articles and did not remain to the last minute in the frigate renders him liable to punishment. I conclude, gentlemen, that M. de Chaumareys should be declared 'Guilty' of not leaving his ships as the last man; and that, in addition to the penalties to which he is already liable for the loss of the frigate, he should be condemned to serve a term of five years in a military prison, if His Majesty so desires."

Le Carlier was compelled to explain why he was asking for a type of punishment which, for this offence, was not laid down in the regulations. He stated that he was aware of various precedents and then took refuge in a variation of de Chaumareys' own plea, that if the 1765 regulations admitted that all offences could not be foreseen, then neither could the penalties.

The third and final charge concerning the conduct

of de Chaumareys after the frigate had run aground
was potentially almost as deadly as that from which
he had just escaped. It was the accusation that he had
abandoned the raft. And here, the captain's ingenious
plea, that he had left his ship while there were still
men aboard her because he had wanted to save the
people on the raft and direct the boats, could with
ease be argued against him.

Le Carlier d'Herlye set out to argue for him, and
at great length. He said there were two ways of looking at the matter. "Firstly, the *Medusa* being entirely
abandoned (sic) by all the men who were now re-
formed on and around the liferaft, should this craft be
regarding as forming, with the men, the physical basis
of a new command under the direction of M. de
Chaumareys? If so, his abandoning of it would imply
that he had infringed the articles already mentioned.
Or, alternatively, should the liferaft and the six boats
which accompanied it be regarded as distinctly separate craft, each one under the command of a particular
officer and forming part of a division under the orders
of M. de Chaumareys? I am utterly of the opinion
that the second way of looking at things is that which
is usual and just. The boats cannot be regarded as
forming part of the liferaft which, anyway, could not
help or protect them against bad weather as a ship
does: on the contrary, it was from the boats that the
liferaft would receive help."

This was extremely dangerous ground, but Le Carlier pressed on. "I therefore consider the liferaft and
the boats as a division of seven craft, whatever their
size or type, following the commands of a chief common to all. One of these boats being in trouble or
sinking, it is certain that the others must give it as
much help as possible. But if bad weather or other
forced circumstances do not allow the rescue attempt
to continue, or even to save the crew of the craft in
distress, the commander of the division is not guilty
of having abandoned it."

As Le Carlier continued, his meaning began to

emerge slowly, underlying what he did not say rather than in his spoken words. De Chaumareys had revealed that, on occasion, his orders had not been carried out; but he had never named the officers whom he said were to blame and had taken all the responsibility himself: he had never accused anyone. Now, Le Carlier was doing it for him.

"In this case, the boats of M. de Chaumareys and his companions were already crowded. Perhaps they could have taken more men from the raft, but it is evident that the boats would have been rushed and sunk in doing so. This fear, well-founded I believe, appears to have been the reason which prevented any of the boats going near the raft. Even in the letter written by M. Schmaltz to the Minister, this motive is revealed. I must observe, however, that M. de Chaumareys made both his own boat and the Senegal boat go about and return to take up the towrope again, but by the time they had done so, they found that the other boats were no longer towing the liferaft and were making no move to renew the tow. Therefore I conclude that M. Duroy de Chaumareys should be declared 'Not Guilty' of abandoning the liferaft."

That was the nearest that His Excellency the Governor of Senegal ever came to being declared "Guilty" of the same offence.

Saturday, March 1, was given over to speeches for the defence. They hardly needed longer, as the prosecutor had done most of their work for them. On March 3 the members of the court voted. Although one was for the death penalty, most votes were cast for three years' imprisonment. In addition the name of de Chaumareys was to be struck from the Navy List and he was to forfeit his orders and decorations.

Le Carlier had previously written to the Minister in confidence, explaining why he intended to be merciful. "I hesitate to pronounce the death penalty because in my soul and conscience I do not judge that the accused deserves death for having left the frigate before he should have done. He did not commit this offence from weakness or to save himself, but to put himself in a place where he would be of use."

No doubt this was a delicate letter to write for, putting politics aside, many believed that the principal fault lay with the government and in particular with the Minister of Marine. As the captain of the *Loire* had noted, "Chaumareys was without doubt truly guilty, but shouldn't' a great part of the responsibility fall on the government which entrusts such men with employment for which they were not fitted."

There were some who thought that even the mild sentence passed on de Chaumareys was too harsh. An officer who was serving at Rochefort and had closely studied the trial wrote to the Minister. He was concerned first to bring out what the trial had concealed, in case Du Bouchage did not know. "The captain committed major errors from the first. He immediately alienated his second-in-command, who in turn involved the other officers, by taking as his confidant in the navigation of the ship a passenger who was to be the poor captain of St. Louis." This was the amazing Richefort, of course.

The writer made the significant point that not a single nautical document, chart or log was produced to show with certainty how the *Medusa* was navigated before the stranding. The implication may be that they were deliberately destroyed or "lost" because they were incriminating.

Impatiently, he short-circuited the endless tale of the errors committed by de Chaumareys and asked: "What do they prove? Failure, unfitness for leadership, inability to cope with difficulties, and a quite unusual lack of safety-precautions. But by no means a coward. At present, he is regarded as solely responsible for this disastrous event, because it was he who was in command and also because he had the generosity not to transfer one part of this fatal responsibility to any of his subordinates. But these men, have they all done their duty?"

He examined the separation in the night of the *Medusa* and the *Echo* and concluded that Reynaud, officer of the watch in the frigate, and de Vénancourt, captain of the corvette, were jointly responsible. De Chaumareys had nothing to do with it. Had the two ships not separated, there might have been a stranding but there would have been no disaster.

He condemned Reynaud again for casting off the towrope to the raft without a direct order from his captain, and asked pointedly: "Was it M. Schmaltz and his entourage who gave this advice? Further, this boat (holding Reynaud and Schmaltz) saved only forty people from the frigate. I have been told that this boat had on a previous occasion carried no less than seventy soldiers with their arms. If this is true, then it could easily have taken off the seventeen men remaining on board the *Medusa*."

The writer concluded by explaining that this was not merely his opinion but that of a number of other officers who were not directly involved and were therefore unbiased. They all thought the sentence too harsh and that, at the least, de Chaumareys should be returned to the Navy List and be given back his rank.

In a sense these three men who sympathised with de Chamaureys were too detached. Neither Le Carlier nor des Touches nor the anonymous naval officer from Rochefort had any real contact with the *Medusa* tragedy.

But to men like Savigny and Corréard who had by a small margin survived the horrors which had been the direct result of the multiple errors and muddles made by de Chaumareys, the Court Martial and its judgements appeared to be mere white-wash; an example of the "old boy net" at work to protect its own. But they were far from blaming de Chaumareys alone. Although the Minister was their prime target, they were extremely bitter about the conduct of Schmaltz, Reynaud and several of the other officers. Charlotte Picard also was to give a very poor impression of the behaviour of some of the officers on whom de Chaumareys had to rely.

It is all very well to point out, as some French academic historians have done, that the testimony of Savigny and Corréard is "biased and suspect"; and to endeavour to discount it because there were political or personal undertones. The affair was indeed political and politics could hardly be avoided, but their original involvement was quite involuntary (except that Corréard chose deliberately to take his chance on the raft with his men). They knew, as few others did, what the results had been. Like Kipling's toad under the harrow, they knew exactly where each sharp steel point had gone home.

Above all they knew, and none better, that the example set by the leader is all-important; and that in this critical aspect de Chamaureys had failed lamentably, as had his co-leaders Schmaltz and Reynaud. They had been tried in the only court that counted—that of a real character-revealing emergency—and had failed miserably. They would have done better to have died with their men.

In Paris they were apprehensive that if all these details leaked out, the French Navy would become the target of unbearable mockery from the English, which would be embarrassing for the new regime. None knew better than the émigrés how arrogantly proud the British were of their record at sea in the last war, how ready to condemn the French out of hand.

By the strangest of coincidences, unknown at that moment either to the French or to the British, as the court martial trying de Chaumareys for the loss of his frigate was actually sitting and arriving at final judgement, an almost exactly similar series of events was taking place many thousands of miles away, but to a British frigate. The conduct of her captain and her crew in a nearly identical situation provided a real-life judgement on de Chaumareys which is far more effective than any discussion, although the British captain also had to stand his trial in due course.

14

A BRITISH "MEDUSA"

The Alceste in the South China Sea, February to March, 1817

ON January 21, 1817, while Le Carlier d'Herlye was still studying the documents in the de Chaumareys case, the British thirty-eight-gun frigate *Alceste* was leaving Whampoa in China carrying 257 persons including a V.I.P. and his entourage. The captain, Murray Maxwell, was a battle-experienced officer. He and his ship had been partly responsible for probably ruining one of Bonaparte's campaigns, by capturing his artillery at sea before he could attack. Although that had occurred in 1811, he was to be reminded of it in the strangest way before he saw England again.

The V.I.P. on board was Lord Amherst, then the British Ambassador to China and a very much more distinguished official than M. Schmaltz, for he was later to become Governor of Canada and later still Governor-General of India.

It is probable that, as with the *Medusa*, some of the *Alceste*'s guns had been removed to make room for passengers. A slightly smaller ship, she carried 150 fewer people than the *Medusa* had done; by French standards, British warships always were undermanned, a fact which reflected the comparative sizes of the populations of the two powers.

The British frigate was bound for home through the South China Seas. In their danger and mystery these more than matched the coast of West Africa. While today the Arguin Bank alone stands out as white and unsurveyed on the charts, the South China Seas contain a space of 100,000 square miles similarly unsurveyed and unknown, labelled simply "The Dangerous

Area." Furthermore, there was no safe route far out from land over deep water, such as the *Medusa* could have taken, had de Chaumareys not obeyed the dangerous instructions issued him by Admiral Rosily from the Ministry of Marine in Paris. For no less than 1,500 miles there was nothing but shallow water, nothing deeper than forty fathoms (240 feet). In an area where typhoons were frequent, this meant that extraordinarily dangerous seas could develop. The time for the passage had been well-chosen, however, and the winds were favourable.

The route recommended then for sailing ships (but not now for steamships) passed through the Bangka Strait, immediately before the Sunda Strait. This is nearer the equator than the Arguin Bank, so that the heat was intense. The route was chosen because it was comparatively known. Nevertheless, Captain Murray Maxwell of the *Alceste* kept the leadsmen sounding continuously, because there were hundreds of submerged shoals in the area, some of which rise so steeply from deep water that neither a sounding lead (nor a modern echo sounder) can give much warning.

On February 17, while de Chaumareys was still being questioned about his stranding, the *Alceste* struck one of these steep-to-reefs at speed. Maxwell let go an anchor at once, to hold the frigate on the reef in case she was badly holed. The British ship proved to have struck on rock, not sand, and was so damaged that the pumps could not control the inflow. Maxwell's plight was worse than that of de Chamaureys, for his ship was doomed to start with. If she was got off, she would only sink. He was, similarly, many hundreds of miles from all help, and off an inhospitable coast populated by potentially dangerous natives. The nearest land was much closer, only three miles distant, but it was merely an island with no obvious landing place.

Significantly, the captain's first thought was for the V.I.P., Lord Amherst, and his entourage; his actions were almost identical to those of de Chaumareys. The

Ambassador and his suite were embarked in a barge and a cutter under the command of the First Lieutenant, Hopper, the equivalent of the *Medusa*'s Lieutenant Reynaud. Hopper was ordered to land this party on the island first of all and then return with the boats. Hopper had to travel six miles to and along the shore, because the mangroves prevented any landing being made opposite the scene of the wreck.

Meanwhile, Maxwell hoisted out the other four boats and ordered the construction of a large raft to be towed by the boats. On this raft, he put no people; only large and heavy stores. The smaller and more important items, such as water, food, arms, ammunition and tools, he had placed in the boats. When the barge and the cutter had returned empty from landing the first party, Maxwell embarked the rest of his crew in the boats and they all headed for shore, towing the raft, the full six miles. By nightfall, they were all safely ashore and setting up a camp.

Next day, it was discovered that the island was waterless. It was known that there was little chance of their being sighted by a passing ship. A council was held and it was decided that the Ambassador and his suite should embark again in the barge and the cutter under Lieutenant Hopper and try to make Batavia in Java, some 200 miles further south. Given good weather, this should take them four days; but it could easily be longer. When they arrived at Batavia, they were to send out a relief ship to pick up the island castaways, who by that time would be very short of water. The men in the boats were given enough water to provide a ration of one pint per man per day for four days only. Little enough for Europeans exposed to the sun in a latitude 3° south of the equator, but more than the castaways on the island would have.

The procedure bears strong resemblance to some aspects of the abandonment of the *Medusa*, particularly that of the second-in-command being given charge of the boats designed to take the V.I.P. to safety as rapidly as possible. But there the similarity ends. Captain Maxwell did not accompany them. He remained behind on the island to control the castaways, who numbered 200 men and one woman. No one was abandoned, not on the wreck, not on the raft, not in the boats, not on the island. The captain was where he should be, with the bulk of his command.

Also, unlike de Chaumareys, Maxwell knew what to do and he saw that it got done. Above all, he was not complacent; he foresaw various hazards, still in the future, and set out to be ready in time. He changed the camp site to the top of a small hill, for better defence; he had the provisions stowed in a cool cave under formal guard by armed Marine sentries; he had his crew digging like beavers in the tropical heat to find water, and when they were twenty feet down into the earth, they found a little water seeping into the clay at the bottom; and nevertheless, he sent out a boat party to the wreck to salvage supplies and arms. His seamen were still digging at midnight and shortly afterwards the first bottle of muddy water was filled and pronounced fresh.

Immediately, there was a rush to the well by the thirsty men. Maxwell stopped it and posted an armed guard over the digging party; he also proclaimed that no-one—no-one—would get any water at all from the well until there was enough to give a ration to everybody. That was hard but fair. By noon next day, February 20, a pint of well water per man was served out.

On the fourth day, February 21, a boat party of unarmed seamen salvaging the wreck were surrounded by several local war vessels—proas armed with swivel guns at the bow and manned by eighty Malays. The British pulled madly for the shore, pursued by the Malays. Maxwell counter-attacked at once. Armed seamen jumped into two of the boats by the shore and rowed out to confront the proas, which gave up the pursuit of the unarmed party. Then a lookout reported more proas, landing armed men on the island about two miles away.

Maxwell assumed that attack was imminent. And

that it would be ruthless. The sea-Dyaks usually murdered everyone aboard any ship they captured and it was rumored that some tribes were suspected of cannibalism. He ordered that all effort be concentrated on defence. A stockade was rapidly built around the hilltop, flimsy but still sufficient to stop a rush. The Marines had thirty muskets and bayonets, but only seventy-five rounds of ball cartridge. The gunner had had the foresight to save the gunpowder charges from the carronades on the upper deck, so there was spare powder; but no shot. He improvised by using broken glass from the bottles instead of lead for projectiles. There were a dozen cutlasses, but most of the 200 men were still unarmed. Again, the British improvised. Spearshafts were made from branches and small trees; knives, chisels and nails were used to give them unpleasant points. Scouts were sent out to keep watch on the Malays and they reported that the Dyaks seemed principally interested in plundering the wreck.

Next day, February 22, was that on which La Tullaye, president of the court at Rochefort, informed the Minister of the French Navy that the officers of his court had agreed among themselves that a moderate judgement should be pronounced upon Frigate-Captain de Chaumareys because it had become clear that the accused was not besmirched by any lapse from honour.

That same morning, thousands of miles away, Captain Murray Maxwell of the British Royal Navy decided to talk peace with the Malays, rather than fight them. He sent an officer down to the landing place to go out in a boat and wave a green bough in token of his pacific intentions. It was a sensible move, for the main interest of the Dyaks lay with the wreck and the metal objects it contained or was built of; to them, this was treasure beyond price. Whereas what the British needed was food and water. But the Dyaks were suspicious and ferocious; it was impossible to negotiate. What they wanted, they would take.

That was exactly Maxwell's own view. He decided to recapture the wreck from the Dyaks, using his best-armed men embarked in three boats under Second-Lieutenant Hay, who was now his second-in-command. As the attack went in, the Dyaks threw their plunder into the proas, set fire to the *Alceste*, and made off. This was helpful, for Maxwell faced the same problem in getting at the stores of the *Alceste* as had Reynaud in his salvage attempt on the *Medusa*. He had decided to burn off the upperworks anyway, so that he could get at the decks below. Reynaud did not do this, perhaps because he claimed that the *Medusa*'s hulk was continuously wave-swept.

All that night the flames from the burning frigate illuminated the eerie mangrove swamps and the improvised stockade with flickering lights and shadows. In just such a situation in the desert the French castaways had been frightened by a lion which proved in the morning to have been a bush waving with the wind. Showing less imagination a British sentry cried: "Halt! Who goes there?" to a hunched shape prowling out in the darkness and pulled the trigger when he received no reply. At the crash of the shot, every man was armed and at his post. Then it was discovered why the intruder had failed to answer a challenge shouted in English—it was a Malayan baboon.

Next day was Sunday, so while the captain took Divine Service in the camp, two boats went out to the charred and smoking hulk of the frigate and obtained a good haul from the opened decks—barrels of flour, cases of wine, and one cask of beer. The latter, for a party of British castaways, was an immense boost to morale.

For several more days, while the Court Martial solemnly assembled at Rochefort, all members in fulldress uniforms, to listen to the prosecutor's presentation of his case against de Chaumareys, the British trial-by-action was still going on. Maxwell was concerned to get as much arms and ammunition as possible out of the wreck and to improve his fields of fire around the stockade. But he did not neglect his boats; he had sentries watching over them all night and his officers, unlike most of those commanded by de Chaumareys, were efficient and alert. At dawn on February 24, Second-Lieutenant Hay sighted two proas with canoes towed astern stealing into the cove where the British boats were kept. He at once manned the boats and went out to attack. The Malays cut loose their canoes to allow the proas to get away faster, and one of the proas brought a swivel-gun to bear as the British ran alongside to board. Fired blindly, it hit nothing and then the British seamen were in amongst the Dyaks with cutlass and bayonet. Within a minute or two, four Dyaks were dead, two were prisoners, five were overboard and vanished.

Later that morning, while Le Carlier was dividing the lamentable story of the *Medusa* into neatly and logically presented "eras" for the convenient comprehension of the court, a second Dyak fleet of fourteen proas was approaching the wreck of the *Alceste*. One vessel was much larger than the others and appeared to be a flagship, carrying perhaps a rajah. They took possession of the wreck and the "rajah" was seen directing their salvage operations.

On March 1, 1817, while defence counsel for Frigate-Captain de Chaumareys were making their final speeches to the court at Rochefort, Captain Maxwell's castaways saw yet another division of fourteen proas join all the others; and during the night yet more were noticed arriving, but the light was too bad to count their numbers exactly. The build-up for a major attack seemed to be taking place.

On the morning of March 2 which, being a Sunday, meant well-earned rest for those concerned in the hearings at Rochefort, twenty of the largest proas approached the shore in line-abreast while the remainder clustered closely around the wreck of the British frigate. Still in line, the twenty approaching vessels anchored as one just offshore and to the beating of gongs and brandishing of spears the Dyaks opened fire with their bow-mounted swivel-guns. But no landing was attempted.

Maxwell believed it would come that night, under cover of darkness, which would render ineffective the fire of those of his men who were armed with muskets. Now it may be that the Malays were merely demonstrating; that, in effect, they were simply saying: "Your ship is now ours, keep off." Or they may have been genuinely enraged by the killing of their men in the raiding proa a few days before, and were itching to get at the perpetrators. Or, because the islands on which they lived were short of protein-food, they relished the thought of meat; and there were two hundred live carcases on the island. All of them British.

The British captain was certainly right to prepare for the worst. He gave them a rousing speech which was also coldly informative. "My lads," said Maxwell, "you must all have observed the great increase in the enemy's force, and the threatening posture they have assumed. I have reason to believe they will attack us this night. I do not wish to conceal our real state, because I do not think there is a man here who is afraid to face any sort of danger. We are in a position to defend ourselves against regular troops, far less a set of naked savages, with their spears and krises. It is true they have swivels in their boats, but they cannot reach here. I have not observed that they have any muskets, but if they have, so have we. When we were first thrown on shore we could only muster seventy-five ball cartridges—we now have sixteen hundred. They cannot send up, I believe, more than five hundred men; but with two hundred such as now stand around me, I do not fear a thousand—nor fifteen hundred of them. The pikemen standing firm, we shall give them such a volley of musketry as they will be little prepared for; and when they are thrown into confusion, we will sally out, chase them into the water, and ten to one but we secure their vessels. Let every man be on his alert, and should these barbarians this night attempt our hill, I trust we shall convince them that they are dealing with Britons." The seamen greeted this harangue with thunderous cheers, which must have carried ominously to the Dyaks and spelt out the message for them.

The speech, obviously a carefully-constructed one, nevertheless reads oddly when compared to the only equivalent recorded comment by Frigate-Captain de Chaumareys in his situation, and this comment had to be wrung out of him by an officer calling out from the raft to ask if all was ready? "Yes, yes, I have provided you with everything that can be necessary." And when asked who was to command replied: "It is I; in a moment I shall be with you," before he disappeared and got into his own barge.

On the morning of March 3 the members of the Court Martial at Rochefort sat down to vote on the appropriate sentence to be passed on the captain of the *Medusa*, one only favouring execution, most voting for three years' imprisonment.

On the same morning, on a waterless island in the South China Seas, Captain Maxwell was reconsidering his position, which appeared increasingly desperate. There had been no attack by the Malays during the night; all had been quiet. But they could now count a further ten proas among the Dyak fleet, which had obviously come in during darkness. The odds against them were increasing every day; and the relief ship was long overdue. He had estimated four days for the two boats to reach Batavia; if all went well, a relief ship might arrive within a week. But now seventeen days had passed, seventeen days on reduced rations of food and water. There was a gloomy feeling in the camp that somehow the two boats had met disaster on the way to Java, so that no help would ever come.

Maxwell decided not to wait, while his men got physically weaker and the Dyaks became numerically stronger every day; because there could be only one end to that. What he needed was to escape and there were not enough boats to take all the men simultaneously without overloading them to the swamping point. Exactly the situation which had faced de Chaumareys seven months ago, although in detail the problems differed. De Chaumareys had evaded his problem, so that a series of forced and unprepared abandonments took place, for which he was now being tried, luckily by sympathetic judges. Maxwell's judges were going to be the savage and ferocious Dyaks with their spears and long, curved knives.

Maxwell was not going to abandon, he was going to attack. He needed boats. The encircling Dyaks had them. Take them from the Dyaks then. The only thing which he would abandon would be the raft. To tow it would slow the boats too much and any men he had to place on it would be exposed without cover to the fire of the proas' swivel-guns. These were the equivalent of huge, heavy shot-guns on swivel mountings which could fire destructive blasts of musket balls, glass, shingle, old nails or any other hard object which happened to be lying around. To tow men on a raft while exposed to a hail of such shot from scores of proas simply could not be done. But neither could he leave some of his men behind on the island to be massacred.

He determined on a night attack by part of the force and began to work out an ingenious and risky plan. Maxwell had originally had six boats and a raft, just as had de Chaumareys. He had sent two boats, lightly loaded and therefore seaworthy, two hundred miles to get help. He had four boats left. He would divide these into pairs and each pair would capture a single proa by simultaneous boarding from both sides. While the boarding party manned the captured proas, the four boats would return to shore to pick up more English seamen. The attack would then be continued, until enough proas had been captured to take all his two hundred men comfortably; and then they would escape. Without the encumbrance of the raft, they would be as fast as the enemy, and to his swivel-guns they could oppose their musketry fire. Some might die, but they would die fighting.

Orders were being issued for this attack when the lookout reported a distant sail in the direction of Java.

A squall obscured it and some thought that it was only a chance glint of sunlight on part of the raincloud which had really been seen. But half an hour later, a signalman with a telescope confirmed that it was not merely a sail but a square-rigged vessel, either a ship or a brig. The Malays, having no hill to climb, did not immediately see the approaching European vessel; when they did, they showed confusion and alarm.

Maxwell instantly decided to turn that to his advantage. He ordered the main body of his men to capture some of the nearest proas by moving towards them unseen through the mangrove swamps and then wading out to the Malay craft. But the Dyaks were alert and, in daylight, could see the British as soon as they left the cover of the mangroves and began to push out through the water holding their muskets at chest level to keep them dry. The swivel-gun of the nearest proa swung round and a blast of shot smashed into the mangroves and lashed the surface of the water. The British Marines, breast-high in the sea by now, stopped and aimed their muskets while trying to keep steady against the slap of the waves and the surging power of the tidal stream. They claimed no hits. But the Dyaks, caught between an aggressively-minded force of British on shore and the British ship approaching from seaward, left the scene entirely, no doubt waiting for a safer time before returning to plunder the wreck.

The rescue vessel, the Honourable East India Company's armed ship *Ternate*, had been sent by Lord Amherst on the same day that he had safely reached Batavia. Captain Ellis, who commanded her, came ashore in the evening and described the scene on the stockaded hill. How wild the castaways seemed, unshaven and in ragged clothes, armed with cutlasses and crude pikes. And how, when the word of command was given, the apparent mob of ruffians fell in smartly under their officers.

On their way home to England in a chartered ship the party touched at St. Helena on June 27, 1817. The ex-Emperor of France received them and when Lord Amherst presented Captain Murray Maxwell to him, Napoleon bowed and said that he recalled the name from the Adriatic where Maxwell in 1811 had helped take two frigates carrying two hundred field guns for the French Army. "Your government must not blame you for the loss of the *Alceste,* for you have taken one of my frigates," he said.

Like de Chaumareys before him, Maxwell was returning home to stand trial by court martial for the loss of his ship. However, he was able to show that soundings were being taken continually before the stranding and that the submerged shoal was not marked on any chart. The verdict was "Not Guilty." When it came to considering the actions he had taken after he had abandoned his ship the court could only express its marked approbation. In a desperate situation, he had not lost a man. Not to the sea, not to sickness, not to the Dyaks (although he had inflicted casualties on them). He had brought them all home. Shortly afterwards, he received a knighthood.

This was admittedly an unusual case, of an extremely efficient and determined captain who not merely coped with all problems as soon as or even before they appeared but aggressively kept his enemies on edge. For this reason the affair has been largely forgotten, although it provided a striking lesson in leadership. Had Maxwell failed, however, had he been complacent, inefficient, half-hearted and utterly without foresight, then most of his men might have been massacred and possibly eaten by the Dyaks. A terrible scandal would have resulted, there would have been calls for vengeance, and a punitive expedition might have been mounted. And the affair of the frigate *Alceste* would have become widely known.

Perhaps fortunately for de Chaumareys, quite a different sort of captain, his court martial had ended by now, the sentence had been reviewed, and he was safely inside the château-prison of Ham. For on April 4, 1817, the hydrographic mission under Ship-Captain Roussin which had been sent out to re-survey the coast of West Africa and in particular establish both the position of the Arguin Bank and the site of the wreck of the *Medusa* sighted a remarkable object to the south-east.

In the corvette *Bayadère* with the small despatch boat *Epervier* in attendance, Roussin was methodically sounding the approaches to the bank and taking bottom samples with the lead at the same time. He was finding a pure sand bottom ten leagues out from the bank giving about fifty fathoms and reducing to forty fathoms as he approached to within five leagues. Closer in still there began to be much broken shell mixed up with the sand and the depth had reduced to twenty-five fathoms. That was quite a considerable slope, leading up to the bank itself. This Roussin reported as: "A vast platform of sand, of the same nature as the surrounding coast and consisting of the same alluviums which had helped to shape it. Its mass, as hard as that of the actual coast, is similarly covered with sand and broken shells. It has an abrupt slope on the seaward side. By taking a large number of measurements, the base of this slope was shown to be eight fathoms deep." As the bank was wholly submerged all that could be seen was league after league of tossing wave-tops, giving to the inexperienced eye an impression of a vast open ocean. And it was anything but that. It was a series of steep terraces, unexpectedly shallowing.

Early in the morning of April 4 the little despatch boat *Epervier*, sounding ahead of the corvette which was her base ship, reported that she was approaching the Arguin Bank. That was at 0330. At 1100, continuing the same course, the colour of the water had changed abruptly and the agitation of the sea clearly showed the presence of a large, submerged obstruction which was causing the waves to rise steeply around it. At 1400 hours, or 2 p.m., the *Epervier* signalled: "Something remarkable, south-east."

Lieutenant Legoarrant of the despatch boat climbed the mizzen mast for a better look. "I saw the wreck of a large vessel on the Arguin Bank and thought it was the frigate *Medusa*. I warned Captain Roussin of the danger. Simultaneously, the bottom over which I was sailing shallowed by three fathoms, which now gave only six fathoms under me, so I turned and came around the corvette's stern." Six French fathoms are thirty-two English feet, but the dark shape of the wrecked vessel was still miles away and inshore of the survey vessels. Roussin determined not to come too near and from the initial sighting at six miles closed in only to four miles, from where the carcase of a ship could be seen clearly through a telescope.

He reported formally: "The frigate *Medusa*, wrecked on the Arguin Bank, appeared in front of us. The colour of the water indicated a shallow area and also that the bottom was very uneven. I only approached to within four miles, but this was enough to fix the site on our chart of the Arguin Bank. She can be useful for a very long time yet, as the waters do not seem to ruin her. There is every reason to believe that her bulk, by fixing the sand around her, will form a kind of islet of which she will be the lower part. Already the reefs appear only in her vicinity and about half a mile from her bow and stern. In addition, her heel to larboard, which faces west towards open sea, is the most favourable one to withstand the waves without damage. The bulwarks only are ruined. The bowsprit is still in place and the entire wreck is very prominent above the water, so that it can be seen from two leagues away. I do not doubt that much can still be salvaged from her—cables, guns, shot, and especially the 90,000 francs in gold. The heel of the ship will make the salvage of her contents easy."

So there it was, the wreck of the *Medusa*, found on the day following the court martial of her captain. He had stranded her on July 2 and abandoned her on July 5, 1816, after about sixty hours. And she had been found on April 4, 1817, nine months after he had abandoned her in haste, without preparation, without thought for the lives of his men, because he was convinced she was going to break up at any moment and drown them all. And now, here she was, high enough out of the water to be seen from six miles away, with only her larboard bulwarks broken down. And add that significant detail, that her bowsprit was still standing. That meant that the internal beams, knees and bracings of her basic structure were still strong.

That the "fix" which Roussin obtained of her position did not agree with either of the two positions de Chaumareys had given was nearly irrelevant in face of the brute fact that she need never have been abandoned. There had been sufficient time to send the two best boats to St. Louis, carrying the governor and his entourage, and for the *Echo* or the *Argus* to sail to the rescue of the remaining men and women left aboard. But that would have meant de Chaumareys remaining, too.

Not one life need have been lost. There were no seagoing Moorish pirates to attack the wreck and anyway there were hundreds of armed soldiers aboard. There were only the waves, the unavailing storms which had proved impotent to crush her hull through nine long months. There had been no need to loose the raft with its crowded cargo of 150 souls to their ghastly and fatal despair under the blazing sun of Africa. No need to put them on the raft. No need for a raft at all.

They had been worried in Paris, when de Chaumareys' first bland report had come in with the *Echo*, of what public reaction might be. They had worried even more, at the Ministry, at what the English would say when they read that disgraceful "leak" by surgeon Savigny in the *Journal des Débats*. They had denied its truth, libelled Savigny, tried to shut him up. They had tried de Chaumareys as secretly as possible and let him escape lightly. Reynaud and Schmaltz had gone virtually scot-free. The conduct of the three principal culprits was not officially and openly repudiated. Instead, Savigny and Corréard and anyone else who tried to tell the full, dreadful story were to be threatened or forced into silence.

And so the English reacted then, and to this day, in the way that the Ministry had thought they might. They passed off the *Medusa* affair with a shrug. In effect, they said: "What else can you expect from the French." Once that attitude had set, it was hard to change it. Yet that too was a libel and again it was a libel on Savigny and his companions. The part they had played in the tragedy was in stark contrast to that of de Chaumareys, Reynaud and Schmaltz. If the Ministry had been more perceptive they might have seen that the reputation of France lay rather with those who had endured and survived, rather than with those who had abandoned and fled.

Instead, they reacted then, as French historians still tend to do now, with a shudder of distaste for the slaughter and cannibalism that marked the raft of the *Medusa*; and indeed with deep suspicion of what Savigny, as effective leader, might have done. This was, and is, an extremely facile and fastidious judgement. How wrong it really was could not be understood for a century and a half, because an ominous mystery then underlay many of the events which had taken place on the raft. The facts were known, but the meaning of the facts was not. There was no comparative experience from which to interpret and explain them; or rather, any comparable event must have lacked the trained mind of a Savigny and his determination to record it.

But they were also wrong in the short term. No doubt they thought that the *Medusa* affair could be quietly disposed of by silencing Savigny with threats and putting de Chaumareys "on ice" for a few years in a discreet château-prison. Executing him would of course have been the worst possible thing for public relations, even if he did half-deserve it. This way, the *Medusa* would soon be forgotten. That proved to be a monumental miscalculation.

15

"SHADOWS OF OFFICERS"

France and Senegal, 1817–1821

ON January 1, 1817, the British handed Senegal
to the French and evacuated their garrison and
administration. This meant a turn of fortune for the
Picard family as M. Picard could now take up his official duties as attorney in the new administration and
begin to receive pay and allowances. He was still a
comparatively poor man, however, because of the
large size of his family, the loss of his fortune and
effects in the *Medusa*, for which he had not been com-
pensated, and the wiping out by war of the fruits of
his work on the plantations at Safal.

The new governor, Schmaltz, now confirmed in his
powers, remained a bitter enemy, determined to crush
all criticism of the *Medusa* affair which could hurt him
personally. Already, his defence to the charge of abandoning the raft, purporting to be a letter from his
secretary, Griffon du Bellay, had reached France in
the *Loire*. The denial of the fact of abandonment, that
the towrope had been cast off deliberately, signed by
six survivors of the raft, all of them then under his
orders, must have made strange reading in Paris. For
all those who were not under the Governor's direct
command, but were in France, had already testified
that the tragedy of the raft had begun with the casting
loose of the towrope by Reynaud, and some had
added that this was done at the orders of Schmaltz
himself. When Reynaud also left the Governor's
sphere of influence and appeared before the Rochefort court in January, 1817, his first-hand testimony
corroborated the evidence of the other officer wit-

nesses. No doubt Du Bouchage recognised another politician at work behind the letter apparently emanating from Griffon du Bellay.

But the public were not to know that. After all, the Minister himself had publicly cast serious doubts on the accuracy of Savigny's narrative. From this flowed a situation which for Savigny and Corréard was to prove awkward, irritating and even dangerous. They were forced to beat vainly at the air against official denial and harassment, in order to prove what they both knew to be true, what the Navy knew to be true, what the Minister knew to be true. Indeed, in some respects the Minister was better informed than they were, for he had at his disposal the machinery of government to carry out the necessary lengthy and extensive enquiries.

As soon as Corréard came ashore from the *Loire* at Rochefort, he was taken to the hospital where he was visited by Savigny. Knowing what was in the Governor's letter which had also arrived in the *Loire*, Corréard warned the surgeon. Schmaltz had done more than construct an edifice of defensive lies. He had sought to focus discredit on Savigny and thus destroy the original published narrative. This had admitted both cannibalism and that, in the later slaughters on the raft, the sick had been sacrificed to save the strong; not at all the sort of admission that a politically minded person was likely to make. As the only doctor present it was likely that Savigny had taken a leading part in the decision and in the selection of the victims. Indeed, whether he had acted rightly or wrongly, Savigny had been the effective leader during those thirteen terrible days. Schmaltz had seized on this fact to accuse Savigny of being the instigator of all the horrors on the raft, instead of a victim fighting back.

It was necessary to counter the Griffon du Bellay letter, with its six signatures, by similar documentation. To start with, Corréard wrote out a personal statement supporting Savigny and, as an eye-witness, giving the lie to Schmaltz. "I certify," he wrote, "that

I have refused to sign a memorial drawn up by M. Schmaltz, which was addressed to his Excellency the Minister of Marine, and tended to disapprove of the conduct of M. Savigny on board the raft, as well as to refute some parts of the narrative of our shipwreck, inserted in the *Journal des Débats*, the 13th of September, 1816. Further, the events related in this memorial appear to me to be so entirely false, and so contrary to all that we owe to M. Savigny, that it was impossible for me to put my name to it."

Armed with this document, Savigny set out to approach those survivors of the raft who were still alive and had reached France. The first two were quickly found.

From Midshipman Coudein, already at Rochefort for the court martial, Savigny received the following: "I, the undersigned, appointed to command the raft of the *Medusa* frigate, certify that M. Savigny, the surgeon who embarked in the said raft, has given on all occasions, in the unhappy situation in which we were placed, proofs of the greatest courage and coolness, and that on several occasions his prudence was of the greatest service to us, suggesting to us means to maintain good order and discipline, of which we had so much need, and which it was so difficult for us to obtain."

Nicolas François, the hospital administrator, certified similarly that "M. Savigny, by his courage and coolness, succeeded in maintaining good order upon the raft and that his prudent arrangements saved the lives of the fifteen unfortunate persons who were rescued by the brig *Argus*."

Savigny applied for permission to lay these documents before the Minister. After a wait of two months a letter arrived from Paris, dated May 10, 1817, but it did not contain the good news he had expected. On the contrary, permission to state his case to the Minister was refused and, further, as long as the present Minister remained in office, Savigny was told that he could expect no promotion. The surgeon was so furious that he resigned.

Corréard, who had lost 10,000 francs by the wreck of the *Medusa* and was now without either means or employment, journeyed painfully to Paris, the marks of suffering still upon him, and sought both compensation and a post from the Ministry of Marine. Compensation was refused and there were only vague offers of possible employment in some distant colony. What hurt as much, as far as Corréard was concerned, was the refusal of a decoration, the cross of the Legion of Honour, for which he had applied. This medal had been granted recently for exceptional conduct in circumstances of peacetime disaster, such as the overwhelming of a frigate by a hurricane and the entombment of a party of miners. What particularly annoyed Corréard was that aristocratic teenage clerks working at the Ministry already wore this ribbon, for meritorious but unknown services.

The unsuccessful application may be an important clue as to how the raft survivors viewed themselves and their disputed conduct. They were of course national celebrities, which was not unpleasant, but one at least felt that the mere fact of survival in those circumstances, let alone a significant contribution to the quelling of disorder, was an achievement in its own right. And indeed it was.

Yet one can see how the civilised cynics of Paris could have exercised their wit, had decorations been awarded to men who had survived by eating their comrades. However, even Charlotte Picard, who had come well out of a somewhat lesser ordeal in the desert, had felt the same sense of being set apart by what she had endured and had lightly mocked her clever Parisian friends. Her faithful description, plus Corréard's action, are a true barometer to the feelings, and therefore the motives, which underlay the coming Savigny-Corréard affair.

They found that their every effort made through official channels to obtain restitution was blocked by inflexible argument. Corréard was told that none of the survivors of the raft had any claim on the Ministry, he least of all. They put their finger on a paragraph of an agreement covering the exploration side of the Senegal expedition, which stipulated that all correspondence with the Minister of Marine should be undertaken through the Governor of Senegal, under whose orders they were and without whose approval they could undertake nothing. In short, Corréard was to be ruined and denied even the chance to protest. Attempts to obtain the intercession of the king were easily blocked by the Ministry. Corréard was so enraged by his treatment that he boiled for years, even to think of it. And the same malignant power reached out for Savigny. The pair were to be harassed, crushed financially, tricked and manoeuvred into silence. They were speedily reduced to poverty and despair. And the cause of it all was the unauthorised printing by a newspaper of part of Savigny's short and confidential report.

The policy of deliberate and unscrupulous oppression by the Minister of Marine drove them into a corner. They reacted violently and logically. There was only one way out, to assume that the Minister was an enemy, to treat him as such, and to strike at him in the way which, he had clearly shown, he liked least. What the Minister wanted was less publicity about the *Medusa*. What he would get would be more, much more.

Together, Savigny and Corréard sat down to rewrite and expand Savigny's original brief narrative to near book-length; and to make it a book by adding further material which had later come to light plus a good deal of general information about the situation in Senegal. Their work was published in November, 1817, bearing some signs of hasty and scrappy compilation by two authors trying to collaborate and finding it easier said than done. The public cared nothing for that. The whole work was sensational and scandalous. It was delightful trying to work out who the villain mentioned as M. —— might be, and then establishing by deduction towards the end of the book, that the authors could only mean M. Schmaltz, or the first lieutenant, or the aristocratic captain. Indeed, it was rather like a crossword puzzle. People compared notes, ideas and impressions. The game spread like wildfire across France. And here and there, but especially in the footnotes, were delightfully ironical and only near-libellous denunciations of M. —— (the Minister of Marine) and M. —— (the present Governor of Senegal).

But it was not a game. France was full of disgruntled veterans of the Napoleonic wars, retired on half-pay or no pay, who hated the aristocratic incompetents who had flooded into the country to take advantage of her final defeat. And recognising how dangerous it was to antagonise them, the king could take wry satisfaction in the storm that was beginning to blow about the ears of M. Du Bouchage. Let it blow a little longer and that man's dangerous policies could be swept away.

The book sold out within a few months and a second edition was prepared, enlarged with further material, which was published early in 1818 and went into English translation almost instantly. The furore and wave of sympathy created by the book brought in assistance from various quarters. When he heard about it, ex-sergeant Lavillette, then recuperating in France, contributed a legally-phrased certificate in support and withdrew his signature from M. Schmaltz's report which he had signed while in hospital. This was deadly for Schmaltz.

On November 1, 1817, Lavillette stated that he had been the chief workman under the orders of M. Corréard, engineer and geographer and one of the members of the commission appointed by the Ministry to survey Cape Verde and its neighbourhood. He went on to certify that, "in the month of November, 1816, a memorial was presented to me to sign, by order of the Governor of Senegal. At this time I was in hospital in

Goree recovering from an epidemic fever then raging on Cape Verde which caused temporary fits of delirium. With my moral strength impaired and not in full possession of my mental faculties, I was made to sign this memorial without even reading it. It appears that it tended to blame M. Savigny for his conduct on the raft, for which I personally owe him only praise. It appears also, according to what I have been told, that I have been made to certify that the towrope broke and was not loosened. I declare that my signature at the bottom of this memorial, having been surreptitiously obtained, is null and void."

In the first edition Corréard had referred to the pressures improperly brought against himself, then also ill in Senegal, by members of the Governor's staff at the orders of the Governor; but he had not named the principal person, Griffon du Bellay, secretary to Schmaltz, because Griffon had been his companion on the raft. Savigny had met Griffon du Bellay again at Rochefort, to find that the man had been horrified by the implications of Savigny's published narrative. He could understand very well what would happen to anyone who associated himself with that. He had therefore been forced to say that it was nothing to do with him and even to join in the attacks on Savigny. Now, however, he wrote an open letter to Savigny, retracting, regretting that he had ever been forced to act against a man "whose firmness did not a little contribute to saving our lives." And he hinted at some of the pressures put upon him, when he added, "I fancied that the account which he (Savigny) had drawn up might render us odious to all our relations and friends." This letter was dated January 7, 1818, for publication in a later edition of the book, and shortly afterwards Griffon du Bellay also found himself without employment from the Ministry of Marine.

Edition by edition, the book grew as confirmatory narratives came in, being added as notes or footnotes. An officer of the frigate, who concealed his identity for obvious reasons, checked the text in so far as it related to matters of seamanship and threw a good deal of authoritative light on the strange manoeuvrings of M. Richefort, the self-appointed "navigational" expert, which had caused the tragedy. M. Landry, uncle of Bredif the mining engineer, contributed a substantial narrative by that witness which had been privately written without political motive or any thought of publication or protest. It was uncritical of the Governor's actions during the evacuation of the *Medusa*, but the panic, disorder and cowardice which were general, though not universal, were described from a different point of view and with additional detail. The group which Bredif had joined, led by Lieutenant Espiaux, had displayed a courage and determination which served to highlight the lamentable performance by the peak of the command pyramid.

There were some discrepancies between Bredif's narrative of what he saw or believed he saw, first from the already abandoned *Medusa* and then from the desperately overcrowded longboat commanded by the only rescuer, Lieutenant Espiaux. He did not see the towrope connecting the Governor's barge with the raft deliberately loosened by the First Lieutenant amid cries of "Let's leave them" or "Let's abandon them." He assumed that it had broken in the general confusion. Indeed, Corréard calculated that only about twenty men were close enough and had a sufficiently clear view to swear to that. He was one of them. But what Bredif did see was the effect the approach of the overcrowded longboat, in which he was seated, had upon the line of rowing boats which had been roped together to tow the raft. He had written to his sister, "The boats, in order to avoid us, cut the ropes which united them together, and made all the sail they could from us. In the midst of this confusion, the rope which towed the raft broke also, and a hundred and fifty men were abandoned in the midst of the ocean, without any hope of relief." There could not have been a more sober and devastating indictment. Raft aban-

doned, longboat abandoned, Governor, Captain and
First Lieutenant fleeing for the horizon.

The veterans of the Napoleonic wars, who had con-
quered all Europe, gritted their teeth when they read
that. Then with bitter relish they turned to the footnotes where Savigny and Corréard had grouped together with devastating effect all their firepower
against the man fundamentally responsible, their
enemy, the Minister himself. They asked him how he
felt at having confided "seven or eight expeditions to
officers who do no more honour to his choice and
discernment than the expedition to Senegal has done."
Then they listed some of the cases which had become
public knowledge.

"Besides the *Medusa*, which was conducted straight
upon the Arguin Bank by the Viscount de Chaumareys, Knight of St. Louis, of the Legion of Honour, and
in the intervals of his campaigns, Customs Officer at
Bellac in Upper Vienne; apart from this, everybody
knows that the *Golo*, bound from Toulon to Pon-
dichery, nearly perished on the coast by the unskil-
fulness of the Captain, Chevalier Amblard, Knight of
St. Louis and of the Legion of Honour, who, in order
not to lose touch with maritine affairs, had become a
salt merchant near Toulon. Neither is the debut of the
Viscount de Cheffontaine forgotten who, on leaving
Rochefort for the Isle of Bourbon, arrived instead at
Plymouth without his masts three or four days later.
Who does not know that it would be in our power to
mention more examples of this kind?"

They quoted from a debate in the chamber of depu-
ties, in which a member had referred memorably to
those "shadows of officers" who had been given
important commands by favouritism. These men,
pointed out Savigny and Corréard, had "had the privi-
lege of losing the vessels and people of the State without it being possible for the law to reach them. It
would be difficult to suppose that they intended their
own destruction; they have proved well enough that
they know how to provide for their own safety. They

could say: We did not appoint ourselves; it is not we who are to blame."

The public did not know, for the Minister had hushed it up, that de Chaumareys had already been punished; but not the man who had appointed him. Some of the émigrés may have felt these comments to be unfair, because more than twenty years ago, the Revolution had had the same distressing effect upon the navy as had the return to command of the émigrés recently.

The venom with which honorary Colonel Schmaltz was pursued was probably to most people's tastes. They wrote of "his great application to business, the numerous occupations, the diverse enterprises which have agitated his life"; of his outstanding record as "an apothecary in Bengal, a physician in Madagascar, a dealer in small wares and land-surveyor in Java, a shopkeeper's clerk in the isle of France and Holland, an engineer in the camp of Batavia, commandant at Guadalupe, chief of a bureau at Paris" and now, "with the orders of St. Louis and the Legion of Honour, the rank of colonel and the command of a colony." There was indeed something extremely odd about the career of Schmaltz; possibly it had involved undercover intelligence work of some kind. And he had proved as Savigny and Corréard hinted, totally ruthless and unscrupulous where his own self-interest was concerned.

The two authors suddenly found that they had acquired a power base. They had written and had published their own book in despair and desperation, as an attempt to lash back at their tormentors. Now, thought Corréard, as they had been so remarkably successful and as there clearly was money in the business, why should they not publish other people's books? He took premises at the Palais Royal and starting with political pamphlets began a new career as a publisher with an established "edge" in the protest market. Above his new bookshop he placed an eye-catching sign: *Au naufragé de la Méduse*.

The appearance of this bookshop in the centre of Paris made it a gathering point for the political opposition. M. Du Bouchage, Minister of Marine, had achieved by the instinctive desire of all authority to stifle, if not harass criticism, the exact opposite of what he had intended. His opponents in his own government and around the throne could now move against the principle Du Bouchage stood for and not only in the navy but as regards the army as well. That year, 1818, the law of Gouvion de St. Cyr was passed. The entire officers corps was thrown open to all men of merit and experience and was no longer to be the exclusive preserve of the émigrés and the aristocracy. The immediate political battle was over, although there was an aftermath of resentment among the émigrés. And in the same year, 1818, M. Schmaltz was recalled from Senegal and another governor appointed in his place. The Minister was defeated, the Governor replaced, the Captain in prison. This had taken two years, but it was not the end of the *Medusa* affair. Far from it.

Of course, there were some errors in the book by Savigny and Corréard. They did not have access to official records, to start with. They give the name of one of the three men found still alive in the *Medusa* after nearly two months as "Dales." The court martial minutes show that it was actually "Dalestre." Like de Chaumareys they made an elementary geographical error in their positioning of a coastal feature, the river St. John in their case. But unlike de Chaumareys, they did not have a chart at the time. However, unlike de Chaumareys, they had their work checked by an officer of the *Medusa*, who really did know what he was about and they printed his correction verbatim. And, finally, again unlike de Chaumareys, or for that matter, M. Schmaltz, they did not cover up by deleting the mistake but left it as evidence for any ill-wisher to quote. This was in character. It chimed with Savigny's original report describing terrible events in which he participated, in spite of the fact that his own narrative could be used against him. This is decidedly more surprising than the fact that a second-surgeon and an engineer-passenger did not understand the navigation as fully as did the officers of the frigate (with the admitted exceptions of de Chaumareys and Richefort).

In expanding their own story the two authors did not offer a strictly impartial overall account. Savigny and Corréard did not pretend to be anything but embittered by their experiences. Indeed, they proclaimed their attack. It is all quite honest. In English translation, their rather mannered and studied tone suggests "stiff upper lip." That is, pride that they had behaved well; contempt for those who had not. This is an excessively normal reaction, however much one may deplore it. The episode, towards the end of the thirteen days, when a few of those still left alive wrote out their experiences on a board, so that their endurance should not be forgotten, even if they were all dead when the raft was at last sighted, again points the fact that they felt pride in what they had done.

However, there were other stories of what happened on the raft of the *Medusa*, which put these terrible events in a different and quite horrible light. They are not first-hand. The directly admissible evidence is that of Savigny, Corréard and Coudein (the midshipman, unlike the other two, was actually required to furnish a report). The contradictory stories were provided by Midshipman Rang, who had escaped in the captain's barge and had no personal knowledge; he merely picked up the stories from two other raft survivors in Senegal. After he had read the book by Savigny and Corréard, he decided to write a narrative of his own and to include these contradictory accounts. His work was not published until more than a century later, however, so that there was no opportunity for an enlightening controversy, at the time, although there may have been whispers in the background.

The stories he heard covered two quite different periods on the raft: the first was that of the "mutiny," the slaughters which occurred early, probably starting on the second day; the second was that of the "mercy killings," which occurred towards the end on conjectural dates, for by that time the few who were left would hardly be in a position to recall the exact sequence of deaths. There was no question that the latter were deliberate, but what is different, and surprising, about one of Rang's witnesses, is that he told the midshipman that the mass slaughters of the "mutiny" were deliberate also; that they had been plotted and sparked off by the officers.

This witness was a seaman called Thomas, whom Savigny and Corréard describe as a "pilot" in their list of raft survivors. Rang describes him by a French term which, confusingly, can be translated into English as either helmsman or signalman. In English "pilot" means navigator or else a set of sailing directions. At a guess, he was probably a helmsman; certainly not an officer. Rang says he was young and not having any responsibilities, unbiased. He obtained the seaman's confidence and was so startled by his version, that he asked Thomas to write it all down for him, briefly. The point being attacked was a passage in Savigny's report reading: "We were not strong enough to prevent them getting drunk as much as they liked." Other than this, Thomas tells of events in much the same way as Savigny, Corréard and Coudein, although he sometimes differs in his sequences, which could be important.

Thomas's note read: "At the beginning of the night, the officers gathered apart and held a small council. When this was over, some of the men belonging to their group set a barrel of wine in the middle of the raft, then, having smashed it open, left it to be plundered. All the soldiers rushed to it and most of them drank so much they lost their senses. From that moment, the greatest disorder reigned on board the raft; drunken soldiers gathered about on every side, some demanding their hammocks, asking the way to the main deck or the battery deck; others screamed that they were lost and threw themselves into the water. Then, some having grasped hatchets or knives, they wanted to cut the ropes and drown everyone. The officers, fearing they might succeed, rushed on them sword in hand and slaughtered a great number. They were deaf to the cries for mercy coming from these unfortunate men, forty of whom were killed."

Coudein's official report is only slightly different, in stating that the officers were attacked. He wrote: "They wanted to cut the ropes that bound the raft together, so as to put an end to their lives; but as they feared the officers might prevent them from doing so, they decided to throw us overboard first. A faithful servant came and warned us. The officers, the second surgeon, some passengers, several craftsmen and myself, anxious to save our miserable lives, decided to prevent this abominable action. We armed ourselves with guns and each watched over a different part of the raft where the most essential ropes were located."

It is highly unlikely that the officers were so foolish as to intend to get the soldiers drunk; this would be a very dangerous proceeding with any soldiers anywhere, let alone a low-grade cosmopolitan French battalion standing on a raft abandoned somewhere off the coast of West Africa. What Savigny says is that a wine ration was organised on the first night, but that the breaking open of the barrel and the indiscriminate drinking occurred on the second night, as a result of the men's growing sense of despair and loss of hope. The long-term interest of Thomas's grumbles, as told to Rang, however, is merely the fact that they occurred. That different groups among the survivors were blaming each other during the period immediately following the rescue. The reason is that, in historic perspective, the comedy of de Chaumareys and Richefort and the stranding of the frigate is indeed a mere "bagatelle," long forgotten and of no importance anyway. But what happened on the raft of the frigate was another thing altogether; that story never died because it held enduring lessons for mankind; indeed, many more than were ever suspected at the time; and the main reason that it did so, was that there was a qualified man, a surgeon, to note exactly and objectively what happened, and, so far as he could remember, in what order.

It is essential to distinguish the "mercy killings" from the "mutiny." Thomas told Rang, and he was probably right, that they were not so merciful as all that. He described the despatching of the canteen manageress. "A soldier having been slaughtered and thrown overboard, they said to his wife, the only woman on the raft, 'Since your husband has gone into the sea you must join him there,' and they forced her overboard."

The other raft survivor to whom Rang talked was Lavillette, whose testimony gives the impression of an organised system of destruction, of groups of men deliberately set against other men, so that the overall numbers on the raft would be rapidly reduced. The ex-sergeant was fever-ridden when this interview took place, but certainly group fought group. And he was to provide that telling vignette of the kissing and prayers to God that took place after every killing and of how, eventually, in revulsion, the guns were thrown overboard. Rang did not know what he was doing in recording these strange tales, some spoken by a man in delirium, others the grumbling confidences of a seaman to an officer. But his motive was exactly that of Savigny: to note as accurately as possible some very strange events which seemed then to defy rational explanation—but do not do so now. For the story of the raft of the *Medusa* did not end with the downfall of de Chaumareys and Schmaltz in 1817 and 1818, nor with the publication in 1821 of a definitive, illustrated edition of the book by Savigny and Corréard, *Naufrage de la Frégate la Méduse faisant partie de l'expedition du Sénégal*. There was a great deal more still to come.

* * *

In 1820 another eyewitness of the shipwreck returned to France and in 1824 published a personal narrative which included the sufferings of those who had trekked through the Sahara. This book was *La Chaumiere Africaine* by Madame Dard, which went into English translation three years later. Madame Dard was the former Mademoiselle Charlotte Picard. Her change of name was the result of a strange love affair which had arisen out of the most appalling tragedy.

The ill-luck which had dogged the family as a direct result of the stranding of the frigate and the loss of her father's fortune and all their possessions had continued. M. Picard's outspokenness had not been forgotten and eventually the family were reduced to poverty and then decimated by illness. His young wife was the first to die. Then the children began to sicken and it was then that M. Dard visited them frequently in order to help. The little girl, Laura, did not recover, and in August, 1819, M. Picard was also stricken. His illness was worsened by a terrible mental depression and a great foreboding of the evil that was to come to his family. War between the Moors and the Negroes had driven them from the cotton plantation into which they had put so much labour and they were now all poor refugees dressed in rags and tatters, living a "Swiss Family Robinson" existence.

On his deathbed her father had asked her to promise that she would look after the children, for only then could he rest in peace. He reminded her of their obligations to M. Dard and his other friends who had helped. He said that he forgave his enemies the evils they had made him and his family endure. He and his eldest daughter were obviously very close and the death of her father made the girl desolate. She contemplated suicide in order to follow her father to the grave. Even after her friends had dissuaded her, she was inconsolable, unable to attend the funeral. Then, although the other children were ill, she felt that she must see her father's last resting place, which was beside his wife on the island of Safal where their plantation had been. Leaving the children to her sister Caroline, she made a lonely pilgrimage. The plantation was a wreck, weeds everywhere, the cotton plants withered, the fields of millet, maize and beans rooted up by cattle, the house plundered: a scene of solitude and desolation.

When she could bring herself to search for her father's grave, she found it beautiful, surrounded by shrubs whose branches overhung and seemed to protect it. The utter quiet was broken only by the sounds of birds or the occasional rustle of foliage by the wind. She fell to her knees and remained still for a long time. When she got up, her resolution was made. As if speaking to her father, she promised to give all her care to the tiny children, her step-brothers and -sisters, who were now orphans; and she promised also to make known the misfortunes which had driven him to the tomb.

The day after her return from the island, M. Dard called to say that he would take upon himself the charge of providing for the whole family until he could get them on board a ship for France. Madame Thomas, in whose house they were then living, took the girl aside and told her in confidence that there was more in this offer than appeared. M. Dard wished to marry her but would not ask her until her grief had lessened.

This revelation was not at all unwelcome to the girl, who was very conscious of the family's fall into poverty. In some circles, poverty is regarded as a disgrace if not an actual crime. And in France especially a girl's family is expected to contribute handsomely. She recalled her father's words: "M. Dard is an estimable youth. His attachment for us has never diminished in spite of our wretchedness. I am sure he prefers virtue in a wife above all other riches." The young man was Director of the French schools in Senegal and his career was not bound up exclusively with the colony. He could find employment in France.

The last days in Senegal were distressing, as the young children died one after the other. Gustavus was old enough to go to school, and when his little brother Charles asked where he was (for he had had to be buried immediately), M. Dard tried to postpone the blow by saying that he was at school. Then the boy asked for a hat, so that he could go to the school and see if Gustavus was really there. Charles died also towards the end of 1819.

When in November, 1820, the time came to sail for France, all that remained of the original family of nine were the eldest daughter Charlotte, now married to M. Dard, her sister Caroline who remained behind in Senegal and married M. Richard, an agricultural botanist, and the young boy Alphonse Fleury, a cousin. After two months in Paris they went to the home of M. Dard on the Côte d'Or, where the bereaved girl found new relations and friends to help her forget her loss. But she did not forget. She settled down to write her book.

16

"HIDEOUS SPECTACLE . . . BEAUTIFUL PICTURE"

The experience as Art, 1817–1824

THE picture was sombre, reddish-brown—and enormous. Ragged clouds poured in a molten sky past the reeling mast of the castaways' raft sixteen feet above the bottom of the canvas on the Salon wall. From the foam on the left where it fretted against the damp timbers to the cadaver on the right, sprawled in the sea with one shrunken leg caught by a beam, was a distance of twenty-three feet. The sheer length and height of the painting seemed to immerse the excited crowd of viewers in the waves, involving them against their will.

"Why, you already feel as though you had one foot in the water!" thought the artist Eugene Delacroix. To this young man the scheme of the picture before him was not new. He had posed for one of the emaciated figures slumped exhausted and barely conscious at the moment of rescue. But the effect of the completed work came as a shock to him.

Other figures on that gigantic canvas were more authentic. That man whose left arm with open fingers is thrust out towards the rescue ship as he turns to his companions. . . . Is that Corréard, you know, the engineer fellow? Savigny the surgeon must be there, too. Perhaps that one by the mast, one of those still upright, not overwhelmed by suffering or despair.

Conjectures flew freely, for although the catalogues in the hands of the viewers described the item merely as a "scene of shipwreck" by Théodore Géricault, everyone knew what raft that was and had heard of the horrors which had taken place upon it. Everyone in Paris was aware also of the political scandal that was threatening the monarchy and the government as a direct result of what might, in other circumstances, have been just another shipwreck among thousands. So intense was the interest in this one picture that the work of painters famous already, such as Ingres, was eclipsed. That artist's sensuously delicate *Grande Odalisque,* so often reproduced today all over the world, was on this, its first showing, largely ignored by the public and censured by the critics.

Ingres himself was critical of that "shipwreck scene" by Géricault. He declared that he wanted no part of such paintings, those "pictures of the dissecting room which show man as a corpse, which show only the ugly, the hideous!" This outburst was caused by nothing so simple as jealousy at the success of a young rival or even an inability to comprehend what we can now appreciate was a startling new approach to art. It proved to be a widespread reaction to the shock effect of the great canvas.

A reviewer took the same line. "All is hideous and passive—not a trait of heroism or grandeur upon which the soul and eye can for one moment repose— nothing to indicate life and sensibility—nothing honourable to humanity. This picture is truly said to be a work to rejoice and glut the sight of vultures."

Because he had a rich father who supported his artistic ambitions, Géricault could paint what he pleased. He could also study when and where he wished. He had spent more time at the Louvre, standing before the old masters such as Titian and Rubens, than in the formal discipline of the studio. In the year of the wreck of the *Medusa*—1816—he had been in Rome, had stood before Michelangelo's *Last Judgement* and "trembled" at the energy and power of that work. In the year of the book of the *Medusa,* Savigny and Corréard's *Naufrage de la Frégate la Méduse faisant partie de L'expédition du Sénégal en 1816,* the young artist was back in Paris. That was late in 1817, when

the two authors were preparing their book for the
press and Géricault was moving in the same artistic
and political circles at Montmartre as they were.
Whether they met by chance or whether Géricault had
already decided upon his subject and deliberately
sought them out is not known.

Much about the artist is still a mystery. His personal
life at this time was kept intensely secret within his family, for he was in the midst of a difficult, stormy love
affair with the wife of a relative. The girl, Alexandrine-
Modeste, was six years older than the young man and
married to one of his uncles. The visit to Italy may
have been an attempt to break off that painful rela-
tionship. But affer his return to Paris in 1817 the girl
became pregnant and the following year bore his child.

Géricault was then about twenty-six, "fairly tall and
of elegant appearance," noted another young artist in
his circle. "His face expressed vivacity and energy, but
it also showed great gentleness. I noticed then, as I often
did since, that he blushed at the slightest emotion."

The young man was in a turmoil, not only in his
personal life, but artistically. A painter for only seven
years, he was still searching for a complete style of his
own, an adequate means to express the imperative
demand within to astound the world with some tremendous statement on canvas. The next Paris Salon,
to be held in 1819—in less than two years' time—
would be his opportunity to grasp or to lose.

Thus far, he was regarded as a promising gentleman-
artist with a flair for outdoor action pictures which
could be bold, even grand. He had exhibited two at a
previous Salon, a *Mounted Chasseur* and a *Cuirassier*.
There was another side to his talent. He could hint at
terrible and dramatic events by the use of a few quietly pathetic human figures isolated from their context.
Lately, he had explored the possibilities of painting a
recent event, the assassination of a notable politician,
but had abandoned the subject when it was shown
that the affair had been merely a murder for gain. He

belonged to no "school" of art and because he was financially independent did not have to.

The Paris tradition was, broadly, either for small-scale chocolate-box easel paintings which could be produced by a private individual or for giant "king-size" propaganda pieces, heavily subsidised by the government. Previously such "subjects honourable for their national character" had been sponsored by Napoleon; in fact, these were "command" battle pictures, public relations art. Under the monarchy, the subjects were different but the intentions and the methods were the same. Indeed, the forthcoming Paris Salon was designed to demonstrate the overwhelming might of French talent, flourishing as never before under the Bourbons, to be shown most spectacularly by the vast number of gigantic "set-piece" canvases, over one hundred, which no other nation could match.

It was this national stream of enormous action-painting which Géricault was now about to join, but made free of sponsorship by his father's support. While other and better-known painters were delving into the legends of Ancient Greece and Rome or studying anew the lives of the Saints, in the hope of an inspiration which might produce a work saleable in the new climate, Géricault was reading the newspapers. The result was to be modern history painting in a new guise. In effect, an item taken from the morning's news and then portrayed in the grand manner.

No one knows when he decided that the Raft would be his subject. Probably he began work on the *Medusa* theme early in 1818. In this, the research stage, he collected "a veritable dossier crammed with authentic proofs and documents." This was not in order to produce a painting accurate in detail but to immerse himself in the story. To depict the experience, he first had to understand it; if possible, as thoroughly as those who had actually suffered, so that when he stood finally before the blank canvas it should seem that he painted as a witness.

There were many stages to undergo before that situ-

ation could be created. In all, they occupied a period
of about ten months. First, he listened to Savigny and
Corréard, and absorbed their story. Then he got the
designer of the raft, the ship's carpenter of the *Medusa*, to make him first a plan and then a scale model,
until finally he had the physical nature of the raft fixed
in his subconscious mind.

He visited hospitals to see for himself what the sick
and the dying looked like, and smelt like. He borrowed the severed limbs of corpses, and sometimes
entire corpses, and took them to his studio, to sketch
them; but he was to use few of those drawings. What
he was doing was to surround himself with objects
which would impress the truth of the experience upon
his own soul. He went to the beach at Le Havre, not
so much to observe seascapes and marine skies (not
at all like the tropic seas where his subject was set),
as to sense the sea.

And while this emotional side of his nature was absorbing the facts, the other, technical side was considering where to stop the action. What, really, could
be considered the most effective scene of the entire
shipwreck story? Had there been a moment which, if
caught, would sum up in one split-second for all eternity the story of the *Medusa*?

One might think first that the fatal moment was the
loosening of the towrope. That was, and is so—but
only when presented in narrative form. There is no
record, in the form of a preliminary sketch, to suggest
that Géricault ever considered this. Indeed, it is a
scene only in the motion picture sense. It took time,
time which could only be suggested visually by a number of pictures linking the various actions together.
The scenario would have to run: panic abandonment
of the frigate, the bungled effort to tow, abandonment
of the tow, abandonment finally of Espiaux's longboat
also. It is impossible to freeze the truth in a single
moment of real time.

What then? The mutiny on the raft? Yes, indeed,
this idea did attract Géricault. He made sketches of

veritable cascades of crowded, tumbling bodies; he produced one without cascades, a viciously vivid close-up of a struggle with naked steel. But perhaps cannibalism? This also Géricault tried out, and horrifyingly effective it is, with men eating men like crouched carniverous apes, and the dead half in the water and the damned crying to heaven. In the end he did not use it, indeed eliminated all outright traces of cannibalism and employed other means, both more subtle and more powerful, to indicate that aspect of the tragedy.

The scene finally chosen, and the way in which it was to be presented, has a power beyond all these. It is the first sighting of the *Argus,* when the brig's crew did not see the raft but passed on in the distance unaware. The castaways are done for. "Last Gasp" might be its title. Only two men can wave, only one can point, two more can pull themselves to their knees. The rest are mostly beyond hope or fear, but slumped unaware; as blindly ignorant of the moment as the crew of the *Argus.* There is only a hint of cannibalism, of what has led up to this moment of false hope. When he outlined this scene, the definitive draft for the final work which was to be done on a gigantic canvas, Géricault was still not quite finished. He altered three things, to oppress the spectator. He raised the horizon high up the picture, he reduced the *Argus* in size to a distant speck, and he cut out the waves which had been in the foreground, between the raft and the spectator. Now the raft drifts less alone on that rough and ragged sea. Marine painters were to criticise this part of his composition. What Géricault had really done by this alteration was to zoom in on the scene, so that we can no longer stand back and look at the raft freely adrift. We are on those soiled and sodden timbers.

These preliminary work stages had taken the artist ten months. The painting of the actual canvas took eight months. It was finished in July, 1819, just in time for the opening of the Salon on August 25. The artist had never done anything like it before and he was never to do anything like it again. The concentration required was terrible not only in intensity but in duration. Géricault hired a large studio and shut himself up for those eight months, shaving his head so that he would not be tempted to go out into the streets.

As the picture grew it acquired an extraordinary aspect. It was as if a frieze of statues was appearing on the canvas. The castaways grouped on the raft were painted individually from models. A few were professional, such as the negro who was to pose as the peak of a pyramid of human bodies, a contorted group which must be fused with the raft at the bottom and the sea and the sky above. Some were friends. Savigny and Corréard visited the studio, to pose for Géricault as themselves.

Few visitors were allowed, but the young artist Montfort was one of them. He wrote: "I was impressed, first of all, by the intensity with which he worked, and also by the quiet and reflection which he needed. He generally started work as soon as there was enough light and continued without interruption until nightfall. What forced him to work in this way was usually the size of the piece which, started in the morning, had to be finished the same day. . . . I was vividly impressed by the care with which Géricault worked. Being still quite young (I was only seventeen), I had trouble keeping still for several hours on end, without getting up and, accidentally, making a little noise with my chair. In the midst of the absolute silence which reigned in the studio, I would sense that this slight noise had disturbed Géricault. . . . I would see him smile at me with a slight expression of reproach. He assured me that the noise of a mouse was enough to stop him from working.

"When evening came Géricault abandoned his palette and took advantage of the last rays of light to contemplate his work. Usually, he was very little satisfied, but on some days he thought he had found the proper way of modelling. The following day, he would confess that he was not on the right track and would have to make a fresh effort.

"Once, he had gone (to the Louvre) to see the *Sabines* and the *Leonidas*. He came back discouraged. What he was doing seemed clumsy to him. Referring to the young warriors in the *Leonidas*, he said to me: 'Ah well! Those are tremendous figures!' And he averted his eyes from his own picture."

This was just the depression and self-doubt of the artist, which may be essential to ensure flexibility and responsiveness during the actual process of creation. Visiting painters had no such doubts. In that small studio the impact of the huge figures did seem tremendous, even terrifying. The painter Delacroix always remembered his first visit. "The impression it gave me was so strong that as I left the studio I broke into a run, and kept running like a fool all the way back to the rue de la Plance where I lived then, at the far end of the faubourg Saint-German."

The composition changed organically, grew on the canvas, became more terrifying. Yet it was artifice. In order to weld his figures together, and they were already sombre, Géricault had to link them by darkness as if they were on a blanket of shadows, with only the edges or contours high-lighted. The only black sufficiently intense to achieve this darkness was bitumen, which is chemically unstable. Over the years, this was to cause the decay of the painting, so that it can no longer be seen as it was originally.

So far, Géricault had seen his canvas only in his own studio, in one particular type of lighting. When the work was finished and the painting had been moved to the Théâtre Italien where all the entries for the Salon were being assembled, Géricault was shaken. He saw now that he had raised the peak of his pyramid of human bodies without sufficiently strengthening the base. Hurriedly, he added two further figures to the raft at the bottom of the picture, using some of the many ideas and studies which he had worked on and discarded earlier.

Eighteen months' continuous work was now over and it had finished the artist. Géricault was mentally and physically drained; dazed; utterly incapable of valid judgement or further emotional effort. In this state, he made a serious and damaging mistake, threw away a great chance. The officials of the Salon had been impressed. They paid him the great compliment, and offered him the great advantage, of allowing the painter to choose for himself where on the walls of the Salon the "Scene of Shipwreck" should be hung. And Géricault made a monumental error. He selected a prominent position, but high up—actually above a tall doorway. Nothing could have been more calculated to defeat the entire effect of the canvas. The raft needed to be low down so that the viewer felt that he could virtually walk onto it, actually enter the scene.

As the vast canvas was lifted higher and higher to his chosen place on the wall above the doorway, Géricault was angered and dismayed. He had the strong impression that as it rose, so it lost impact. But perhaps that was just because he had failed, because it was a poor painting. His judgement blurred and wearily incapable of decision, he left matters too late. By the time he had convinced himself that he had made a mistake, nothing could be done to change the position of the canvas before the opening of the Salon. That was to be on August 25. And three days later the King himself would visit the exhibition and be introduced to some of the artists.

The critics were divided. They were more than divided, they were puzzled. Even when hung at the wrong height and in the wrong place, the painting still had emotional impact. But what did it *mean*?

Unable to examine the work closely, the reviewers often contradicted each other on matters of fact as well as opinion. The man on *La Gazette de France* condemned it outright as "a work for the delight of vultures," while his colleague writing for the *Revue Encyclopedique* complained that the painting could hardly represent the raft of the *Medusa* as the really convincing details, such as half-devoured portions of human bodies, were nowhere to be seen.

There was a glut of gratuitous advice. It would have been better if M. Géricault had shown the castaways fighting each other to eat a corpse, wrote the man on the *Revue.* Others advised the artist to moderate his enthusiasm and to study carefully the draughtsmanship of Girodet and David. They assumed that he had dashed off the work in a weekend or so and pointed out that the young man would do better when he became an old man and could devote more time to a subject.

There was much praise, too, most of it in exclamation marks. "My heart trembled" . . . "I shudder while I admire" . . . "What movement, what verve!"

A few expressed mixed feelings with a deliberate objectivity, actually seeking to understand. An aristocrat, Count O'Mahony, who on religious and political grounds should have condemned the work outright, wrote instead: "On a raft which is about to be engulfed by a wave, the painter has assembled the most revolting aspects of despair, rage, hunger, death and putrefaction, and he has expressed them with an abundance of verve, a truth of touch, a boldness of handling and of colour which multiply their effect a hundredfold. All must die, there is no chance of salvation, since none of them raises his arms towards Him whom the winds and seas obey. . . . For as they have forgotten God, so they have also forgotten one another. . . . Each sees only his own death and laments only for his own life. . . . Is it possible that suffering should not have joined two souls, two brothers, a father and his son? What a hideous spectacle, but what a beautiful picture!"

The cause of the confusion was in the preconceived ideas of the critics. They failed to fathom its politics. The subject was clearly the infamous raft of the *Medusa.* Therefore it was an anti-government painting. While one set of critics sought to defend the government by attacking the painting, others attacked the government by praising it. Almost invariably, the views of the art critics coincided with the politics of the paper for which they were writing. Count O'Mahony was an honourable exception. The basic assumption common to them all was that because of his subject matter and because of his friends, especially Savigny and Corréard, Théodore Géricault must be a politically "committed" artist.

Nevertheless, in their clumsy attempts to unlock the meaning of that "shipwreck scene," some stumbled perilously near the truth. While O'Mahony had looked for belief in God and failed to find it, others scanned the various grouped figures for those ideas and emotions usually expressed by Napoleon's painters, such as David, in their depiction of the battlefields of Marengo, Austerlitz, Jena, and so on, short of Waterloo. Not surprisingly, they failed. They concluded that Géricault's picture showed nothing except a spectacle of "men jostled between life and death." And that troubled them.

The truth was the painting had no "message" in the political sense.

But as this amazing fact was grasped by hardly anyone in France, the expected visit of the King to the Salon on August 28 was awaited with relish. How would the monarch react to a quite scandalously antiroyalist, anti-government picture and what, if anything, would he have to say to the young man who had painted it?

Painfully, because he suffered from gout, Louis XVIII limped round the great exhibition, from painting to painting, and being introduced to the artists. When he came to the "scene of shipwreck" he stayed studying it for a long time and according to the official *Moniteur Universel* said a pleasant word to M. Géricault which combined encouragement with judgement. It was reported unofficially that his comment was: "Monsieur Géricault, vous venez de faire un naufrage qui n'en est pas un pour vous!"

"You've made a shipwreck which isn't for us!"
This can be read two ways. That the monarchy was
not going to be shipwrecked (the story of the *Medusa*
had served the King well, politically, although this was
not generally appreciated at the time). But it could
have been a really perceptive comment: that the painting compelled the viewer to share an experience which
was not to his liking.

The public acclaim and the public criticism, the cau-
tiously favourable reception of his work in official circles, did not break Géricault's black despair. He was
exhausted, drained. He felt he must go abroad, go to
the Orient, have exotic adventures; wash himself clean
of the *Medusa*. The country he went to, however, was
England; and there was no escape from the raft. He
must still suffer with those suffering men.

An enlarged, revised edition of the book by Savigny
and Corréard had already been translated and published in London during 1818 as the topical *Narrative
of a Voyage to Senegal in 1816*. It had proved much
to the taste of a public then peculiarly fascinated by
the sea and also by the records of great maritime disasters. Although little England could not match France
in private patronage or bureaucratic subsidies, there
existed a democratic alternative. The "nation of
shopkeepers" had found its own solution to the
problem of feeding the creative artist: the box office
exhibition. Mr. William Bullock, owner of the Egyp-
tian Hall in Piccadilly, arranged to show "Monsieur
Jerricault's Great Picture" in 1820. Fifty thousand
people are claimed to have seen it and both men
profited financially.

Being ignorant of any political implications, the English reviewers judged the painting purely as a work
of art. "A tremendous picture of human suffering . . .
one of the finest specimens of the French school ever
brought to this country," was the judgement in the
Literary Gazette. That he had not imitated David was
here a point in Géricault's favour. He was praised for
breaking free of that "cold, pedantic school."

The critic of the *Globe,* reacting to the vainglory of Napoleon's propaganda painters, stressed both the problems and the achievement. "Monsieur Jerricault has selected for his first great historical effort a subject of the utmost difficulty, and with singular absence of the national vanity ascribed to his countrymen, one which it would be well for the naval character of France to have blotted from her maritime annals. The story of the *Medusa* records a narrative of the most criminal ignorance, pusillanimity, and individual suffering, which has no parallel in modern history. . . . The artist, however, has selected the subject on account of its difficulties, and he has triumphed over many in the completion of his design. In the first place, to embody and concentrate the interest of this appalling subject, he has selected the time when the ruin on the raft may be said to be complete, and when the wretched survivors were first raised from their state of despair, by the appearance of the vessel that rescued them from their perilous situation. The personification of horror which his grouping exhibits baffles description; there is one figure of an old man, who still retains at his feet the dead body of his son, that is full of appalling expression. It is the very countenance of Ugolino's despair, which Reynolds portrayed with an effect finely forcible indeed, though without the haughty distinction which Michaelangelo gave the Italian Nobleman."

To be mentioned in the same paragraph as Michelangelo, before whose *Last Judgement* he had "trembled," must have made the young painter breathless with the realisation of what he had achieved.

After London came Dublin. The press ignored Géricault's painting although the *Medusa* as a subject was an oddly popular topic. The sensation of the day there was an exhibition of a series of *Medusa* paintings totalling 10,000 square feet of canvas. In an inventive and novel anticipation of cinema technique the spectators were seated, a full orchestra played appropriate "mood music," and the pictures moved to portray the story of the wreck scene by scene.

Géricault returned to France in 1821, was seriously ill in 1822 and died in 1824, aged only thirty-three. He had never recovered from the black despair which had afflicted him at the end of the exhausting one-and-a-half-year's work on his monumental canvas. In his last days, wasting away, he bitterly condemned the uselessness of his short life. He had not produced even so much as five good paintings to justify his life and to be remembered by. He seemed now to dismiss even the "shipwreck" as a vignette, an achievement of little real worth. But it tormented him and his mind always returned to his memories of the canvas. Confined to a sickbed now, all he could study was a small copy of the original work. Again and again he examined this, anxiously searching for any defects, and finding them; but also clearly asking for contradiction from his friends. His only hope of immortality lay on the raft.

In the year of his death the "shipwreck" was put up for auction. A rich Englishman was among the bidders as were a group of French businessmen who planned to chop the painting into a number of small, more easily saleable scenes. The prospects were that the canvas would go abroad to foreigners or be cut to bits by Frenchmen. It was the King and the court who stepped in, bought the picture for the nation, and saw it hung in the Louvre where it is today.

Géricault's self-doubt and despair proved unjustified. It was the King who was right. Out of more than 1,300 paintings submitted to the Paris Salon of 1819, 208 sculptures, 157 engravings and 27 architectural designs, little now is remembered. Time's perspective shows most to have been mediocre works in a tired tradition.

That "scene of shipwreck" by Théodore Géricault is the great exception. It is regarded as a key work in the history of art, ending one tradition and marking the start of another. Everything to do with it, including preliminary sketches, is regarded as important. The most recent exhibitions of Géricault's work were held in 1971 and 1972 at Los Angeles, Detroit and Philadelphia. The life and work of the artist were the subject of a masterly study by Professor Lorenz Eitner published on both sides of the Atlantic in 1972 under the title *Géricault's Raft of the Medusa*. One hundred and fifty years after the death of the painter, his work still lives, as relevant now as it was then.

It might be thought that the actual ship, the real raft, the personal witness of the survivors might be forgotten, overshadowed by what one great artist had made out of their experiences. That is not true either. What Géricault achieved with oils and brushes and canvas, Savigny and Corréard attained in their writings, based on first-hand observations. Those experiences, so closely and accurately noted, have achieved a different type of immortality. The story of the *Medusa* was not relegated merely to stirring accounts of adventures and survival at sea, to be read casually in front of a winter fire. It was to be increasingly studied in the middle of the twentieth century, as it was realised how much the two authors still had to say to modern man. The story of the *Medusa* did not end with the court martial of de Chaumareys or the excitement of the Paris Salon of 1819. It has continued to the present day.

But there has also been a "twist" to the story. Certain elements are seen in a different light, the real truth behind them fully realised at last. The English art reviewer of 1820 had stated his honest belief that the tale of the *Medusa* "has no parallel in modern history." He was wrong. We now know that it is far from being unique.

17

REPETITION IN THE SOUTH ATLANTIC

The rafts of the Rio Azul, *June 29 to July 14, 1941*

GÉRICAULT'S painting should have been the end of the *Medusa* affair, a terrible moment of time stilled for eternity on canvas. But it was not.

Artists and writers went back to the subject again and again, fascinated—or inspired—by some aspect of what they felt was a unique experience which still held some monumental message for mankind.

When T. E. Lawrence wanted to describe the hardships of a desert journey in Arabia, he invoked the thirst-image of those suffering men on the raft. When Hans Werner Henzes wished to raise a political storm in the modish manner of the 1960s, for his subject he went back to the raft. His audience disapproved of his politics, and *Das Floss der Medusa* was hissed off the stage.

The word "Medusa" had gone into the universal language of thinkers as a kind of shorthand, vivid and unmistakable because there never could be again such a unique sequence of pure horror.

Writers on disasters at sea inevitably included the story of the *Medusa* and almost invariably agreed that the events were unique. English historians, particularly, dismissed the horrors and hysterias as being especially French, or at least foreign.

Common to them all was the horrified assumption that the tragedy of the *Medusa* must—must—represent a special set of circumstances. Yet what is really interesting is how universal it actually is; the fact that we can still learn from it lessons applicable to ourselves.

These were rammed home by countless events at sea during the Second World War. The unfortunate Corréard is forgotten but Surgeon Savigny is still remembered and quoted, precisely because he was a surgeon. That is, a naval doctor of experience who was a direct witness of the events he describes.

Nor was he merely a technical witness who collaborated in a popular book. That book is still regarded as important, but its medical aspects were enlarged upon by Savigny in a paper which he submitted to the Faculty of Medicine in 1818 and had published the same year.* Some 150 years later a German student of the subject, Professor Dr. Hans Schadewald, wrote another paper in which he discussed Savigny's testimony in the light of much recent, practical experience.†

Professor Eitner, the art historian, following recent French verdicts, believed that Savigny and Corréard were far from being impartial chroniclers because they desired to incriminate the frigate's captain while attempting to minimise or explain their own part in the "atrocities" which occurred on the raft.

Professor Schadewald, the student of survival at sea, took the opposite view. He regarded Savigny's technical paper as admirably objective, even surprisingly so, and he rejected any attempt to turn the subject into "Art." He had in mind that political play by H. W. Henzes which collapsed in riot during its premiere in 1968.

This medical professor considered the tragedy too horrible to be "warmed up again in any kind of artistic manner" and that justice could be done only through a commonsense and scientific objectivity. He stressed that the raft did hold a message and that it could not be repeated sufficiently often. It was what Savigny

---

Observations sur les Effects de la faim et de la soif éprouvés après le naufrage de la frégate du Roi le Méduse en 1816.

†*Patho-physiologische und psychologische Beobachtungen des Schiffsarztes Jean-Baptiste-Henri Savigny beim Schiffbruch der Fregatte "La Meduse."*

himself had concluded as a result of his experiences: "Moral strength is of greater importance for survival than physical strength." This, of course, was to deny the validity—except as a personal statement—of Géricault's painting. And it is not accepted by some modern French historians who conclude that, on the raft, the officers sacrificed the others to save themselves.

The observations and actions of Savigny and his companions are still being debated, sometimes with bitterness, more than 150 years after the event. And everything centres on the question: was the sequence of events on the raft truly unique? Or are there more modern duplicates and parallels?

Although my own father was a naval surgeon (in the British Navy), I can claim no medical knowledge. It was therefore all the more important in tracking down evidence to limit myself to witnesses who did have the requisite technical background. Yet as a professional assessor of eye-witness evidence, I had to note that Savigny's narrative was necessarily defective in one respect. No man being able to be in two places at once, it was essentially that of the sufferer looking out—not that of the objective observer surveying the whole scene from an outside vantage point. I felt that some French historians were being unfair in not allowing for, let alone criticising him for, this involvement.

Therefore I sought first for a "control." An event of absolute and even staid normality which would pick out those points of conduct on the *Medusa*'s raft which really were strange; although not necessarily unique. It seemed an exacting if not impossible requirement. The circumstances would have to be almost exactly the same. The place would have to be off West Africa, the time of the year would have to be July, the period spent adrift before being found would have to be about two weeks, hope of rescue should have been glimpsed and then dashed at least once, and somewhere there had to be a medical witness.

The story I chose eventually is unknown. I found

the evidence in my own files, dating back fifteen years to a time when I had been studying the technical problems of survival at sea.

The raft of the *Medusa* had drifted off the coast of West Africa for thirteen days from July 5 to 17, 1816, after which time fifteen men only were still alive, five of whom died shortly after.

The two rafts of the *Rio Azul* had drifted off the coast of West Africa for sixteen days from June 29 to July 14, 1941, after which time only eleven men were alive, one of whom died at the moment of rescue and another a few days later.

The similarities were startling, but the discrepancies would be even more telling.

The *Rio Azul*, 4,000 tons gross, carrying a cargo of "Pepel" iron ore from West Africa, was in convoy until 1800 hours on June 28, 1941, when she received a signal ordering the convoy to disperse. The following day at 1740 hours, alone in the South Atlantic, she was torpedoed.

The torpedoes struck her on the port side below the bridge, breaking the ship in two. The port lifeboat was smashed by the explosion. The falls of the starboard lifeboat went over the side and there was no slack which could be paid off. Both lifeboats were therefore useless and the only hope of the crew of forty-four men lay in the rafts which she carried on deck. There was no time to launch these. In less than sixty seconds after the explosion, the bows and stern cocked up in the air and sank. The crew jumped overboard.

Two rafts floated clear of the wreckage, one of them damaged. They were crudely constructed and consisted of a platform of planks laid on and lashed to metal drums. Most of the supplies they carried, together with the signal flares and other distress signals, had been torn away or destroyed. The damaged raft had lost the drums which would normally have supported one end, so that it floated in a lopsided manner, the planks sloping towards the water. Any man clinging to this would be likely to roll off.

There were a large number of men in the water, some swimming and the non-swimmers clinging to wreckage. The swimmers gradually made their way towards the rafts and tried to help others to reach them. While this was going on, a large U-boat surfaced about three hundred yards away from the rafts.

The survivors reported her as being in excellent condition. From her general appearance and the fact of her paint being new, they concluded that she was fairly recently from the shipyards. They counted two guns, one forward and one aft of the conning tower, but were unable to estimate their calibre. The U-boat commander hailed them, saying he would try to have some assistance sent to them. He did not, however, offer to leave them any supplies. The submarine then departed, leaving the rafts with some men on them to drift with the currents—for there were no paddles or oars—and an undetermined number of men clinging to wreckage or trying to swim.

By nightfall eighteen men had reached the rafts. They huddled there, very cramped and uncomfortable, their sodden clothes clinging to them. The most senior of the survivors were the Third Mate, the Senior Radio Operator, the Chief Steward (an old man of sixty-nine), and the bo'sun. Three seamen, two greasers, a fireman and a trimmer had arrived at the rafts, as well as an apprentice, a cabin-boy, a deck-boy, and a galley-boy. Of the trained gunners carried by all merchant ships to man the defensive armament, three had survived—two of them were soldiers, men of the Maritime Regiment, R.A., and one was a navy gunner of the D.E.M.S. organisation.

As they sat there shivering they could hear out in the darkness the sound of shouting. The cries died away gradually and no more men reached the rafts. At dawn the next morning they were alone on the sea. A number of men who at nightfall had been seen clinging to wreckage, but too far away to be either rescued or identified, were no longer there.

The eighteen men on the rafts then set about check-

ing what supplies were left and also collecting what
they could from the litter of floating wreckage in
which they were drifting. The sun, with a blazing and
pitiless intensity, began to burn the moisture out of
them.

Lashed to one of the rafts they found a container
holding 1¾ gallons of fresh water. Among eighteen
men exposed to the sky for every hour of every day
for an unknown number of days to come, this quantity
was minute. As a measure for rationing the water they
used the brass stopper of a paraffin can. It held the
equivalent of about three tablespoonfuls. They decided that this would have to be the ration of water
for each man each day.

From the drifting litter in the sea they salvaged what
treasures they could. Cigarettes and tobacco were
picked up—but no matches. Three objects of more
vital use were found—one tin holding about ten tablespoonfuls of molasses, one tin of egg substitute, and
one tin of cocoa. Apart from this, there was nothing
to eat. They rationed these items also. The method of
issue was to moisten a stick and then insert it into a
tin, so that a little of the molasses, egg substitute or
cocoa stuck to it.

Once only was there a shower. This occurred one
night. They hurriedly spread out a tarpaulin and succeeded in catching about half a gallon of rain water.
During the entire time they were adrift they had no
more to drink and eat than this—a total of 2¼ gallons
of water and the contents of the three tins. When men
are exposed to the direct blaze of the sun they lose
five times more moisture by evaporation than they
would do under some form of overhead protection.
Literally, these men were by degrees sucked dry of
moisture. At the same time they starved, suffering the
headaches and stomach cramps that go with it. And
during daylight their exposed arms and legs were
flayed by the scorching sun.

On the fourth day they saw a ship. Probably a tramp
steamer, it was hull down on the horizon, only its

masts, bridge and funnel visible. The rafts floated low in the water. Certainly they would not be seen from that distance away. The bo'sun, who had assumed much of the leadership, had foreseen this possibility. As a substitute for the lost flares and distress signals he had hit upon the idea of employing the useless tobacco tins as heliographs. Flashed in the sun, their light would carry for miles. Under his leadership, they had also constructed a rough flagpole, with an improvised flag attached, which could be held up and so increase by many miles the distance from which they could be seen.

Excited and hopeful, they waved their flag and flashed the tobacco tins at the vessel on the horizon. But as she passed steadily on her way and at length sank out of sight, their sudden hope burnt out into a reaction of lethargic despair.

There was no ease on the rafts, for they were very cramped. As day succeeded day, this became a torment which could only be alleviated by going into the sea. All of them bathed at intervals to stretch their limbs, with the single exception of the elderly Chief Steward. But otherwise they kept as still as possible, lying down for long periods in order to conserve their energy which continued to ebb away. They were continually thirsty, but found that there was slight relief to be gained by splashing each other with seawater, which they did from time to time.

The temptation to drink seawater was always present. Some of the men succumbed to this, and the unanimous opinion of those who survived was that the practice was harmful. Some of the men also began to drink their own urine. About the effects of this, opinion was divided.

They slept fitfully and nervously, falling off into a sleep which was usually filled with fantastic dreams. Often they saw visions of fresh, clear water.

When not asleep, no-one was unduly despondent and prayers were said regularly every day. They were all surprised to find that the craving for food and water did not increase to an unendurable extent. Indeed, it was less than they expected. This was in fact the first sure sign of approaching death.

Less and less were they aware that their arms and legs were cruelly burnt by sun and salt water and covered with sores; that they were cramped and thirsty and hungry. As life ebbed they became dull and apathetic, not fully conscious of their condition.

On the thirteenth day adrift, which was July 11, the Radio Officer died. He was the first. He was followed next day by the Chief Steward, the oldest man among them.

On the fifteenth day, one of the gunners went mad. He was one of those who had drunk his own urine. He dived off the raft into the water and was unable to get back. The same day, two others died quietly from exhaustion. These were the trimmer and the cabin-boy. Their bodies were pushed overboard during the night and although they were not weighted, by morning they had disappeared. It was assumed that they were eaten by sharks and possibly it was this which first attracted the sharks to the rafts.

By July 14, the Third Mate also had become mentally deranged. He died very early that morning. During the day it was noticed that one of the seamen had died also. The bodies were pushed overboard. With deaths now taking place in rapid succession, it is clear that even the toughest of the survivors had not long to live. At this point, another ship was sighted and use was made again of the bo'sun's tobacco tins as a heliograph.

This time—unknown to the survivors, by the narrowest of margins—the device worked. The ship, which was actually on escort duty, turned away from the vessels she was protecting to investigate what could have been merely the sun flickering on distant wave-tops.

Within the next few minutes, while actually being rescued the eighth man—the fireman—died. Even the toughest of the survivors admitted that if their hopes of rescue had again been dashed, three or four days more would have been their limit. Sheer disappointment and loss of hope would have finished them off.

They owed their lives, some probably by a matter of hours, to three men: an alert young signalman, an approachable captain, and the bo'sun who had devised the method of signalling. His death, ten days after being rescued, was a tragic piece of irony.

The remaining nine men were landed at Scapa Flow a few weeks later and although their wounds and sores took long to heal, they all eventually recovered. Like the survivors of the *Medusa,* they were almost destitute.

This time the medical witness was not among the feeble spectres on the raft. Instead he was the doctor of the rescue ship, the man who treated the survivors, who saw them as they surely could not have seen themselves.

When the armed merchant cruiser *Esperance Bay* left Freetown in Sierra Leone, six hundred miles south of Senegal, as escort for a convoy headed north up the coast of West Africa her captain was a retired naval commander, Geoffrey Holden. He was "one in a thousand," a captain who was approachable, to whom the crew were intensely loyal. Five or six days out of Freetown a new and inexperienced signalman was coming down from the bridge when he noticed something flashing in the water at some distance from the convoy.

It is no small thing for a young seaman to beard the captain of a warship on his own bridge, particularly when he only thinks he has seen something and none of the regular lookouts have reported it. He hesitated a moment. He knew that this captain was not given to biting people's heads off, but it was with some trepidation that he went back to the bridge where Captain Holden stood with his officers. Holden listened, complimented him for drawing his attention to what he thought he might have seen, remarked that it would perhaps be appropriate to warm through the engines. The *Esperance Bay* increased speed and began to turn away from the ships she was protecting. Now Holden would have to justify his action if the momentary flashing proved to have some innocent cause or even been a trick of the light on a wave. But when the convoy had fallen a few miles astern, two objects were sighted, floating low in the water.

They were rafts. It was realised with chilling apprehension by all aboard that they could only be from the previous convoy, which had been dispersed by U-boat attack in this area more than two weeks before. If there were men on them, then they had been exposed without shade or cover of any kind to the broiling sun of the South Atlantic for at least fifteen days.

There were men on them still. Eleven blackened travesties of human beings were stretched out on the bare planks. They were all alive, at that moment, for they twitched feebly. Round them, patiently in the deep water, undulated the bodies of the sharks; nearly one shark in the water to every man on the rafts.

With care and great difficulty the utterly exhausted men were helped aboard. One man, alive when on the raft for he was seen to move slightly, was dead by the time he had been taken below to the sick bay. It was impossible to say at what precise moment he had died, so close to death were they all.

They were a difficult problem for Doctor C.* because, apart from severe sunburn and saltwater burns of their arms and legs, their vitality had almost flickered out from intense deprivation of fluid and food. A light diet of egg custards and light food was given to them but they had to be encouraged to eat; the craving for food had gone. They hardly knew what was happening to them. They did not know that, while on the rafts, a school of sharks had been keeping them company a few feet away. Their injuries, burns that

---

*The doctor, who was in private practice in Portsmouth when interviewed, wished to remain anonymous.

would normally have made a man writhe in agony, now caused them hardly any pain. They had gone beyond that. It was hard to bring them back.

One man, their leader, sank fast into a coma. This was the bo'sun, who had saved all their lives by making a reflector out of tobacco tins. It was this flickering, flashing light which had caught the eye of the young signalman. The truth was, the bo'sun was suffering from kidney failure. If he had been in normal health, it would have been a terrible truth, for this is one of the most agonising ways of dying that can be imagined. But the bo'sun felt no pain. So far towards death had he sunk already, in the closing days on the raft, that now he merely became more and more drowsy; and, after ten days, he died.

From the others, as they slowly gained in strength, the doctor bit by bit pieced together their story. The crew of the *Esperance Bay* were intensely curious about what had happened to them, but in the men's shocked and exhausted state, they could not be disturbed by casual visitors. So the doctor put down on paper what he learned from them and had it typed and sold to the crew. The proceeds were given to the nine destitute survivors. It is from this document, amplified by the doctor concerned, that the story of the British rafts has been told.

Tens of thousands of such reports were made and exhaustively studied during and after the Second World War. The curiously conservative sailormen were made to understand that their standard forms of life-saving apparatus were virtually useless, simply because no one had bothered to find out what the survival problems really were. For instance, the Royal Navy's regulation life raft stood condemned on every count. Only ten percent of these rafts ever got into the water at all and most of the men on them died anyway. Flotation was all very well, but it was very far from being enough. Battle casualties amounted to one-third only of the total war losses; for two-thirds died by drowning or by exposure. Exposure of the unprotected body to biting wind and cold or to burning sun and heat. (Report of the Talbot Committee, 1946)

At the same time the Americans were also studying the problem from their own bitter experiences. They produced a chart showing the expectation of life for men in the sea, using lifejackets or rafts. This varied with temperature, but in average conditions survivors had lasted less than sixty minutes. It is as well to remember this when some well-meaning but amateurish Safety Committee next sloganises the lifejacket as a panacea for survival.

To quote from an article I wrote in 1958: "The result of these detailed studies of survivors' reports was to show that there was not one problem—but three. The first was to devise life-saving equipment which could actually be launched, even in adverse conditions. The second was to ensure that this equipment kept the survivors insulated from the three killers: the sea, the sun, and the wind. The third was to make sure that the survivors could be located and rescued."

The answer which had by then been newly arrived at and was just being introduced was based on the aircraft dinghy, which had had a good war record, unlike lifejackets, liferafts and lifeboats. The new type of liferaft was a light inflatable dinghy with overhead cover called an "Arctic tent" which could be completely closed by flaps at both ends. Like most good inventions, it was more than a century old. The first inflatable liferaft was invented by Lieutenant Halkett, R.N. and tested by him in the Bay of Biscay under winter conditions in 1844. The Admiralty turned down the idea but similar craft were used for Arctic exploration in the 1840s and 1850s.

The emphasis was on North Atlantic conditions— cold wind and cold water—rather than on those of the South Atlantic, where the sun may be a torment, but survival time is likely to be a matter of days or weeks rather than hours or minutes. Nevertheless, the use of the tent as overhead protection against the sun in the tropics is nowadays regarded as critical for survival, to prevent dehydration. Here also a modern innovation had been "invented" more than a century earlier, for in their last days on the raft the survivors of the *Medusa* had indeed erected a tent as sun-cover, fashioning it out of their useless sail. Had they thought to do so earlier, more of them might have lasted until the moment of rescue. Nevertheless, it took 140 years and two world wars before Ministries relearnt that lesson.

The basic difference between the improvised raft of the *Medusa* and the unofficial non-regulation rafts of the *Rio Azul* was that the former lacked flotations. Wooden ships are generally less likely to sink than iron or steel ships, which is why they carried few boats, but in the last resort every sailor knew that he could always make a raft out of the materials to hand, buoying them up with empty casks, for solid wood floats low in the water. It is to the eternal discredit of de Chaumareys and Schmaltz that they made a quick, botched job of the raft. Consequently, we must regard the immersion to their waists in salt water as an adverse, agonising factor for the survivors of the French ship which was not duplicated in the case of the *Rio Azul,* although one raft came near to it by the loss of half its oil drums.

Some experiences were clearly common to the survivors of both vessels. The drinking of seawater and urine, the relief obtained by bathing, the habit of formal prayer (in spite of the slight difference in religion). The sharks also exhibited standard reactions— a small group took station on the floating objects but did not attempt to attack the men. Even mullet do this in hot weather in the English Channel, so it may have been a matter of shade and temperature combined perhaps with the mass of the rafts which for small fish are protection and for large fish an ambush position. While the British seem not to have thought of the sea under them as a source of food containing liquid, the French did try to catch fish, although unsuccessfully. The French also showed initiative in erecting

a tent, although it is true that the British could not
have done this because no canvas was available.

However, it was a French doctor, Alain Bombard,
who in 1952 set out to prove that with only a little
equipment it was possible to subsist for many months
in the South Atlantic on a diet of seawater, plankton
and fish. His introduction to the problem the previous
year had been in its cold water aspect, the delivery to
the hospital where he worked of forty-three trawl-
ermen, still wearing their lifebelts, who had been in
the sea off Boulogne in springtime for a very short
period. They were all dead. One answer to this problem was technical and not always convenient—the use
of a buoyant, insulating "survival suit" to replace the
almost useless and in some designs actually dangerous lifejacket.

Bombard's research began in 1951 with the classic
case of the *Medusa*'s raft in 1816 and included Bligh's
voyage in a boat from the *Bounty* in 1789. He concluded that Savigny was correct in his basic statement,
many survivors died from despair and not from any
physical cause, in comparable conditions of excessive
heat rather than excessive cold. The first step was to
combat despair with reason in order to prolong life to
its physical limit; and then to extend the physical limit
by showing how men could live from the sea. Again,
it was not necessary for him to invent the basic statement. The work had already been done by 1888, and
was described by Prince Albert I of Monaco, an
oceanographer, in a report to the Academy of Sci-
ences in Paris. In July and August of that year an
oceanographic vessel operating in the South Atlantic
had proved that simple nets, lines and harpoons could
extract ample food from the ocean, particularly at
night. In that part of the ocean, at that time of the
year, no castaway should die of starvation. Provided
that he had the will to live and this elementary
equipment.

The third requirement was for liquid to combat
thirst and here Bombard was to make an original con-

tribution by putting forward theories, proving them in the laboratory, and then drawing attention to the fact by a practical test in which he drifted like a castaway across the southern part of the North Atlantic roughly on a line opposite West Africa.

The first of his propositions is that the body of a fish contains much fresh water. Catch enough fish and you will not die of thirst. His second proposition was more controversial. It was based on the fact that fish do not always immediately gravitate towards a floating object; it may be three days or more before they begin to do so. Without water, a survivor may become irreversibly dehydrated during this initial period. Bombard's solution was to drink seawater at first, before the fish arrived and provided fresh water. It will be recalled that the men of the *Rio Azul,* while having no definite opinion on the effects of urine drinking, were all agreed that the drinking of seawater had proved harmful. This is indeed the consensus of opinion of centuries.

Bombard, being a doctor, knew that better than most. Drunk in great quantities it inflames the kidneys and this causes death (as in the case of the bo'sun). The doctor decided to drink seawater but to limit his intake to a daily 1½ pints, because this amount contained the salt which the human body actually requires in that period. Further, he decided to limit the drinking of seawater to the first five days, the critical period when there might be no fish to catch. Clearly, there was an element of risk, but the doctor was confident that he would survive. At the time he was in a minority of one. There was even strident opposition, mainly from old mariners turned bureaucrats whose ancient expertise was being derided (to their minds) by a layman.

The craft which Bombard used was an inflatable dinghy, which provided insulation from the sea only (not from the wind or the sun). For sixty-five days he drifted in the north equatorial current, living on fish which he caught and plankton scooped up with a net.

Plankton consists of both vegetable and animal life in almost microscopic forms—fish, lobsters, prawns, all these in their early stages are part of the great fields of plankton in the sea. Although accused as a charlatan, Bombard had made his point unforgettably to practical people. The two most spectacular examples, both from the South Pacific, were the survival of the Robertson family after thirty-eight days in 1972 and the endurance for 117 days of Maurice and Marilyn Bailey in 1973. These were genuine castaways who followed Bombard's example and fished for their food; they went further, and put up overhead cover to protect themselves from the extremes of cold and heat.

The only real scientific objections to Bombard's own demonstration of his theories seem twofold. Firstly, that he was a doctor and knew exactly what he was doing. An ordinary man might not be so confident in his ability to judge just how much sea water was enough, when taken as drink. Secondly, there stands the awkward fact that there are no ordinary men. Each individual, from his finger-prints to his breathing-patterns, is different from every other individual.

A much better test is the survival of a group, and better still the survival of different groups at widely spaced intervals. The differences which occur between them are probably even more important than the similarities in pin-pointing vital evidence. An exception appears to be those hallucinations which affected equally the men of the *Rio Azul*, the men on the *Medusa*'s raft and in at least one recorded case, that of M. Bredif, in one boat of the *Medusa* also. Savigny's opinion was that these were not due entirely to the sun and the heat, as hallucinations occurred at night also; and that there must be another factor, probably a lack of certain nutrients in the food, which affected the minerals in the body. Somehow, he thought, the system is put out of gear and so the hallucinations start.

Both diets, the French and the British, certainly were unbalanced. There was a difference which could be important, however. The French flour, water and wine came from the unsavoury hold of a nineteenth-century sailing vessel in the tropics and three weeks out of port, while the British molasses, egg substitute, cocoa and water were in twentieth-century tins.

Professor Schadewald put the question: was there a specific poison present on the raft of the *Medusa*? Before considering this critical point, one must admit the truth of his statement that Savigny's narrative is a "document unique in medical history." This is the main reason why the case of the *Medusa* is still studied even in a century remarkable for its advances in the field of medical knowledge. There was no doctor on the rafts of the *Rio Azul* to give close-up testimony, and the leader who emerged naturally was the bo'sun who did not long survive rescue. On the raft of the *Medusa,* however, not only was there a ship's doctor but he was the man who emerged as the leader and quickly recovered from his ordeal. We know therefore that he had realised from the first the necessity for strict military discipline, careful thought, and above all an emotionally hopeful note to the leadership (even if the leaders did not always believe it), because they saw despair as the deadliest danger of all.

The British report does not stress this to the same extent because, comparatively, morale on the British rafts was much higher; indeed, highly satisfactory. The tougher men would not admit defeat. In face of all the evidence, they were convinced that they could have gone on for another three or four days, even if the *Esperance Bay* had disappointed them as cruelly as the earlier ship. They had already lasted two days longer than the men of the *Medusa* were required to do and their losses, proportionately, had been much less. They had managed this without resorting to cannibalism, a factor which must have contributed greatly towards the survival of the last fifteen men on the French raft.

They had not eaten each other, they had not fought each other and although crowded, there is no record of their having become even exceptionally irritated with each other, although some irritation might be expected on medical and nutritional grounds alone. The voyage of the boat from the *Bounty* in 1789 provided a famous case, in which a near-mutiny broke out, almost resulting in a cutlass duel between the emaciated Lieutenant Bligh and one of his equally emaciated officers. Bligh was a bad officer and a worse captain and no doubt morale was well below normal to start with.

This was certainly the case with the *Medusa* and is a central fact of the whole affair. Firstly, she was wrecked in peacetime, not sunk by an enemy. Secondly, she was wrecked by bad management. Thirdly, her abandonment was marked by cowardice as well as incompetence on the part of her captain. Fourthly, she was carrying a large number of passengers. Fifthly, these passengers were not acclimatised to the tropics. Lastly, these passengers were of mixed origins and included many convicted felons who were virtually slaves. It is a formidable list.

The difference between a peacetime disaster and a wartime tragedy is immense. In peace, one does not expect to be sunk and there is both shock and protest. In war, one is mentally prepared in advance to face the worst; if you're still alive afterwards, you're lucky.

The crew of the *Rio Azul* were a small, homogeneous body of men crossing the South Atlantic with essential war supplies at the height of the U-boats' success in the area. The soldiers aboard were gunners, manning the defensive armament and therefore part of the crew. Their chances to start with were not good, but then the U-boat crews were not likely to survive the war, either. Nobody had a guaranteed ticket to life, liberty or the pursuit of happiness at that time. The ship broke in two and sank in sixty seconds which, considering the cargo it was carrying—iron ore—was what you would expect. The lifeboats went down with it—of course. That two rafts floated free was blessed good luck. That many men lived to jump overboard and that eighteen of them actually managed to reach the rafts was amazing good fortune. Now all they had to do was help themselves, endure—and hope. The British tend to be rather good at this.

The *Medusa,* on the other hand, was undertaking a commonplace voyage which, properly conducted, held few hazards. By a series of perverse stupidities the captain deliberately left his convoy behind and when the frigate was completely alone, despite clear warnings, drove her ashore on a well-known sand bank. He then bungled the process of getting her off and shamefully mismanaged the subsequent premature abandonment of a ship which could not sink and was unlikely to break up. Through personal weakness, incompetence and cowardice he deliberately condemned most of the men on the raft to death.

The basic difference in morale between the two groups of castaways may be appreciated. Quite apart from the fact that the high-strung French tend to be more nervous and aggressive anyway. Even so, there were critical differences between the components of the very large group on the *Medusa's* raft. The soldiers were not defensive gunners; they were passengers, pure victims, unaccustomed to the sea, unaccustomed to the tropics, placed in an unexpected and terribly unfair situation. The sailors were less downcast and resentful, because their profession did involve the possibility of shipwreck and no doubt they comprehended that not all captains were immaculate navigators and shiphandlers. The engineering workmen under Corréard represented a third closed group while the officers themselves formed yet another, with similar backgrounds, mental outlook and training.

The men on the British rafts were crowded, too crowded to lie down until death had created a space. The men on the French raft were more crowded still and in addition were standing to their waists in salt water, until death lightened the raft and gave them space also.

The British had a water ration only. The French had wine as well as water and some of them got drunk on the wine. The fighting which broke out may in part have been due to the wine and the result was to inflict sabre, bayonet, knife and musket-butt wounds on many as well as to expend energy. British soldiers and sailors, when only mildly drunk, also tend to become quarrelsome and if no pretext for a fight is to hand will soon invent one. It has been suggested that there may have been a poison in the *Medusa*'s water casks (such liquid was often putrid and alive with organisms), but water was drunk in the *Medusa*'s boats without producing anything more than mild hallucination (if in fact it was the cause at all).

On the French raft such symptoms were incomparably more severe. Instead of merely seeing visions of flowing water, men acted on the strength of their delusions. They demanded and fought for non-existent portions of chicken. One man was found about to cut a slice off Captain Dupont's leg, believing that the leg was a loaf of white bread. Savigny himself pointed out that this state was far from being unknown. It had been described by the French doctor François Boissier de Sauvages in 1763, as usually occurring in the tropics, but had been identified long before that in reports by the early Spanish seamen in southern waters. They had called it Castilian fever and sometimes attributed the state to sunstroke, although others believed it was due to the bad air in the lower decks of their cramped and crowded vessels.

Savigny doubted both these theories on the ground that there was all too much air on the raft and that the severe hallucinations occurred at night. His own conjecture was that the special conditions of the tropics affected the supply of blood to the brain with results not dissimilar to encephalitis or meningitis. Professor Schadewald considered that a poison in, or a deficiency of, the diet was the likely cause.

He observed, however, that only three men—Savigny, Corréard and Dupont—had apparently kept a clear head all the time, for this was partly a matter of willpower, and that a group of twenty or so men which included most of the officers had managed to control the rest. The majority, however, had shown some symptoms of insanity which, under the influence of alcohol, hunger, sleeplessness and the general hopelessness of the situation had produced an extreme state of excitement—a "temper tantrum"—which had resulted in the mutinies and riots.

This was the reading of a German medical specialist. A French historian, writing even more recently, suggested an artificial and sinister interpretation of these same events. In his view the pattern could fit the theme of "survival of the fittest." The officers and their juniors had moved to the centre of the raft so as to reduce the danger of their being swept overboard and by climbing onto the barrels had managed to keep dry. They had started the fighting in order to clear people off the raft and so obtain more room for themselves. And they had killed people in order to eat them.

It is absurd to take this as being literally true in the sense of selfishly reasoned conduct. The officers went to the centre of the raft and when possible placed themselves on the barrels because this was necessary in order to control such a large body of men tightly packed. In the armies of the time, officers of about the rank of major and above were issued with a horse because the animal provided them with a mobile eminence on which they could be seen by all and from which their commands would carry more clearly and compel more attention. After twenty years of war, the conduct of the officers on the raft can be seen as no more than a sensible reflex action, and one which was to be expected of officers. That the nominal commander of the raft, the injured midshipman Coudein, was soon superseded by the older, more experienced and perhaps more forceful Savigny and his friend Corréard, is only to be expected. Exactly the same happened on the British rafts of the *Rio Azul.* It was the experienced seaman, the bo'sun, who assumed most of the leadership rather than the Radio Officer, theo-

retically his senior. And, it is important to note, it was
not leadership in the sense of bullying domination but
in spreading the gospel of hope and suggesting means
by which they could help themselves and perhaps even
save themselves; and were fully justified in the event
because they did just that. In such situations a leader
or leadership group is necessary and these usually tend
to be the people who think they know best what ought
to be done in given circumstances. This implies a measure of knowledge and experience. In a sea survival
situation it was the senior seaman, the bo'sun, who
took over. The Radio Officer's knowledge was irrelevant in this context, as the bo'sun's might have been
in another.

But the British experience did high-light the extraordinary "temper tantrums" on the *Medusa*'s raft,
amounting almost to insanity. Was this just the result
of wine, hunger, heat, hopelessness and lack of sleep?
Or was there a specific poison present? Or was there
another cause altogether?

18

IN THE DESERTS
AND THE MOUNTAINS

The age of aviation, 1970–1973

A PURELY medical explanation appeared reasonable enough until in September, 1970, three airliners were hijacked to the Middle East and hundreds of passengers kept prisoner for a week inside them, after the huge aircraft had been landed in the Jordan desert. The first aircraft to be seized was an American Jumbo Jet, a Boeing 707 of TWA, hijacked over Brussels at the start of a flight to New York with nine crew members and 149 passengers—a group almost identical in numbers to those isolated on the raft of the *Medusa*. In conditions of extreme heat by day (the nights were cold) they were occupying a confined and completely covered space, forced to remain in their cramped seats by armed guards for seven days as a result of no fault of their own. Like the wreck of the *Medusa*, this was a totally unexpected situation, not covered in the small print. And like those from the *Medusa*, the castaways had been brought together by chance. Instead of unity, there was an infinity of potential divisions.

And, as with the raft, there was among the castaways a qualified observer who noted what happened and later presented a paper on the subject.* This was Sylvia R. Jacobson, Associate Professor of Social Welfare at the Florida State University, Tallahassee. When

---

*"Individual and Group Responses to Confinement in a Skyjacked Plane," *Amer. J. Orthopsychiat*, 43(3), April 1973, and *Schwallbacker Blatter*, 98, Jahrgang XXIV, Heft 2, 1.6.73, Wiesbaden. Also personal communications and discussions with the author.

I first read a summary of this report, it seemed that there was a definite sequence to the psychological and physical deterioration which took place and I was amazed to see how closely it appeared to parallel many of the events on the raft of the *Medusa*. There were only slight differences and these were all caused by the varying nature of the outside events which impinged upon the castaway communities. There were no jellyfish or butterflies in the cabin of the Jumbo, for instance. But there were equivalent incidents to torment on the one hand and to raise hopes, often illusionary, on the other.

The actual moment of the hijacking was not mentally critical. There was an element of stunned disbelief, similar to that experienced by soldiers in their first battle or civilians under air attack for the first time. The impact of what had happened only began to be realised at about the time when, according to the original flight plan, the passengers should have been arriving at their destination, Kennedy Airport, New York. There they were due to meet their relatives and friends. Now, they thought, they might never see them again. Some became very worried and swapped names and addresses with other passengers in the hope that if they were unlucky, news of what had happened to them might still get through. This moment seems to approximate to the stranding of the *Medusa*.

The equivalent to the casting off of the raft was the landing of the Jumbo in a remote place in the desert which was garrisoned and controlled by armed Arabs of the Popular Front for the Liberation of Palestine. That was very final. Once on the ground, at the mercy of their captors for an indefinite time, there arose a conflict *between* the passengers. The sub-division of the passengers had already begun during the flight, but then it had been hardly more than latent, less marked than the conflicts and suspicions which had occurred at the time of the *Medusa* stranding, for some of these went back three weeks to their original departure from Rochefort. In the Jumbo there was time during the five-hour flight only for the first tentative appearance of this phenomenon.

"Sub-groupings began subtly to form," wrote Sylvia Jacobson. "Families clung more closely to their children. Seatmates and those adjacent, hitherto strangers for the most part, dropped normal psychological barriers; in the sudden sense of unity in danger they whispered together in sudden communion, exchanging conjectures, anxieties, fears. The fourteen college students scanned seat-pocket maps, speculating among themselves, trying to foretell destination, evidencing a sense of adventure. Almost at once, they formed and remained a sub-group. A voice hissed harshly that this was as it had been in the Nazi Holocaust: 'People were led helplessly to their deaths, like sheep.' "

Preliminary lines having begun to form during the flight, the first dangerous division occurred almost immediately after landing and sparked the first actual conflict, approximately equivalent to the agitation concerning Lieutenant d'Anglas which preceded the first mutinous riot on the raft of the *Medusa*. Inside the Jumbo, of course, there could be no question of the passengers physically fighting among themselves. They had guns pointed at them. Their rapidly building antagonisms could not be worked off by strength-sapping hand-to-hand fighting but had to take the internally corrosive form of vicious argument, snapped replies and general nagging.

What Sylvia Jacobson called "the first divisive wedge" came with the Arab demand for passports. This revealed the basic fact of their captivity: that, although all were hostages of a sort, some were in greater danger than others. Much greater danger. She heard the Arabs openly declare that the mass skyjack was an effort to impress the world with the plight of the Palestinians, to ransom their imprisoned "brothers," to express their anger at America for supplying fighter planes to Israel and to demonstrate their protracted and intense resentment and hatred of Israel.

The hunt was for people with Israeli passports. It set apart those who held dual passports of two different nations and families in which parents and children held passports of different nations. "With the demand for passports, an apprehension that was never to leave flooded the cabin," noted Sylvia Jacobson. She herself had queried the demand for passports but had been silenced by murmurs of "Sshh—don't make trouble" from other passengers. Next morning this division was deepened when some passengers asked an Arab doctor to let them get their personal medicines from the baggage in the hold. Other passengers who, although travelling on American passports had a second, Israeli passport in their luggage and feared that these might be found during a search of the cases in the hold, became extremely alarmed. "This evoked a fierce, whispered quarrel," noted Sylvia Jacobson. Eventually, those who wanted medicines gave in, but "subgroups existed in uneasy, distrustful proximity to one another."

This initial situation may be thought to parallel the preliminary lines on the raft, with the officers, sailors and engineering workmen broadly on one side and the mass of the soldiers—but by no means all of them yet—on the other. Also paralleled were the fluctuations between hope and anxiety brought about by outside stimuli, which resulted in alternating periods of calm succeeded by violent quarrelling.

A visit by Jordanian Army officers brought momentary unity and quiet to the cabin, although they could offer little real promise of help apart from an offer to send in food. But when the food actually arrived, it triggered off yet another half-suppressed explosion. Some Jewish parents urged their children to eat and were sharply criticised by other Jewish parents for accepting non-Kosher food. Yet another divisive element had been introduced, cutting across two previous boundaries, that of the dual-passport holders and that of age, for the adolescents continued to be "a definite, almost closed sub-group, immersed in companionship and self-organisation for available satisfaction. They continued to evidence a certain sense of adventure." This was similar to a preliminary war situation, which may well be enjoyed by the young, who have few ties or responsibilities, while causing nothing but concern to older people and particularly the elderly.

"By noon, however, the mothers of babies had spontaneously become another sub-group, concerned with the practical problems of caring for their infants and themselves. Formula preparation, bottle heating, the improvisation of cribs against the cold night engaged them. While most passengers continued to speculate on their fate, to read, to pray, to doze, half-heartedly to play cards, the mothers, with busy hands, remained purposefully and enviably engaged and united. Along with the stewardesses, women passengers moved to look after the six children who were travelling alone. It seemed as though this, as other life crises of birth through death, called upon the work of women and their hands."

Some loose parallel may be suggested with the officers on the raft, engaged in the intricacies of rationing or stepping a mast, and also perhaps with the Negroes. These latter had originally divided between the small command group and the large mutinous group, but had eventually withdrawn from both groups to form their own self-seeking mutinous party which, by suggesting that they could help the mutineers survive in the desert, tried to influence the side with the greatest numbers.

That evening some of the passengers were ordered out of the Jumbo in order to be evacuated to hotels in Amman. The Indians went first, then other nationals, then mothers and their children, then all the remaining women. But first, they had to sign forms which revealed, one way or the other, whether or not they could be considered Jewish. All Jewish women were ordered back into the cabin, together with two non-Jewish women who pleaded not to be separated from their husbands. Sub-conscious fears of a new Bu-

chenwald rose to the surface and were openly expressed now.

The arrival of the International Red Cross on the
third day changed matters. Spirits rose and there was
a feeling of general unity among the passengers.
"Sighting-seeing" visits by armed men of various
North African armies had the same effect. The passengers felt as if they were on display, resented it and
united to put on a show of indifference. "Divisiveness
was subdued," noted Sylvia Jacobson. Then "suddenly, all passengers were ordered off the plane, os-
tensibly for air." In their absence there was a search
of cabin baggage, in which Israeli passports were
found. The Arabs suspected that there were others
and demanded that these be given up. The airline
stewards advised the passengers to comply.

The main lines of division immediately hardened.
There were hostile remarks: "If it were not for the
Jews, none of us would be in this spot." This antagonism was reciprocated. Passengers who had got into
curious and apparently friendly conversation with the
Arab doctor and the female Arab guards were the
targets. They were attacked for "fraternisation with
the enemy."

The opposite line of natural development—attempts
to impose a command set-up to carry out agreed measures for organisation and survival—failed almost entirely. Tentative beginnings were met with contempt.
"Who gave *you* any special right?"

There may have been a Savigny or a bo'sun who
saw what had to be done and could think out detailed
measures; but, if so, he did not appear. This may have
been because a command staff—and a very inferior
one—already existed in the aircraft. It was composed
of the stewards and air hostesses, trained to act as
waiters, waitresses and wet-nurses, not leaders or or-
ganisers. Their traditional role as reassurers of naïve
and nervous passengers in this instance boomeranged.
The cabin became a "rumour factory." This emphasised the fact that commands and information must

emanate from a single dominating point, whether that be a couple of barrels in the centre of a raft or from the aircraft captain's cockpit by loudspeaker.

The outbreak of general irritation on the third day, starting with anti-Jewish remarks, was repeated more aggressively on the fifth day. Some non-American passengers began to agree with the anti-Jewish and anti-American sentiments of the Arab guards and became more forceful in doing so. One American, of recent European origin, said that he despised American customs and values and was only waiting for retirement to leave the place for ever. These outbursts were countered and quelled by the aircraft crew and a black American soldier who was among the passengers.

Although this developing conflict could not be physically indulged in and had to be restricted to abuse, there does seem to be a pattern closely similar to that which developed on the raft of the *Medusa*. The first burst of general irritation was marked by a period of angry posturing, with some reluctance to actually fight, followed by single combats between particular pugnacious individuals or "champions" of both sides, followed—one is tempted to say inevitably—by a general combat between the two sides.

On the fifth day in the desert the passengers found out that the aircraft had been wired for demolition. "The only reactions seemed numbness, apathy, depressed isolation on the part of some, increased tendency among affiliates for relatively idle talk, bolstering of self defences in fitful scapegoating, and the ongoing bickering around eating." Where the French castaways had fallen into desultory converse on their worst memories of the Napoleonic wars, here there was a certain "gallows humor." "Veterans of Buchenwald scorned the complaints of others. Compared with what they had lived through, this was a 'Hilton Hotel.'"

They were of course perfectly right. However, what one may call "concentration camp superiority" is not new but rather one form of a trait well known in war contexts, exhibited in Normandy in 1944 where it was identified and classified as "D-Day Snobbery" ("If you'd been here on D-Day, you'd have been dug in by now"), familiar also as the theme of earlier British civilian air raid experience ("My bomb was bigger than your bomb"). The attitude can perform a useful service in lending perspective and particularly in introducing "green" personnel to active and dangerous realities; but, undeniably, it can also be irritating.

On the sixth day the confined passengers in the aircraft began to crack emotionally; they lost their perspective. "There was a general sensing of the rapidly spreading deterioration of health and morale. The atmosphere grew more physically and emotionally oppressive. The remaining men were paler; those of military age showed and complained of gastric disturbances; vomitings increased. Babies were irritable: half-hearted attempts at card-playing and checkers were abandoned or increased; more sudden sobbing occurred and stopped; more intimate expressions of loss of hope and longing for death by older ones were heard. Grief over guilt towards others in the past emerged with a seeming lack of coherence." On the raft, the younger men could have fought; in the plane, with their emotions held in check by armed guards, their feelings were deflected internally. Instead of sabre wounds, they suffered stomach disorders.

The crazy suspicions which showed early on the raft did not become really marked on the aircraft until this same, sixth day. When a guard became ill and was taken off the plane by another Arab guard, even Sylvia Jacobson was alarmed. "Was this a ploy to get the *fedayeen* off the plane before it exploded? When, some half hour later, he was returned we were newly disquieted. Having been ill, was he thought worthless enough to be blown up with us?" There followed what she wrote of as an "access of paranoia," suspicions which a cool look round would have discounted. Whatever move was made, whether by their captors or by a sub-group, was interpreted by the remainder as a plot to kill them. Given a little more confinement there might have been actual killing. Had the cause of their close detention in unbearably hot circumstances been purely natural, rather than the muzzles of Arab guns, there might have been killing already.

Next day, the seventh, was the last day. The remaining passengers in all three aircraft were taken to Amman, while the planes were blown up. But the affair was far from being over emotionally. "In subsequent rescue stages and on the long flight westward to America, recriminations were more open and bitter. . . ." Just so had Thomas complained to Rang about Savigny and the other officers.

What now remains of that French historical view which accuses Savigny of deliberately causing antagonisms on the raft in order to get rid of many of the occupants and so let him and his friends have more space and better rations? Does anything remain even of the long-held view that the strange occurrences on the raft of the *Medusa* were unique, unrepeatable? On the contrary, it may now be said that the *Medusa* narrative continues to be relevant in the twentieth century; that the technological differences between an early-nineteenth-century wooden sailing ship and the latest jet airliner are utterly irrelevant. The subject is not transportation methods but the study of groups of people under stress. The *Medusa* case, where everything went to extremes, is therefore still the most valuable piece of evidence we have.

But just as the *Medusa* must be corrected and "controlled" by equivalent incidents, such as that of the *Rio Azul,* so must the experience of the American Boeing 707 be compared to that of the other two skyjacked aircraft—the Swissair DC 8 and the British VC 10. Sylvia Jacobson was told by the Arab guards that conditions were far worse in the other planes. "I learned that the contrary was true. We, on the American plane, had the worst of the three situations. Aboard another plane, greater total cohesiveness was sustained, and a passenger was heard to say: 'Our fear was controlled; our anxieties uncontrolled.' "

Professor Jacobson is still engaged in a comparative study of these illuminating differences. In the interim, she believes that the determining factors may be: (1) the nature and character of the leadership maintained (or not maintained) by each captain, together with the degree of direct contact he had (or did not have) with the passengers; (2) indigenous passenger leadership fluctuations; (3) the greater degree of efficiency and technical competence in a crisis of this sort of one crew over the others; (4) the presence or absence of women (other than female crew) and children; (5) the behaviour of the captors and the vulnerability of the captives to their explicit threats; as well as their nationality.

In the case of the *Medusa* it must be said that the initial leadership was appalling, amounting to abdication. The captain, who should have commanded, had bolted. The senior naval officer was only a midshipman (literally a novice trainee) who was already virtually incapacitated by injury. A vacuum existed which clearly had to be filled by someone. As some later testified, the survivors owed a debt of gratitude to Savigny and Corréard for actually forming an effective leadership group. Clearly, this is not so easy to achieve as one may think.

However, the basic underlying cause of the irritation which leads to sub-division and the breakdown of physical and mental health has yet to be explained. Climate, helplessness, confinement to a limited space are obvious critical factors. It is difficult to decide the order of their importance. But it may be that space is the real key: that the over-crowding of any type of creature, whether human or not, tends to result in a conflict which is resolved only when there is space enough for the survivors to lie down and stretch out.

In all the raft narratives, both French and British, the sense of relief once death had removed a sufficient number of persons to make life bearable is a subconscious theme easily detected. The French, but not the British, hurried on the removal by butchering each other; but then the French were even more crowded and vulnerable to begin with. And, like the passengers of the American Jumbo Jet, they were mostly a miscellaneous collection of individuals brought haphazardly together. The British were the close-knit survivors of a small, organised crew.

If these observations are fundamental, then the *Medusa* may have a lesson even for the conditions of modern urban life. It is possible that high-rise, high-density "tower blocks"—as opposed to a rather crowded but still close-knit community of slum dwellers who may have occupied the site previously—may lead to alienation and rioting, purposeless or with only an apparent purpose.

One basic aspect of the *Medusa*'s story, however, yields to modern perspective. The eating of human flesh, condemned as an "atrocity," and used as a political weapon against Savigny and Corréard, is not now seen in the same light. There is no reason to doubt the genuineness of the immediate revulsions at the discovery of how the survivors had really survived; the confusion in people's minds as to whether they were confronting savages or heroes. For once again, an episode of the *Medusa* has repeated itself in modern times, amid the glistening wonders of twentieth-century technology which have changed nothing basic and can again be dismissed as irrelevant.

For a long time the French experience was thought to be unique. Later in the century, it was true, a comparable event resulted from the stranding of the Donner party in a snowbound pass during the covered-wagon days of the American West. That, too, was thought to be exceptional and scandalous. This was largely because the historians of the sea and the historians of the "Wild West" operated in separate compartments, so to each, each event appeared uniquely horrifying.

However, in the early 1970s two instances of community cannibalism occurred and were widely reported, for they were the result of aircraft accidents—one in Canada, one in South America. Like that of the Donner party, they were cold-climate occurrences; that is, thirst was not a factor but food most certainly was. The small group in Canada were faced with the choice: eat human flesh or die. An Eskimo boy resolutely refused to consume human flesh. He died. The German pilot ate from a body killed in the crash. He lived. With air travel now so common any one of us might tomorrow be faced with this dilemma.

The crash in the Andes took place in October, 1972, and was particularly well covered by the media.* It was also especially interesting because, although many of the basic factors were utterly different from those which had acted on the crew and passengers of the *Medusa,* nevertheless certain patterns of behaviour were repeated. Consequently, although it is not necessary to tell the whole story in any detail, some aspects need to be considered. Those which appeared to transcend physical differences which occurred in spite of the contrast between the climate of the tropics in summer at sea level and the climate at 12,000 feet in the Andes in winter.

One has to ignore, to begin with, the quite amazing coincidence regarding the causes of the accident. The pilot of the Uruguayan Air Force Fairchild turboprop in 1972 made what was in principle exactly the same navigational error as the captain of the French frigate in 1816. Both machines, incidentally, were Service-owned and operated but being used for passenger carrying. The Uruguayan had taken his machine through a particular pass in the Andes (because it lacked the performance to go over the top), which meant careful navigation to a check point on one side, a large change of course to fly through the pass in cloud, followed by another large change of course over a navigational "fix" on the far side of the pass. By some mental

*Including two documentary books, *Survive!* by Clay Blair, Jr. (Berkley, U.S.A., 1973) and *Alive* by Piers Paul Read (Alison Press Secker & Warburg, 1974).

aberration the final turn of the "dogleg" was made much, much too early and instead of flying north on the far side of the mountains he flew north right into them. Just so had de Chaumareys turned when only half the required distance had been covered and sailed right into a sandbank.

However, as the Fairchild was going a good deal faster—about 240 miles an hour faster—than the *Medusa* when it met a solid object, many of the five crewmen and forty passengers were killed instantly or died soon after. But after seventy-two days in the mountains in winter, sixteen young men survived. It was almost miraculous.

The composition of the passenger group was extraordinary; it could hardly have been more homogeneous, more different to that of the *Medusa*. Basically, it was a school rugby team and its supporters. They were almost all men: young, tough, physically fit. As it was a Catholic school, they were all Catholics. And as it was an exclusive school they were all from the top and upper classes of their nation. Politically, all bar one were "liberal" or left-wing. Four were medical students, one of whom was to survive to play an important part in their protracted endurance and eventual rescue. The "command" structure of the military plane did not survive the crash by long, the pilots dying of their injuries pinned to their seats. It was all up to the students now.

They had hope on their side to begin with, for an accurately directed search pattern put one aircraft right over the scene of the crash a day later. The survivors saw it clearly, but they did not know that the pilot had not seen them, for the wrecked machine was painted white and was lying in and partly buried by snow.

The first night was the most horrible, spent crammed inside the wreckage with the dead, the dying and those who had been terribly injured but might live if help came soon. The cold was bitter. Wine was passed around and many of the boys took a drink or two.

Some, mercifully, went to sleep. Others could not sleep at all. Others again were irrational. One boy kept crying out that he was President of Uruguay; another said he was going out to find a bar and fix himself a coke. In short, in the intense cold and thin air of the Andes, exactly the same sort of hallucinations which had been common on the raft of the *Medusa* was repeated. Here, there could be no question of tropic heat or of water poisoned by long storage in the hold of a wooden sailing ship. The *Medusa* survivors had drunk wine too, which may have contributed, but the essential similarity seems to be shock. The shock of the crash—or of being fatally cast adrift in a raging sea. That is to say, a sudden and awful change of circumstance, which would also disturb a disciplined human system accustomed to a long-standing routine of sleeping and waking, eating, resting, and working. And here climate *would* contribute to the existing psychological and physical disturbances of the system, because both climates, although opposites, were *extreme*. Cold and thin air which made breathing difficult on the one hand, suffocating heat and lifeless air impregnated with desert dust which also made breathing difficult on the other. In sum, a series of shocks, of fundamental disturbances affecting both the nervous system and the breathing system as well as the digestive system.

None of this is really very surprising and certainly it is not alarming. Given time, all systems would adapt to some extent. But, terribly, the crash of the Fairchild did parallel the *Medusa*'s raft in respect of the dangers of restricted space. Originally there were twenty-eight survivors, some injured, who—in order not to die of cold—had to withdraw to the fuselage at night. This wreckage gave a usable space only fifteen feet long for the twenty-eight people. They had to sleep in "stacked" formation, limbs intertwined or draped over someone else. This, plus the cold, led to cramps and the sufferer would move; often he would disturb, or hit, or kick someone in the face or on a wound, involuntarily. There would be a cry of pain, perhaps wild cursings, sometimes blows; occasionally a fight between two individuals which would bring on mêlée involving several others. Clay Blair wrote: "As a result of these fights, so much anger and hostility built up during the nights that they instituted a rule that everybody had to shake hands all round every morning." Just so, in his delirium, Tousche-Lavillette had told of how, on the raft, "after each slaughter, they would kiss, thanking God; after the last one, all the guns were thrown overboard." These clashes occurred in spite of the fact that all the aircraft survivors could in fact lie down, if uncomfortably. On the *Medusa*'s raft, for many days, no-one could lie down, or even sit; they were tightly packed even when all were standing up.

In the Andes, initially, they burnt money in order to melt snow for drinking purposes. Paper currency was much more valuable than coinage in these circumstances. Later, they found more efficient ways of melting the snow and there was never a thirst problem. Consequently, hunger tended to dominate above all other desires. It was the medical student Roberto Canessa, a determined nineteen-year-old, who rationalised the problem for them. Their situation was very long-term. If they were not seen from the air, then they would have to walk out of the Andes. There was no other alternative. And to do that, they would have to wait until the late spring when the snows would melt. Their food supplies would not last nearly so long and anyway it would not be enough merely to stay alive. They would have to be physically fit at the start of the march out in the spring or they would not make the distance.

He explained exactly what malnutrition was and how they were all showing the symptoms of it. There were now twenty-six left alive, with ten bodies near by, shallowly buried in an improvised cemetery. Another boy pointed out that to eat these bodies would not be wrong, because their friends were already dead;

it was not as if they were murdering each other to stay alive.

The pattern which followed was exactly that which had been enacted on the raft of the *Medusa*. Initial reluctance, then a few became involved and as they grow stronger and the abstainers become obviously weaker, one by one all become involved. All bar one, that is—and he died. It was a grimmer version of the argument in the Jumbo concerning non-Kosher food. There were still certain taboos which dictated the choice of corpse. The dead wife of a still-living survivor, by mutual agreement, was not consumed. Certain dead friends were not eaten.

The survivors never were found, for the search had long been abandoned. Further, their situation was far worse than they had thought because while they believed themselves to be merely in the foothills of the Andes they were in fact in the middle, surrounded by mountain ranges. Nevertheless, in the spring Roberto Canessa the medical student and Fernando Parrado, a twenty-two-year-old engineering student, were still fit enough to walk and climb out of the icy mountains into the green foothills and bring help. The fourteen men who were still alive in the plane were rescued by helicopter. The rescuers were stunned by the scene. Pieces of human bodies, particularly feet, lay around. Feet contained too many bones and too little flesh to be worth eating. The rescuers thought: what have we saved—heroes or savages?

Just so had the French reacted to the fifteen survivors of the *Medusa*'s raft in 1816.

During my preliminary study for this book, I made a note: "In almost all disasters at sea, historians like to point out, there is some enobling or moving feature. They decline to give the story of the *Medusa* the status of a tragedy because, they conclude, the victims were largely responsible for what happened to them. *I wonder how true that is?*"

INDEX